This book belongs to

country Friends

all through the Seasons

ISBN-13: 978-0-8487-3713-9
ISBN-10: 0-8487-3713-X
Library of Congress Control Number: 2009925826
Printed in the United States of America
Second Printing 2012

Oxmoor House, Inc.
VP, Publishing Director: Jim Childs
Executive Editor: Susan Payne Dobbs
Assistant Brand Manager: Terri Laschober Robertson
Managing Editor: L. Amanda Owens

Gooseberry Patch All Through the Seasons
Project Editor: Diane Rose
Senior Designer: Melissa Jones Clark
Director, Test Kitchens: Elizabeth Tyler Austin
Assistant Director, Test Kitchens: Julie Christopher
Test Kitchens Professionals: Kathleen Royal Phillips,
    Catherine Crowell Steele, Ashley T. Strickland
Photography Director: Jim Bathie
Senior Photo Stylist: Kay E. Clarke
Associate Photo Stylist: Katherine Eckert Coyne
Production Manager: Tamara Nall

Contributors
Designer: Nancy Johnson
Proofreader: Donna Baldone
Interns: Emily Chappell, Angela Valente

Parts of this book were previously published as *Gooseberry
Patch Celebrate the Seasons* and *Gooseberry Patch Family
Favorite Recipes*.

To order additional publications, call 1-800-765-6400.
For more books to enrich your life, visit oxmoorhouse.com
To search, savor, and share thousands of recipes, visit
myrecipes.com

*Front cover: Farm-Style Birdhouses (page 480); Cranberry Slush
(page 173); Ornament Keepsake (page 480); Roast Turkey with
Sage Butter (page 215)*

all through the

Seasons

recipes & crafts

Four seasons fill the measure of the year. ~Keats

How Did Gooseberry Patch Get Started?

You may know the story of Gooseberry Patch...the tale of two country friends who decided one day over the backyard fence to try their hands at the mail order business. Started in JoAnn's kitchen back in 1984, Vickie & JoAnn's dream of a "Country Store in Your Mailbox" has grown and grown to a 96-page catalog with over 400 products, including cookie cutters, Santas, snowmen, gift baskets, angels and our very own line of cookbooks! What an adventure for two country friends!

Through our catalogs and books, Gooseberry Patch has met country friends from all over the world. While sharing letters and phone calls, we found that our friends love to cook, decorate, garden and craft. We've created Kate, Holly & Mary Elizabeth to represent these devoted friends who live and love the country lifestyle the way we do. They're just like you & me... they're our "Country Friends®!"

Your friends at Gooseberry Patch

Mary Elizabeth · Holly · Kate · Spotty

A friend can touch your heart from across the world or across a room.

Table of Contents

Spring

There's a hint of warmth in the air, the trees are budding, and there's a red-breasted robin singing in the back yard...spring has arrived at last! It's time to pack away the heavy quilts and open the windows to enjoy the fresh air while you prepare for warmer weather. Why not greet visitors to your home with a lovely profusion of spring color? Dress the porch in sunny tulips, pretty pink petunias, crimson phlox and other blossoms; finish with a lush floral wreath on the door.

Spring has Sprung!

Celebrate Easter and the arrival of spring with Sunday brunch…and don't forget the decorations! Trim a twig tree with dyed eggs and colorful buttons, or plant grass in a painted pot and "hide" eggs for visitors to discover. For pretty little gifts, make candy eggs and embellish them with icing. Egg tree how-to's are on page 122.

HAM, BROCCOLI & CHEESE QUICHE

For my 20th birthday, my mama, Lorry Bates, gave me an heirloom cookbook. She had various relatives and close friends write out their favorite recipes. I am sure this will be one of my treasured possessions as the years pass. It includes this recipe, which Mom has made for years.

1 c. half-and-half
5 eggs, beaten
$\frac{1}{2}$ t. dry mustard
$\frac{1}{4}$ t. pepper
1 c. cooked cubed ham
1$\frac{1}{2}$ c. shredded Cheddar cheese
1 c. broccoli, blanched and
    chopped
1 onion, finely chopped
9-inch pie crust

To make quiche filling, combine half-and-half, eggs, mustard and pepper; set aside. Layer ham, cheese, broccoli and onion in prepared pie crust. Pour egg mixture over layers and bake at 350 degrees for 45 to 50 minutes. When a knife inserted comes out clean, remove from oven and let cool 5 minutes before slicing.

Alicia L. Bates
Kent, OH

PAINTED EASTER POT

Spring has sprung and Easter's on its way! How about growing your own Easter grass in a springtime flowerpot? Paint a large pot (this one is 6¾" tall) with primer, then pale yellow. Use a 1" wide flat brush to paint pastel pink stripes around the pot. Trace the flower pattern from page 137 onto tracing paper, then use transfer paper to transfer flowers randomly onto the pot. Referring to *Painting Techniques*, page 134, paint the flowers purple and green with a pale yellow center, then add the green dots to the pink stripes.

To grow the grass, spread rye grass or wheat seed in a shallow dish that fits down in the pot. Lightly mist the seed with water, then place in a resealable plastic bag in a warm spot (this will create a terrarium). Now watch the seeds sprout. When the grass is the desired length, place the dish in the pot on a cake stand or can.

CANDY EGGS

There's nothing like a big candy egg for Easter, and they're oh-so simple to make! Follow the manufacturer's instructions to melt 8½ oz. of white melting chocolate...add ½ oz. to 2 oz. of colored candy wafers until you have the color you want. Pour the melted candy into a clean egg-shaped soap mold that has been sprayed with non-stick vegetable spray. Allow the candy to harden and remove the egg from the mold. Use royal icing and a decorating bag with a small round tip to decorate the eggs as desired. To make the royal icing, mix together 3 tablespoons meringue powder, 4 cups powdered sugar and 6 tablespoons warm water in a medium bowl. Beat with an electric mixer for 7 to 10 minutes until stiff...this will make 3 cups of icing.

spring rides no horses down the hill, but comes on foot, a goose-girl still.

⌐ EDNA ST. VINCENT MILLAY

MILK BOTTLE VASES

You can make enough of these quick & easy vases to give as party favors for your garden club meeting. Start by painting each bottle with faux etching paint. After the paint is dry, apply springtime stickers around the bottle. Tie a ribbon bow around the neck of the bottle, then fill with fresh-cut flowers from your own garden.

MILK CARRIER CENTERPIECE

Place glass milk bottles in a wire carrier. Using a continuous length of wired ribbon, tie one end of the ribbon into a bow around one bottle. Crinkling the ribbon between bottles, tie the ribbon into a bow around the next bottle. Continue until you have tied a bow around each bottle. Glue the free end of the ribbon behind the loop of the bow on the first bottle to finish the centerpiece.

BASKET OF BLOOMS

Choose a wire basket made to hang on a door. Line the basket with Spanish moss, then fill it with potting soil. Following the planting instructions for your climate, fill the basket with your favorite spring bulbs. Now, keep it watered…before you know it, you'll have springtime color that will brighten your home!

EMBROIDERED PIN

Trace the background pattern, page 138, onto tracing paper, then the basket onto paper-backed fusible web. Using the pattern, cut three backgrounds from muslin; cut five 1" diameter flower circles from assorted fabrics. Fuse the basket to brown fabric and cut out. Center and fuse the basket appliqué onto one background; layer the basket piece onto another background. Referring to *Embroidery Stitches*, page 133, and the stitching key on page 138, work the embroidery design through both layers of fabric. For each flower, work *Running Stitches* along the edge of one fabric circle. Pull the threads to gather, then flatten the circle to form a yo-yo. Tack the flowers to the embroidered piece. Matching right sides and leaving an opening for turning, sew the embroidered piece and remaining background together. Clip the curves, turn the pin right-side out and sew the opening closed. Beginning at the top of the pin and leaving a long ribbon streamer, work angled *Running Stitches* to attach ribbon along the edge of the pin. Tie the ribbon ends into a double bow at the top of the pin and tack to secure. Glue a pin clasp to the back of the pin.

Rabbits have symbolized birth for many centuries and as such, represent the new life that Easter celebrates.

You'll have gifts for all ages with this cuddly chenille bunny and embroidered pin! See page 122 for the bunny instructions.

SPRING SALAD

Pick the dill for this salad early in the morning, just after the dew has evaporated.

2 c. spiral pasta
1/2 c. sliced black olives
1/2 c. red onion, chopped
10 cherry tomatoes, sliced in half
3 carrots, sliced diagonally
1 zucchini, thinly sliced
1/2 c. green pepper, chopped
1/2 c. mayonnaise-style salad
   dressing
1/4 c. sour cream
1/2 t. garlic powder
2 t. fresh dill weed, chopped
salt and pepper to taste

Prepare spiral pasta according to directions on package. Drain, rinse and allow to cool. Combine vegetables with pasta. In a small bowl, combine salad dressing, sour cream, garlic powder and dill weed, mixing well. Blend into pasta and vegetables, coating thoroughly. Add salt and pepper to taste. Cover and chill salad one hour before serving.

Simple pleasures are Life's Treasures. ~enjoy~ the first day of spring

Studded with sweet golden raisins and prettily decorated with colored eggs, braided Italian Easter Bread is sure to become a family favorite.

ITALIAN EASTER BREAD

Our family loves this bread served warm with butter.

1/2 c. warm water
2 pkgs. active dry yeast
1/2 c. shortening
1/2 c. milk, scalded
1/2 c. sugar
1 t. salt
2 eggs, beaten
2 t. lemon extract
4 to 5 c. all-purpose flour
1/2 c. golden raisins
Optional: 1 doz. uncooked eggs,
   dyed

Pour water into a large mixing bowl; add yeast and stir until dissolved. Add shortening to milk and stir until melted; cool to lukewarm.

Add to yeast mixture. Add sugar, salt, eggs and lemon extract. Blend in flour and knead until dough is smooth and elastic, about 10 minutes; knead in raisins. Shape dough into a ball and place in an oiled bowl. Cover with a towel and let rest in a warm place about 2 hours or until double in size. Divide dough into 3 portions. Roll out into equal lengths and braid. Form braid into a circle and place on a greased baking sheet. If desired, place dyed eggs between each braid or "nest" (the eggs will cook while baking). Cover and let rise 40 minutes. Bake at 350 degrees for 25 to 35 minutes.

Barb Bargdill
Gooseberry Patch

HomE ...tweet... HomE

There are so many ways to turn a simple birdhouse into something fun! Search flea markets for old cabinet hardware and other vintage finds. You can even top your birdhouse with wallpaper scraps; we used solid-color embossed paper, but a colorful pattern would look charming, too. Turn to page 122 for some clever ideas…we've made it easy for you!

"I meant to do my work today — But a brown bird sang in the apple tree, And a butterfly flitted across the field."

— Richard LeGallienne

grow all sorts of interestingly-shaped

Gourd BIRDHOUSES

Follow instructions on the back of a package of **BOTTLE GOURD SEEDS**. Bottle gourds grow very well on a trellis, and enjoy lots of water & sunlight. Cure your gourds by placing them on a wooden rack where air can circulate around them freely. Be sure to turn them occasionally. Gourds are dry when they turn brown, beige or cream & seeds rattle loosely inside. (It may take 3 to 6 months!)

To make a birdhouse from your gourd:

1. Wash gourd in soapy water to remove dirt & mold. Let dry.

2. Using a sharp knife or fine-toothed craft saw, cut a hole in the gourd's side 1" to 1½" in diameter. The size of the hole will determine which birds will "rent" your house.

3. Remove seeds & any remaining pulp. clean inside with soapy water.

4. Spruce up the house with a painted finial, a wooden ring around the door or a wooden perch.

5. Attach a hanger and enjoy!

Nothing adds flavor to your favorite dishes like freshly harvested herbs. Even if you're not a gardener, you can easily grow small pots of fragrant herbs on the kitchen windowsill, then snip what you need as you cook!

FLOWERPOT PLANT POKES

Use your old broken flowerpots for these fast & fun plant pokes. For each plant poke tag, *Dry Brush*, page 134, a pot piece with a "cottage" color of acrylic paint…you can paint the pots you'll be planting in at the same time. Use a permanent marker to label the tag with the name of your plant. For a stem, using pliers and starting at one end of a length of heavy-duty copper wire, twist wire around the tag to hold it in place, make a loop in the wire and trim to desired height for the pot.

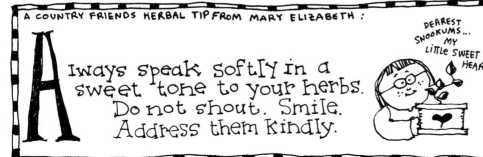

A COUNTRY FRIENDS HERBAL TIP FROM MARY ELIZABETH :

DEAREST SNOOKUMS... MY LITTLE SWEET HEART...

Always speak softly in a sweet tone to your herbs. Do not shout. Smile. Address them kindly.

Good choices for a culinary herb garden include basil, chives, dill, garlic, oregano, marjoram, mint, parsley, rosemary, sage, tarragon and thyme.

HERBED PIZZA BREAD

This delicious fresh-from-the-garden, herb-flavored pizza bread goes great with salads. It's so quick and easy…the herb spread can be made up ahead of time and kept in the refrigerator for days.

¾ c. unsalted butter, softened
¼ c. olive oil
3 T. bread crumbs
1 T. fresh parsley, chopped
1 T. fresh chives, chopped
1 T. fresh basil or tarragon, chopped
1 or 2 cloves garlic, finely minced
salt and pepper to taste
12-inch, ready-made pizza crust
Optional: Parmesan cheese

Combine butter, olive oil, bread crumbs, parsley, chives, basil, garlic, salt and pepper until well blended. Spread 3 to 4 tablespoons herb butter mixture over pizza crust. Bake at 375 degrees for 8 to 10 minutes or until golden brown. Sprinkle with fresh Parmesan cheese, if desired. Makes 1 cup spread.

Edwina Gadsby

RAW VEGETABLES WITH ARTICHOKE DIP

Surround this dip with an array of fresh vegetables…carrots, radishes, celery and peppers.

½ c. low-fat mayonnaise
½ c. non-fat sour cream
½ c. artichoke hearts, chopped
⅓ c. roasted red pepper
1 clove garlic, minced
2 T. fresh basil, chopped
    (or 1 t. dried basil)
⅛ t. dried oregano
⅛ t. salt
raw vegetables, cut up

Blend all ingredients together except cut up vegetables. Cover and chill one hour. Makes 1½ cups.

Herbed Pizza Bread

Down the Garden Path

The garden can be a comforting hideaway, especially when you add accents like a rustic bench or brightly colored pots. You can even spruce up the potting shed with a handy organizer! Help a friend start her own garden with bulbs or plantings tucked in painted pots. Instructions for the bench, tool rack and large painted pots are on page 123.

Interesting planters: Fill baskets, crocks, sugar buckets and galvanized tubs with flowers and herbs. If you want a really old-fashioned touch in your garden, add a weathered barrel to catch rainwater…it's so handy for watering your plants!

Add whimsy to your garden shed…the sprinkling head from a watering can makes a fun doorknob, and an old trowel can become a clever door knocker!

Cultivate the garden for the nose, and the eyes will take care of themselves.
—ROBERT LOUIS STEVENSON

FRIENDSHIP FLOWERS

Share some of your favorite flowers with your special friends. Prime a clay pot and saucer, then paint them a springtime color. Decorate the pot and saucer with painted-on motifs of the season (we used butterflies, swirls, dot flowers and sprinkles of dots). Check out the *Painting Techniques* on page 134 for some tips from your Country Friends®. You can fill the pot different ways. In our yellow pot, we tucked a bulb and a cellophane bag of potting soil into the flowerpot, placed the saucer on the pot as a lid and tied it closed

with ribbon. Follow *Making a Tag or Label*, page 132, to add a handmade tag. For the green pot, we placed a bag of soil, tied closed with ribbon, in the pot. Now, this is easier than it looks; make a free-form butterfly-shaped plant poke using 1/8 dia. soft, pliable wire…make sure you form a loop that will hold your seed packet. Photocopy the packet pattern, page 138, onto card stock; cut out. Color the label if desired. Fold on dashed lines to assemble packet; glue flaps. Fill the packet with seeds, then attach it to the plant poke; "plant" the poke in the pot.

For memories Mom will treasure long after she's enjoyed her breakfast in bed, display the kids' artwork on a handmade tray. A tiny pin-on vase keeps a little flower bouquet fresh all day long, and the children can help craft a pretty card trimmed with pressed flowers and buttons (instructions on page 123).

MOTHER'S DAY LAP TRAY

Turn an everyday picture frame into a Mother's Day memento keeper. Prime and paint a 16"x20" wooden frame (set the glass aside), four 9" wooden legs and 4 corner leg mounting brackets white; lightly sand the wooden pieces. Using the backing from the frame as a pattern, cut pieces of hardboard and fabric to fit in the frame; apply spray adhesive to the back of the fabric and smooth onto the board.

Arrange and glue keepsakes from the kids on the board. Secure the glass and the board in the frame…you may want to use screws or finishing nails to add some extra support. Attach the legs, then take the tray to Mom with her Mother's Day breakfast.

mother knows best!

BACON & CHEESE WAFFLES

For something different at breakfast, try these delicious waffles.

1 egg, beaten
1 c. milk
1 c. sour cream
1 T. butter, melted
2 c. biscuit baking mix
6 to 8 slices bacon, crisply
    cooked and crumbled
1 c. shredded Cheddar cheese

In a medium bowl, blend together egg, milk, sour cream and butter. Stir in biscuit baking mix; blend well. Mix in bacon and cheese. Pour in enough batter to fill a preheated waffle iron and cook until steaming stops and waffles are crisp and golden. Makes 12 waffles.

Jennifer Ash
Piffard, NY

What sweeter bouquet could a mother receive than a bunch of dandelions clutched in the hands of a child?

— Nancy Campbell

I picked these for you, MOM!

BAKED APPLE PANCAKE

So easy to prepare. While it's baking, the table can be set, sausage cooked and coffee made…perfect!

$^{1}/_{4}$ c. butter
4 to 5 apples, peeled, cored
    and thinly sliced
$^{1}/_{2}$ c. sugar
$^{1}/_{2}$ t. cinnamon
6 eggs, beaten
1 c. all-purpose flour
1 c. milk
$^{1}/_{2}$ t. salt
Optional: maple syrup

In a 10$^{1}/_{2}$" cast-iron skillet, melt butter. Add apples, sugar and cinnamon; sauté until apples begin to soften. In a mixing bowl, blend together eggs, flour, milk and salt; pour over apples in iron skillet. Bake, in iron skillet, at 375 degrees for 30 minutes or until puffed and pancake tests done in the center. Serve with maple syrup, if desired. Makes 6 servings.

Debbie Beauchamp
Murrells Inlet, SC

Perfect Planters

April showers might bring May flowers, but these country planters let you enjoy their beauty anywhere you like! You don't have to start with a new container…try painting an old metal washtub or trough, or attach holders to a worn wooden gate.

INDOOR/OUTDOOR GARDENS
Refer to Painting Techniques, page 134, before beginning your garden project.

Planter Centerpiece
Prime a metal planter, then paint it pale yellow; *Dry Brush* with soft green paint. Using the same green, paint a band around the planter, then a wavy vine over the band. Paint leaves randomly along the vine and highlight with pale yellow accents. Spray on a clear sealer to protect the surface.

Blooming Garden Gate
An old wooden gate makes the perfect backdrop for spring flowers. Lightly *Sponge Paint* a wrought-iron plant holder, a decorative wire door basket and the hinges and handle of the gate with a mossy color of green paint. Using vintage drawer pulls as the hangers, attach the plant holder and basket to the gate. Line the basket with moss, then fill the basket and plant holder with flowers.

Washtub of Flowers

Mask the top and bottom edges to make a 7" wide band around a metal planter. Paint the band cream, then *Dry Brush* with brown. Mask 1" wide borders on the top and bottom of the band; paint borders brown and remove tape. Trace the patterns, page 139, onto tracing paper. Using the patterns, cut the petal, flower center and leaf from compressed craft sponge. *Sponge Paint* flowers and leaves along the band.

Use a cotton swab to paint yellow dots on flower centers. Transfer the words along the borders…white or yellow transfer paper will show up the best. Use a liner paintbrush and cream paint or a cream-colored paint pen to draw over the transferred words.

No time for gardening? Create a Friendship Garden! Find a place for a flower or veggie patch, and with a bunch of friends, plan, prepare and enjoy the fun of gardening. Everyone should be willing to work a little every few days to keep the garden weeded and watered; plus, you should get together once a week just to chat over a glass of icy lemonade. Share the harvest...and the fun!

Decorate your hearth for spring with a flowering garden! Instructions for the "picket fence" fireplace screen are on page 123.

DON'T JUDGE EACH DAY BY THE HARVEST YOU REAP BUT BY THE SEEDS YOU PLANT. ~ROBERT LOUIS STEVENSON

PAINTED WINDOWBOX

To brighten an indoor windowsill, prime, then paint a wooden windowbox a pale green with soft cream stripes…a 1" wide paintbrush will do the trick! Use a pencil to lightly draw little flowerpots with heart flowers on the cream stripes. Paint the hearts red. Thin the red paint with a little water, then paint the pots. Use a fine-point black marker to outline the pots and flowers and to add stems for the flowers (don't forget to add detail lines to the pots). Finish your box with sprinkles of blue paint dots and fill it with potted flowers.

Friendship warms the Heart

GROUP HUG

Just as flowers brighten our gardens, friendships brighten our lives. When a good friend is under the weather (or even if she just has "spring fever"), a caring gift can bring sunshine to her day! Some thoughtful ideas… chicken soup, citrusy tea in a painted teapot, a new novel and a handmade bookmark. To make the bookmark, turn to page 123.

Liberal doses of garlic and onion add flavor (as well as healing properties) to Comforting Chicken Noodle Soup. To help relieve a stuffy nose, toss in a pinch of cayenne pepper.

Fun little friendship gifts: a framed snapshot of the two of you, a bottle of scented lotion, the latest book by her favorite author, coupons for free babysitting, housecleaning or lawncare.

COMFORTING CHICKEN NOODLE SOUP

Feeling under the weather? Grandma was right…chicken soup helps ease a cold.

3½ to 4-lb. chicken, halved
2 stalks celery, halved
1 onion, quartered
2 cloves garlic, minced
1 t. salt
¼ t. dried tarragon
4 c. water
3 c. chicken broth
1 onion, chopped
2 stalks celery, sliced
salt and pepper to taste
¼ t. dried parsley
4 oz. egg noodles, uncooked

Combine chicken and the next 7 ingredients in a large soup pot and bring to a boil. Reduce heat and simmer 45 minutes or until chicken easily pulls away from the bone. With a colander, strain the broth into a large container and discard vegetables. Remove skin and bones from chicken, chop chicken meat and set aside. Skim fat from broth and return broth to the pot. Add remaining uncooked vegetables, salt, pepper and parsley to broth. Bring to a boil, reduce heat and simmer 15 minutes. Add noodles and bring to a boil. Cook 8 to 10 minutes or according to package directions. Add cooked chicken and simmer the soup another 5 minutes.

SOOTHING TEA SET

Turn a plain white teacup & pot ensemble and a matching spoon rest into a heartfelt, thinking-of-you gift for a friend with a case of spring sniffles!

Only use Pebeo Porcelaine 150® paints to paint items and follow the manufacturer's instructions to cure the paint.

Paint the cup amber...gently rub paint to give it some texture. Paint the teapot lid and the flat area and sides of the spoon rest yellow. While the paint is drying, refer to

Stenciling, page 134, and use the lemon pattern on page 139 to make a stencil. Use the stencil to paint yellow lemon wedges around the cup.

Use your fingertip to stamp green "leaves" around the teapot and down the handle, on the lid and on the spoon rest. Use black paint and a liner paintbrush to outline the wedges and leaves, draw dotted-line stems and tendrils and to write a message around the top of the pot.

CITRUS MINT TEA
This tea is also delicious served over ice.

3 regular-size tea bags
4 to 6 sprigs fresh mint
4 c. boiling water
⅔ c. sugar
⅔ c. grapefruit juice
½ c. lemon juice, freshly squeezed
Garnish: lemon slices

Place tea bags and mint in a 2-quart heatproof container. Add the boiling water; cover and steep for 5 minutes. Discard tea bags and mint. Add sugar; stir to dissolve. Stir in grapefruit juice and lemon juice. Serve warm garnished with lemon slices. Makes 1½ quarts.

Sheri Berger

The only thing to do is to hug one's friend tight and do one's job.

—EDITH WHARTON

COUNTRY FRIENDS™ EMERGENCY KIT

PAINT AN OLD SUITCASE OR TOOLBOX TO HOLD "EMERGENCY" SUPPLIES:

chamomile Tea

Tissues

Chocolate Candy

Fuzzy Slippers

Teddy for hugging

GOOD FOR 1 ERRAND

Coupons for casseroles, errands & chores

DELIVER YOUR KIT TO A FRIEND WHO NEEDS SUPPORT OR A HELPING HAND ~ *that's what friends are for!*

Instructions for our "emergency" kit begin on page 123…what a great pick-me-up for a friend who's not feeling her best!

FRIENDSHIP JARS

Celebrate spring with all of your friends, co-workers, secret pals or neighbors...just hand them one of these sweet little treat jars and watch the smiles! To decorate the lid, remove the wires from an 11" length of 1½" wide wired ribbon; work *Running Stitches*, page 133, along one long edge, then glue the opposite edge around the edge of a standard-size canning lid. Pull the stitches to gather the ribbon tightly over the lid; tie the threads together and trim the ends. Use paint pens to draw lines or details on the ring part of the lid. For the handle, center an 18" length of the same ribbon over the top of a 4-oz. treat-filled jar, then twist the ring onto the jar. Knot ribbon ends together and trim with pinking shears.

Treat yourself to a good friend.

TEACUP CANDLES

What to do, what to do with all of those only-one-left, too-pretty-to-throw-away cups and saucers? Turn them into "tea-lious" candleholders for yourself or for your friends! All you have to do is purchase waxed wicks and creamy wax in your favorite springtime scent and color, then follow the manufacturer's instructions to add the wick and wax to the teacup. Simple, beautiful and quick!

Forget about the chores and go to the park with a friend. Take along a bag of popcorn and share it with the birds. The vacuuming will wait!

...all's dear that comes from a friend.

~ HORACE

BANANA ORANGE BREAD
Really a treat to give and eat!

2 c. all-purpose flour
1 t. baking powder
1 t. baking soda
1 t. pumpkin pie spice
6-oz. can frozen orange juice
    concentrate
2 ripe bananas
2 eggs
1 c. raisins
1 c. walnuts

Mix dry ingredients together. Blend orange juice, bananas and eggs; add to dry ingredients. Stir in raisins and walnuts. Pour mixture into a 9"x5" greased loaf pan and bake at 350 degrees for 35 minutes. Cool on a rack before cutting into 9 one-inch slices. May be served hot or cold, plain or with cream cheese and butter.

Ruth Palmer
Glendale, UT

Welcome new neighbors with a batch of cut-out cookies. Cut a card stock tag, sew on a quilt snippet and buttons, then add your message. Be sure to include your name and phone number! Watch garage sales and flea markets for vintage linens to line the basket.

some of our **best friends** live right next door...

tHANK your lucky stars for a great neigHBor.

Show your appreciation for an extra-special friend with a simple cross-stitched bouquet...and don't forget to share your handmade calling cards! See page 124 for the instructions.

HOME SWEET HOME COOKIES

What neighbor wouldn't like these heartwarming cookies?

Cookies:
1 c. butter or margarine, softened
²/₃ cup shortening
2 cups sugar
½ cup honey
2 eggs
2 t. vanilla extract
6 c. all-purpose flour
½ t. salt

In a large bowl, beat butter, shortening and sugar until fluffy. Add honey, eggs and vanilla; beat until smooth. In another large bowl, combine flour and salt. Add dry ingredients to butter mixture; stir until a soft dough forms.
On a lightly floured surface, use a floured rolling pin to roll out dough to ¼-inch thickness. Use a 4½"x3¾" house-shaped cookie cutter to cut out cookies. Use a 2" heart-shaped cookie cutter to cut out cookies. Transfer to a greased baking sheet. Bake house cookies at 350 degrees for 7 to 9 minutes and heart cookies at

350 degrees for 3 to 5 minutes or until bottoms are golden. Cool on baking sheets 2 minutes. Transfer cookies to a wire rack to cool.

Glaze:
3 c. powdered sugar, sifted
4 to 6 T. milk
Red food coloring

Combine powdered sugar and milk in a small bowl; tint red. Place wire rack with heart-shaped cookies over wax paper. Spoon glaze over heart-shaped cookies. Use a small amount of glaze to "glue" to house cookies.

Flea Market Finds

In spring, the Country Friends® can't think of anything that's more fun than making a run for the flea market! Now's the time to plan your "spring cleaning" projects…transform worn or outdated items into brand-new treasures like candlesticks, clever containers, even shelves! *How-to's continue on page 124.*

GLASS GLOBE CANDLEHOLDERS

Craft these beautiful yet functional candleholders with common flea market finds…wooden candleholders and glass light globes. Allowing paint and wax to dry after each application, apply primer, then brown acrylic paint to the candleholders; randomly apply paste floor wax, then paint them white. Lightly sand the candleholders over the waxed areas for an aged look. Place one globe on each candleholder. Trim taper candles shorter than the globes and place them in the candleholders.

to make the common marvelous is the test of a Genius.

– James Russell Lowell –

EverYone LOVeS a bargain.

you are my sunshine !

KNOBBY COAT RACK

Antique glass doorknobs that used to open doors can make an oh-so charming coat rack.

For each knob, drill a hole in the center of an unfinished decorative wooden accent piece. *(Drill bit should be the same size as a bolt that will fit each knob.)* Wipe accents with a tack cloth, then lightly *Dry Brush, page 134*, each accent brown.

Arrange accents on an unfinished wooden plaque and mark the mounting hole placement; drill holes, then wipe plaque with a tack cloth. Apply a thick coat of red pre-colored crackle medium to the plaque and let it dry. Apply a layer of green acrylic paint over the crackle medium and let it dry.

Thread bolts, from back to front, through the holes in the plaque. Thread one accent onto each bolt, then twist one knob onto the bolt.

Attach heavy-duty sawtooth hangers to the back of the rack.

VINTAGE

GO SHOPPING with a FRIEND.

While you're at the flea market this weekend, keep an eye out for a little red wagon to paint for the Fourth of July (turn to page 43 for a sneak peek)!

Things may come to those who wait, but only the things left by those who hustle. —Abraham Lincoln

SALE TODAY→

Dye a battered basket a pretty color…just mix a packet of dye in an old washtub, following packet directions. Wearing rubber gloves, dip basket into the dye, constantly moving it. Remove from dye bath and let it dry on several layers of newspaper over a sheet of plastic. When dry, add decorative hand-painted ants, stars or flowers on each strip…a wonderful picnic basket idea!

You won't believe how simple it is to create this handy message center using an old frame and wooden shutters! The complete instructions are on page 124.

*S*ummer

Oh, the long, lazy days of summer,
with its sunny skies and outdoor
adventures! Take time to enjoy the
beauty of nature…go for walks
(or bicycle rides!) early in the morning,
nurture your garden in the afternoon
and spend the evenings relaxing on the
porch. You can create a welcoming
mini-garden at your front door with
pots of colorful zinnias, periwinkle and
yellow kalanchoe; wind mandevilla vines
'round the columns and plant plenty
of four-o'-clocks and other flowering
plants along the walkway.

Just for DAD

Handmade Father's Day gifts are a terrific way to say, "Dad, you're the best!" Decorate a lapboard with the kids' artwork, make a handyman's snack caddy or fill a big, personalized bowl with munchies...try our zesty mix of popcorn & peanuts. Instructions for the bowls are on page 124.

Of all nature's gifts to the human race, what is sweeter to a man than his children? ~ CICERO (106-43 BC)

Hey, Mom! Now's the time to "clean up" the refrigerator door...use the kids' drawings to decorate a lapboard for Dad.

DAD'S LAPBOARD

Dad will love showing off the kids' artwork on a lapboard he can use while watching television this Father's Day!

Paint a wooden lapboard the desired color, then paint stripes along the edges...remember to let the paint, sealer and glue dry after each application. Spray the fronts and backs of your selected artwork with clear acrylic sealer, then use decoupage glue to fasten them to the board...you may want to glue black photo mount corners to a few of the treasures, or have the kids use paint pens to write endearing words on the board. Paint polka dots randomly on the board, then apply 2 to 3 coats of sealer to the entire board.

CARRY-ALL JAR TOTE

Give Dad a treat and a handy portable storage tote, too!

Use screws to attach the lids from 3 jars to the bottom of a wooden plaque...be sure the screws do not go all the way through the plaque. Use decoupage glue to adhere paper cut-outs to the top of the plaque, then apply 2 to 3 coats of clear acrylic sealer. Use screws to attach a door handle to the top center of the plaque. Fill the jars with treats or goodies Dad will enjoy and twist the jars onto the lids. Refer to *Making a Tag or Label*, page 132, to make a tag to go with the tote.

DAD'S POPCORN & PEANUTS
A quick snack for Dad and the gang!

1/3 c. butter, melted
1 t. dried dill weed
1 t. Worcestershire sauce
1/2 t. garlic powder
1/2 t. onion powder
1/4 t. salt
2 qts. popped popcorn
2   1 1/2-oz. cans potato sticks
1 c. mixed nuts

In a large mixing bowl, blend first 6 ingredients together well. Add popcorn, potato sticks and nuts. Toss mixture and place on an ungreased baking sheet. Bake at 350 degrees for 3 minutes; stir mixture and bake another 4 to 5 minutes. Makes 9 cups.

Shelley Turner
Boise, ID

Red, White & Blue
S·A·L·U·T·E

Give an all-American salute to summer with an old-fashioned picnic! You'll need plenty of red, white & blue decorations…how about a super-simple porch swag or an easy-to-paint mailbox cover? Or you can fix up that little red wagon to use as a patriotic planter. The porch swag instructions begin on page 124.

PATRIOTIC MAILBOX COVER

Your home will shine with American pride when you decorate your mailbox with this easy-to-do wooden cover.

Start by cutting 14 wooden lattice strips the same length as your mailbox. Spacing ¼" apart, arrange the strips wrong-side up on a flat surface; leaving about 10" at each end of the wire free, staple 16-gauge wire 3" from each end to hold the strips together. Apply wood-tone spray to the strips, then randomly apply paste floor wax (when sanded, this will create an aged look). Paint half of the middle 6 strips blue; alternating colors, paint the strips red or white. *Sponge Paint, page 134,* white stars on the blue strips. Randomly sand the strips, wipe with a tack cloth and apply 2 to 3 coats of clear acrylic sealer. Arrange the cover on the mailbox; twist the wire ends together under the mailbox to secure.

To create a whimsical planter-on-wheels, use white acrylic paint to dry-brush stripes on a red wagon, then use a liner brush to add blue stars and write patriotic sayings around the rim…like "God Bless America," "Land That I Love," "United We Stand," "Freedom For All" and "My Home Sweet Home." Read our Painting Techniques on page 134 before you start.

PICNIC BARBECUED CHICKEN SANDWICHES

These are delicious hot or cold, depending on where you'll be enjoying them.

3 lbs. chicken thighs and breasts, skinned, cooked, boned and shredded
1 c. catsup
1¾ c. water
1 onion, finely chopped
1 t. salt
1 t. celery seed

1 t. chili powder
¼ c. brown sugar, packed
1 t. hot pepper sauce
¼ c. Worcestershire sauce
¼ c. red wine vinegar
6 kaiser rolls

Combine all ingredients except rolls in large saucepan and simmer for 1½ hours. Pile onto rolls. Serve warm or chill meat and make into sandwiches. Pack in a thermal container with ice and serve cold.

Summertime is cookout time and there are plenty of patriotic occasions to celebrate while school's out. Invite your family, the neighbors and all the kids for a day of fun in the sun and serve traditional barbecue, potato salad and deviled eggs (Celebration Deviled Eggs recipe is on page 46). You can show your independence with a rick-rack flag pin (great for favors, too), a star-spangled tablecloth and painted flowerpots. The craft instructions are on page 125.

GARDEN-FRESH NEW POTATO SALAD
Watch it disappear!

1½ lbs. new potatoes, cubed
¾ lb. fresh green beans, snapped
1 sweet red pepper, chopped
1 red onion, chopped
½ c. vegetable oil
¼ c. cider vinegar
2 T. Dijon mustard
1 t. fresh parsley, chopped
1 t. fresh dill weed, chopped
1 t. sugar

Cook potatoes in boiling water 10 minutes; add green beans and bring to a boil. Continue boiling until potatoes are tender. Drain and allow to cool. Place in a large serving bowl. Add sweet red pepper and onion to cooked potatoes and beans. Combine remaining ingredients and pour over vegetables. Toss to coat; chill thoroughly before serving. Serves 12.

FRESH TOMATO SALAD
This dish is at home with a more elegant meal or your basic backyard gathering!

4 yellow tomatoes, chopped
4 red tomatoes, chopped
2 cucumbers, peeled and chopped
1 red onion, thinly sliced
3 to 4 sprigs fresh basil, chopped
salt and pepper to taste
1 c. vinaigrette dressing
Garnish: fresh basil

Combine all ingredients except garnish in a clear glass bowl; toss. Serve immediately at room temperature. Garnish with basil. Makes 6 to 8 servings.

Carla Meredith
Belchertown, MA

Use colorful cotton bandannas instead of paper napkins at your picnic. Tie one around each set of utensils. After the party, just toss them in the washer.

Summertime favorites...Fresh Tomato Salad, Picnic Barbecued Chicken Sandwiches, Garden-Fresh New Potato Salad and Home Run Bean Bake (recipe on page 46).

QUICK SUMMER SLAW
A GUARANTEED PARTY PLEASER... EVERYONE WILL WANT THE RECIPE!

PACKAGE OF COLE SLAW MIX
1 BUNCH GREEN ONIONS, CHOPPED
½ c. SHELLED SUNFLOWER SEEDS
½ c. ALMONDS, SLIVERED & SLICED
½ c. OIL
3 T. SUGAR
3 T. CIDER VINEGAR
PACKAGE CHICKEN-FLAVORED NOODLES

TOSS SLAW MIX, GREEN ONIONS, SUNFLOWER SEEDS & ALMONDS TOGETHER IN A BOWL. IN A SMALL BOWL, WHISK TOGETHER OIL, SUGAR, VINEGAR & SEASONING PACKET FROM NOODLES 'TIL WELL BLENDED. POUR OVER SLAW AND MIX. CHILL. JUST BEFORE SERVING, STIR IN DRY, CRUSHED NOODLES.

★VARIATIONS~ TRY BALSAMIC, HERBAL OR RASPBERRY VINEGAR IN PLACE OF CIDER VINEGAR. SUBSTITUTE HOT & SPICY CHICKEN-FLAVORED NOODLES FOR A ZINGY FLAVOR.

CALIFORNIA LEMONADE

Cardamom is a fragrant spice from India that tastes much like cinnamon.

1½ c. sugar
1 c. lemon juice, freshly squeezed
5 cardamom seeds, ground

Combine sugar and lemon juice in a small saucepan. Boil at medium heat for 8 to 10 minutes. Add cardamom seeds and store in refrigerator. To prepare lemonade, mix one tablespoon of concentrate with one cup sparkling water.

CELEBRATION DEVILED EGGS

Between me, my 4 brothers and sisters and our children, there are 10 birthdays and 3 anniversaries in the summer months! Along with graduations, Father's Day and the 4th of July, we do a lot of celebrating...any excuse to get together!

12 eggs, hard-boiled
½ c. mayonnaise
2 T. onion, chopped
1 t. fresh chives, chopped
1 t. fresh parsley, chopped
1 t. dry mustard
½ t. paprika
½ t. dried dill weed
¼ t. salt
¼ t. pepper
¼ t. garlic powder
milk
Garnish: paprika and parsley

Remove shells from eggs. Cut eggs in half lengthwise and remove yolks. Place yolks in a shallow bowl and mash with a fork. Add rest of ingredients, except milk and garnish, to egg yolks. Stir. If necessary, stir in a little milk to achieve the desired consistency. Spoon the yolk mixture into the egg-white halves. Cover and chill before serving. Garnish with paprika and parsley. Makes 24.

Barb Bargdill
Gooseberry Patch

HOME RUN BEAN BAKE

Baked beans are always a favorite side dish at our home. Great served with bratwursts or hamburgers...always a hit!

1 lb. dry red kidney beans
1 lb. dry Great Northern beans
1 T. salt
1 lb. Kielbasa, sliced
2 T. water
3 onions, chopped
2 10-oz. bags frozen lima beans, thawed
2 baking apples, peeled, cored and chopped
4 cloves garlic, chopped
¾ c. molasses
¾ c. tomato sauce
½ c. Dijon mustard

Rinse and sort beans. Place beans and salt in a large saucepan, cover with water and bring to a boil. Boil 2 minutes, turn off heat and cover pan; let stand one hour. In a heavy skillet, cook Kielbasa and water over medium heat 10 minutes. Add onions and continue to cook until Kielbasa is browned, about 10 minutes. Remove from skillet and set aside. Drain soaked beans, reserving cooking liquid. Place beans in a 6-quart casserole dish, add lima beans, apples and garlic. Stir in Kielbasa mixture. Combine molasses, tomato sauce and mustard; stir well. Pour evenly over bean mixture. Add just enough reserved bean cooking liquid to cover the beans. Cover casserole dish and bake at 350 degrees for 1½ hours. Reduce heat to 275 degrees and continue to bake for another 6 hours. Add more liquid to beans to keep them moist during baking. Serves 16 to 20.

Helen Murray
Mount Vernon, OH

Be sure to save room for dessert! For rave reviews, try treats like Deluxe Ice Cream Sandwiches, refreshing Fruit Compote or My-Oh-My Peach Pie.

My Oh My Peach Pie

We declare! The best peach pie I ever did eat!

4 c. peaches, quartered & peeled
1/2 c. sugar
1/2 t. nutmeg
dash salt
1 egg
2 T. cream

1/2 c. all-purpose flour
1/4 c. brown sugar, packed
2 T. butter
9" unbaked pie shell

Arrange peaches in pie shell ~ sprinkle with sugar, nutmeg & salt. Beat egg & cream ~ pour over peaches. Mix flour, brown sugar & butter 'til crumbly, then sprinkle over pie. Bake at 425° for 35 to 45 minutes.

FRUIT COMPOTE

Perfect for summer's delicious bounty of berries, peaches, nectarines, melons and cherries…refreshing endings for any picnic!

Syrup:
1 c. water
1/2 c. sugar
3/4 c. fresh mint, chopped
1 T. fresh lemon juice
Optional: 1/4 c. bourbon

Compote:
1/4 cantaloupe, seeded
1/4 honeydew, seeded
1/2 lb. sweet cherries, pitted
3 ripe peaches, thinly sliced
3 T. fresh mint, thinly sliced
Garnish: fresh mint sprigs

To make syrup, combine water and sugar in a medium saucepan over low heat until sugar dissolves. Add mint and boil 5 minutes over medium heat. Let cool completely. Strain mixture into a bowl, pressing firmly on the mint to extract flavor. Discard solids. Mix the lemon juice and bourbon into the syrup. Cover and refrigerate; can be made ahead of time. For compote, scoop melons with a melon baller. Combine all fruits and sliced mint; add syrup and toss. Refrigerate for 30 minutes. Spoon into pretty pedestal glasses or into a watermelon half and garnish with mint sprigs. Serves 6.

DELUXE ICE CREAM SANDWICHES

We like these chewy, thin oatmeal cookies.

Cookies:
1 c. butter, melted
4 c. long-cooking oats, uncooked
1 c. all-purpose flour
1 t. salt
1 1/2 c. sugar
1/2 c. brown sugar, packed
2 t. vanilla extract
2 eggs, lightly beaten

Sandwiches:
1/2 gallon natural vanilla ice cream
Garnish: sprinkles

Combine butter, oats, flour, salt, sugars and vanilla; stir well to combine. Add eggs and mix thoroughly. On a baking sheet that has been covered with parchment paper, spoon 1 1/2 tablespoons of batter for each cookie, leaving about 3 inches between cookies. Flatten cookies into 3" circles. Bake until golden, about 10 minutes. Let cool. Makes 2 dozen. Unwrap block of vanilla ice cream and slice into 1-inch-thick slices, cutting into squares big enough to slightly overlap edges of cookies. Sandwich ice cream between cookies. Dip edges of sandwiches into sprinkles. Wrap individually and freeze until ready to serve.

Make pretty raspberry ice cubes for your lemonade! Halfway fill each compartment of an ice-cube tray with water; freeze. Place a fresh, whole raspberry on each ice cube, fill compartments with water and freeze until solid.

Hey BATTER • BATTER • BATTER

PLAY BALL!

Enjoy some old-fashioned fun with your neighborhood friends! Set up an area outside for a game of horseshoes, softball, tug-of-war, scavenger hunt or Red Rover. It's a terrific way to play together.

Put together kid-safe party packs for the youngsters to enjoy! Decorate a white pail with stickers (you may need to use spray adhesive and finish with clear acrylic sealer if you're using a metal bucket), then fill with goodies…noisemakers, plastic bubble wrap for popping, mini flags, flashlights with fiber-optic sprays, silly sunglasses, etc.

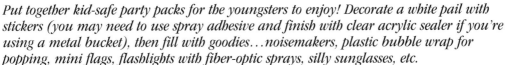

Host the "Summer Olympics" for neighborhood kids. Keep the events fun...have kids balance feathers on their heads while carrying water balloons, run races holding inflated beach balls between their knees and target-shoot with the garden hose! Make fun "medals" for all!

★ROLL BEACH BALLS WITH YOUR NOSE ⌒ RACE ACROSS THE LAWN! ★ PICK UP PENNIES WITH YOUR TOES OFF THE BOTTOM OF THE SWIMMING POOL ★ WASH YOUR BIKES IN THE HOSE ⌒ GET GOOD & WET! ★

Backyard
★ FUN ★
Waterpark

★ RUN THROUGH THE SPRINKLERS ★ WATER·BALLOON TOSS ★ GET PRUNY-TOED IN THE POOL! ★
EAT DRIPPY ORANGE POPSICLES AND RINSE OFF IN THE GARDEN HOSE ★ MAKE MUD PIES & WET SAND CASTLES

Gather 'round a bonfire! Just make a quick phone call to invite the neighbors, and before you know it, you'll have your backyard filled with eager kids and parents! Everyone will love an evening spent together under the stars playing flashlight tag, hide-and-seek, telling stories and toasting marshmallows. If you live in an area where you can't have open fires, use the barbecue grill instead!

Simple Garden Pleasures

Capture the simple beauty of an old-fashioned summer garden with a bouquet of fresh ideas…a trio of stitched flowers, "sew-simple" pillows, a dried rose wreath and a charming topiary in a pastel-striped pot. To make the pillows and framed florals, turn to page 125.

Create your own romantic summer hideaway right on your very own porch. Decorate with white wicker, white tablecloths, crocks full of flowers, candles and white trellises on the sides of the porch. Create as much shade as possible. Add some old flowery cushions and some iced tea or lemonade, and sit there as much as possible with those you love!

— Deb Damari-Tull

SUMMER WREATH

Simple & elegant is what this wreath is. We used dried flowers and naturals on our wreath, but if you grow a garden chock-full of summer offerings, feel free to use them instead.

Begin with a wreath made from dried naturals. Arrange and glue shelf fungi (spray the fungi with sealer before adding it to the wreath), dried flowers and grass along the bottom of the wreath. Fill in any holes with more dried flowers. Tie one yard of ribbon into a bow with several loops and glue it to the wreath. Thread craft wire through the top back of the wreath and twist the ends together for a hanger. Now, you're ready to display this natural beauty for all to enjoy.

SUMMER TOPIARY

The delightful scents of summer are beautifully displayed in this handpainted clay pot...oh-so simple to make, and you can enjoy them for a long time!

Prime, then paint a 6" diameter clay pot light yellow; paint darker yellow vertical stripes around the pot under the rim. Lightly sand the pot, then wipe with a tack cloth and apply a coat of clear acrylic sealer.

Fill the pot with plastic foam. Use a craft knife to cut a hole at the center of the foam. Gather a layer of dried white daisies around a bunch of larkspur, then a layer of dried lavender around the daisies; secure stems with a rubber band. Place the stems in the pot, then glue dried sheet moss over the foam. Tie a length of ribbon into a bow around the stems, covering the rubber band.

Use pretty ribbons to bundle stems of Sweet Annie and hang them on your fence posts or gate. Every time you brush against them, they'll release a sweet fragrance.

CHeerY CHerrieS

Who could resist the colorful appeal of orchard-fresh cherries?
Give your kitchen a sweet summertime makeover…add accessories
like a painted teakettle and stitch up pretty towels, an apron and
a whimsical pot holder! Instructions are on page 125.

Make "instant" kitchen curtains from print cotton dish towels! Place a tension rod across the lower half of the window and use clip-on café curtain rings to hang towels lengthwise. To make a matching valance, simply hang towels horizontally from a second tension rod.

Cheery Cherry Tea

a recipe from Michelle Campen
★ Peoria, IL

15-oz. jar orange drink mix
1 c. sugar
1 c. unsweetened instant tea
½ c. lemonade powder
0.13-oz. pkg. cherry drink mix
2 t. cinnamon
1 t. nutmeg

Blend all ingredients together well and store in an airtight container. Makes about 5 cups of dry mix.

CHEERY CHERRY
TEA

Stir 1 to 2 tablespoons of tea mix in 1 cup of hot or cold water.

CHERRY TEAKETTLE

No patterns needed…using acrylic paint for metal, you can turn a plain old white teakettle into a cheery kitchen accessory.

Using a flat brush in the desired width for your squares, paint a checkerboard border along the bottom of the teakettle. Paint plump red cherries with green stems around the kettle…add green leaves to the stems. Paint a small highlight of white on each cherry, accent the leaves and stems with yellow and add a black highlight at the base of each stem. Use the end of the paintbrush to add dots randomly around the teakettle and let the paint dry.

HAND TOWEL

Transform a purchased kitchen towel with checkerboard stripes into one that looks like you spent hours on it. Sew jumbo rick-rack along the inner edge of one border, then work embroidery floss *Backstitches*, page 133, along the opposite edge and the edges of the next stripe.

For the cherries, cover three 1⅛" diameter buttons from a covered button kit with red fabric. Sew the cherries to the towel, then work embroidery floss *Backstitches* for the stems. Fold a length of green grosgrain ribbon into 3 loops, then sew the center of the loops at the top of the stems.

Add cheer to the breakfast table with a table topper and matching chair pads...trim them with jumbo rick-rack and oversize buttons just for fun! Instructions for the chair cushions and covers are on page 126.

CHERRY TABLE TOPPER

Our topper fits a 20" square table...if your table is a different size, cut your square to fit and cut your border pieces the same length as one side of the square.

Cut a 28" square of fabric; cut four 28" long pieces from border fabric. Turn the short and bottom edges of the border pieces 1/4" to the wrong side and sew in place. Matching right sides and raw

edges, center, then sew one border piece to each side of the square...sew jumbo rick-rack over the seam lines and a button at each corner of the topper.

Cherry Pie

...UNBELIEVABLY GOOD!

INGREDIENTS:

- PASTRY FOR A DOUBLE-CRUST PIE *or* TWO ALREADY-PREPARED PIE CRUSTS
- 1-1½ C. SUGAR
- 4 T. MINUTE TAPIOCA
- 4 C. PITTED TART RED CHERRIES — FRESH, FROZEN OR CANNED
- ½ t. ALMOND EXTRACT OR ½ t. CINNAMON
- 1 T. MARGARINE
- OPTIONAL: RED FOOD COLORING

Combine sugar & tapioca in saucepan. Fold in fresh or frozen cherries; blend well. (If using canned cherries, drain juice from fruit and mix juice with sugar & tapioca in saucepan. Set aside cherries.)

Cook over medium heat, stirring constantly, 'til mixture has come to a boil. Remove from heat.

Add extract & butter. (Add canned cherries at this time.) One drop of food coloring may be added to enhance color. Cool mixture before placing in pie crust shell.

While filling is cooling, prepare pie crust according to recipe if making from scratch.

Line bottom of 9" pie pan with one rolled pie crust dough. Place cooled filling in pie shell. Cut slits in second pie crust and place on top of cherry filling. Seal & flute edges.

Bake at 400° for 30 - 35 minutes.

When selecting fresh cherries, choose the ones that are firm, plump and blemish-free with bright, glossy skin. Store fresh cherries in the refrigerator for no more than three days (use a plastic bag with holes to allow air circulation). Remove stems and wash just before eating...what a sweet treat!

PIE BIRD FAN PULL

Oh-so clever...a fan pull to catch the eye!

Choose a colorful ceramic pie bird, then cut 20" lengths of chenille yarn, rick-rack and ½" wide fabric strips in colors that coordinate with the bird.

For the tassel, bundle the strips together and wrap a length of craft wire several times around the middle, leaving the wire ends long. Fold the bundle in half and secure the wire ends tightly around the end of a pull chain; trim the wire ends. Thread the opposite end of the chain up through the pie bird, pulling the tassel up into the bird.

G·A·R·D·E·N MEDLEY

The summer harvest provides a fresh medley of flavors that make it easy to add a little home-grown zip to your menus. If you're not a gardener, visit the farmers' market for a wonderful selection of fruits & veggies. Here are some of our favorite garden treats…enjoy the tastes of summer!

Clockwise from lower left: Hot Peach Jam, Fresh Corn-Tomato Salsa, Confetti Salad with Herbal Dressing, Bread & Butter Pickles, Summer Tomatoes

CONFETTI SALAD
You may use bottled dressing, or make our Herbal Dressing.

1 zucchini, shredded
1 carrot, shredded
1 green pepper, shredded
1 yellow squash, shredded
1 sweet red pepper, shredded
⅓ c. vinaigrette or sweet-and-sour
    dressing

Combine vegetables and toss with dressing. Serves 4 to 6.

HERBAL DRESSING
Try this tasty dressing on Confetti Salad or a mix of fresh greens from the garden.

½ t. pepper
½ t. fresh chives, finely chopped
½ t. fresh parsley, finely chopped
½ t. fresh tarragon, finely
    chopped
1 clove garlic, finely minced
10 T. olive oil
3 T. wine vinegar
1 t. Dijon mustard
½ t. salt

Combine all ingredients. Blend with wire whisk. Serves 6 to 8.
Marlene Wetzel-Dellagatta

Some herbs can help your vegetables grow! Plant basil, borage, chives and parsley near tomatoes to enhance flavor and repel pests. Mint drives away white cabbage moths, but keep it contained or it'll take over your garden! Dill helps your cabbage grow, but keep it away from carrots and tomatoes. Thyme stimulates overall growth in the garden.

"To get the best results, you must talk to your vegetables."

— *Charles, Prince of Wales*

EASY PICKLED PEPPERS
A mix of hot and mild peppers that's great in salads or on sandwiches.

1 qt. vinegar
3 c. water
2 c. oil
⅔ c. salt
¼ c. dried oregano
¼ c. celery seed
4 cloves garlic, minced
8 qts. mixed hot and sweet
    banana peppers, sliced into
    rings
1 stalk celery, sliced

Combine vinegar, water, oil, salt, oregano, celery seed and garlic in a heavy saucepan; bring to a boil. Place peppers and celery in a large heatproof bowl; pour boiling mixture over peppers and celery until just covered. Cover and let stand at room temperature for 8 hours, stirring occasionally. Put into jars and keep refrigerated. Makes 8 quarts.

Kristie Rigo
Friedens, PA

SUMMER TOMATOES
There is nothing better in the summer than tomatoes…home grown with loving care on a patio or in a backyard garden.

4 tomatoes, sliced
1 red onion, sliced into rings
1 green pepper, sliced into rings

Alternate layers of above vegetables in a big, wide bowl.

Marinade:
¼ c. lemon juice
2 T. fresh parsley, chopped
½ t. sugar
1 t. salt
½ c. oil
⅛ t. dried savory
1¼ oz. blue or Roquefort cheese

Mix lemon juice, parsley, sugar, salt, oil and savory. Pour over layered veggies. Sprinkle crumbled cheese over top. Marinate overnight in refrigerator to blend flavors. Serve as a side dish. Serves 6 to 8.

Ruth Kangas

Summer Tomatoes

ZESTY ONION RELISH

Use the grill to make this relish and grill the main course…a wonderful condiment for chicken, pork or beef.

2 lbs. onions, thickly sliced
¼ c. canola oil
3 T. balsamic vinegar
2 T. brown sugar
¼ t. cayenne pepper

Lightly brush onion slices on each side with oil. Place onions on grill and cook over low heat for 15 minutes or until tender and golden. Turn onions to brown each side, coating again with oil as needed. Remove onions from grill and allow to cool. Chop onions and set aside. Simmer vinegar and brown sugar in a saucepan over low heat. Stir until sugar has dissolved then pour over onions. Sprinkle cayenne pepper over top and stir again. Serve warm, refrigerating any leftovers.

TOMATO-PEPPER RELISH

This makes a delicious Christmas relish to share during the holidays.

1 gal. green tomatoes, chopped
8 red peppers, chopped
2 onions, chopped
2 c. white vinegar
2 c. sugar
2 T. salt
1 T. celery seed
2 sticks cinnamon
2 T. whole allspice
2 T. whole cloves

Combine green tomatoes, peppers, onions, vinegar, sugar, salt and celery seed. Stir in cinnamon, allspice and cloves or add to mixture in a spice bag. Bring vegetables to a boil. Reduce heat and simmer for 15 minutes. Ladle into hot, sterilized pint jars, leaving ½" headspace. Wipe rims and adjust lids. Process in a boiling water canner for 15 minutes. Makes 10 pints.

GARLIC DILL PICKLES

For a really different pickle, try substituting fresh rosemary or tarragon for the dill.

13½ c. white vinegar
13½ c. water
2¼ c. pickling salt
1½ c. pickling spices
10 lbs. cucumbers, 2" to 3" long, thoroughly cleaned
12 cloves garlic, peeled and minced
15 stems of fresh dill

Combine the vinegar, water, salt and spices to make a brine and bring to a boil in a large pot. Fill 2 hot, sterilized pint jars with the cucumbers, garlic and dill; cover with the hot brine. Leave ½" headspace at top of each jar. Wipe the rims and adjust the lids. Process in a boiling water canner for 15 minutes. Makes 2 pints.

FRESH CORN-TOMATO SALSA

A delicious, spicy chip dip…or spoon on top of Spanish rice.

1 c. fresh corn, cooked
1 ripe tomato, peeled, seeded and chopped
1 cucumber, peeled, seeded and chopped
1 onion, finely chopped
1 stalk celery, chopped
1 jalapeño pepper, chopped
3 T. lime juice, freshly squeezed
½ t. cumin
1 garlic clove, minced
½ t. salt

In medium bowl, stir together all ingredients until mixed well. Cover and refrigerate, allowing flavors to blend for at least an hour.

HOT PEACH JAM

Delicious on crackers with cream cheese, as an ice cream topping or a glaze for ham!

1½ c. cider vinegar
¼ c. jalapeño pepper, quartered, or other green chile pepper
5 c. fresh peaches, finely chopped
6 c. sugar
1 t. celery seed
1 t. ground allspice
2 3-oz. pouches liquid pectin

Combine vinegar and pepper in blender. Process to desired fineness. Combine with peaches, sugar, celery seed and allspice in large pot (not aluminum) and bring to a boil. Reduce heat and simmer 50 minutes, stirring often. Let cool 2 minutes, then add pectin. Ladle into hot, sterilized pint jars, leaving ¼" headspace. Wipe rims and adjust lids. Process in a boiling water canner for 5 minutes. Makes 5 pints.

Sonia Bracamonte
Tucson, AZ

Get an early start on Christmas gifts…set aside some of your best home-canned goodies to share!

Basic Recipe *for making flavored vinegars:*

Spiced Vinegar, Raspberry Vinegar

HERBAL VINEGARS
½ to 1 c. fresh herbs
2 c. vinegar
other seasonings such as garlic, shallots, spices, etc.

FRUIT VINEGARS
1 c. fruit
1 c. vinegar
other seasonings such as citrus peel or spices, etc.

HOW TO S·E·A·L A CORKED BOTTLE
½ PARAFFIN TO ½ BEESWAX
GROUND CINNAMON OR OTHER SPICE
CRAYON FOR COLORING

Melt paraffin & beeswax in a small tin or coffee can placed in a pan of simmering water. Be careful – paraffin is flammable! Use low heat. Add crayon & cinnamon. Dip top of corked bottle into warm wax. Allow excess to drip back in can. Rotate bottle slowly as wax cools for even distribution. You may need to dip the bottle several times to get a thick seal.

There are TWO methods for flavoring vinegar:

METHOD #1
Heat vinegar & herbs in a non-metal pan (metal reacts with vinegar causing a tarnished taste) to almost boiling. Do Not Boil! Pour into large clean glass jar.

Herb Lady

METHOD #2
Place herbs or fruit in bottle. Pour vinegar over items in bottle. Do Not Heat vinegar. Cork and allow flavors to blend for 3 to 4 weeks. Cover with wax paper or plastic wrap if using a metal lid to seal jar. Vinegar should rest, unmoved & undisturbed, in cool, dark place 'til steeping process is complete.

SPICED VINEGAR
A very flavorful vinegar.

3" cinnamon stick
1 whole cracked nutmeg
1 T. whole cloves
1 T. whole allspice
1 T. black peppercorns
4 c. red wine vinegar

Place spices in a glass jar and cover with vinegar. Place in a cool place for 4 weeks. Strain the mixture and bottle. Store in a cool dark place. Makes 2 pints.

Marlene Wetzel-Dellagatta

RASPBERRY VINEGAR
A favorite way to preserve fresh summer berries!

2 c. fresh or frozen raspberries
2 T. sugar
2 c. white wine vinegar

Heat raspberries and sugar in a saucepan over low heat until sugar dissolves, stirring often; cool. Add vinegar; strain, discarding solids. Store in an airtight container in refrigerator until ready to use. Makes about one pint.

Gail Prather
Bethel, MN

PICKLED BEETS

They're not only tasty…their deep red color makes the table look so pretty.

4 beets, trimmed, cleaned
   and peeled
1 yellow onion, peeled and sliced
1 clove garlic, peeled and sliced
1 c. cider vinegar
1/4 c. sugar
1 T. cardamom seeds
1 T. whole cloves
1/8 t. salt

In a medium pan, cover the beets with cold water and bring the water just to a boil. Reduce heat and simmer, partially covered, 30 minutes, or until tender. Reserve about 2 cups of the cooking liquid. Slice the beets and put into a quart jar along with the sliced onion and garlic. In the reserved beet juice, add the vinegar, sugar and spices. Heat just enough to dissolve the sugar. Pour the mixture into the jar, over the beets. Allow to cool to room temperature; then cover and refrigerate at least 8 hours before serving. Makes one quart.

BREAD & BUTTER PICKLES

Everyone's old-fashioned favorite!

1 gal. cucumbers, unpeeled
8 onions
2 lbs. green peppers
1/2 c. coarse salt
5 c. vinegar
5 c. sugar
2 T. mustard seed
1 t. turmeric
1 t. whole cloves

Slice cucumbers and onions into thin slices and peppers into strips. Dissolve salt in water and pour over sliced vegetables to cover. Pour ice on top of cucumbers. Let stand 2 to 3 hours. Drain. Combine vinegar, sugar and spices and bring to a boil. Add drained vegetables and heat to boiling point (do not boil). Ladle into hot, sterilized pint or quart jars, leaving 1/2" headspace. Wipe rims and adjust lids. Process in a boiling water canner for 10 minutes.

Pat Husek
St. Joseph, MO

GARDEN VEGETABLE JUMBLE

A great way to use the last veggies from this year's garden.

2 T. oil
4 c. zucchini, chopped
1 c. onion, chopped
1 c. carrots, chopped
1 green pepper, sliced into strips
1 tomato, chopped
2 t. fresh basil, diced
salt and pepper to taste
1/2 c. shredded Cheddar cheese

Place oil in a skillet, turning to coat bottom. Add zucchini, onion, carrots and green pepper and cook over medium heat until crisp-tender. Stir in tomato, basil, salt and pepper. Add cheese on top. Cover skillet and allow cheese to melt. Serves 6 to 8.

Take Zippy Vegetable Casserole to your family reunion…everyone will want the recipe! *To make the casserole cozy, turn to page 126.*

RADISH JELLY

Serve with cream cheese and crackers or spread on a roast beef sandwich.

2 c. radishes, finely chopped
2½ c. sugar
¾ c. water
1¾-oz. pkg. pectin
2 t. prepared horseradish

In a large saucepan, combine radishes, sugar and water over medium-high heat, stirring constantly until sugar dissolves. Bring to a rolling boil. Add pectin; stir until dissolved. Bring to a rolling boil again and boil 1 minute longer. Remove from heat and skim off foam. Stir in horseradish. Ladle into hot, sterilized jars and seal; cool. Store in refrigerator. Makes about 2 pints.

Marie Alana Gardner
North Tonowanda, NY

Zippy Vegetable Casserole

MAKE IT AHEAD OF TIME & STORE IN THE FRIDGE UP TO 24 HOURS... YUM!

3 c. fresh plum tomatoes, seeded & chopped
3 c. zucchini, chopped
3 medium onions, chopped
3 cloves garlic, minced

¼ c. fresh parsley, minced
¼ c. fresh basil, finely chopped
1 c. mozzarella cheese, shredded
2½ c. bread crumbs

Coat two 7"x11" baking dishes with nonstick vegetable spray. Place tomatoes, zucchini, onions, garlic, parsley & basil in baking dishes. Mix together cheese & bread crumbs. Toss 1½ c. of the crumb mixture with veggies. Sprinkle remaining crumbs over top of veggies. Refrigerate until ready to bake. Bake at 350° for about 45 minutes.

The time to Relax is when you don't have time for it.

~ Sydney J. Harris ~

ZUCCHINI RELISH

Zucchini is always a favorite from my garden. This relish is great served on steak sandwiches, hamburgers or hot dogs. It's also a perfect hostess, teacher or Christmas gift!

10 c. zucchini squash, chopped
4 c. onions
4 T. salt
2½ c. vinegar
3 c. sugar
1 t. turmeric
½ t. pepper
¼ t. dry mustard
½ t. mustard seed
3 peppers (2 green and 1 red)

Grind squash and onions; add salt. Refrigerate overnight. Drain. Run clear water through the zucchini mixture several times. Drain again. Put ingredients in a large kettle. Add vinegar, sugar, turmeric, pepper, dry mustard and mustard seed. Grind green and red peppers. Add to squash mixture. Stir gently. Bring to a boil and cook 3 minutes. Ladle into 8 hot, sterilized pint jars, leaving ½" of headspace. Wipe rims and adjust lids. Process in a boiling water canner for 10 minutes. Makes 8 pints.

Janet Myers
Reading, PA

Be sure to follow the USDA-recommended water-bath method when canning. Your local Cooperative Extension Service will have the most up-to-date information on canning, and may even offer canning workshops!

When canning, always select fresh, healthy, ripe fruits and vegetables; wash well.

Use real sugar only...don't use artificial sweeteners, sugar substitutes or sugar blends when canning. Never double jam or jelly recipes, as the mixtures may not set properly.

Making Memories

Make the most of a summer afternoon…gather your friends for a scrapbooking party! Ready-to-use pressed flower stickers make it easy to give the invitations a cottage garden look. Ask your guests to bring along their family photos and creative supplies, then spend the afternoon sharing ideas and memories.

FLOWER INVITATION

Announce your memory-making day with this beautiful invitation.

Tear a piece of handmade paper into a rectangle to fit on the front of a blank card; use a craft glue stick to adhere the paper to the card. Overlapping and gluing ends at front, wrap a length of ribbon around the front of the card. Use decorative-edge craft scissors to cut a tag from card stock. Write a message on the tag, then glue the tag to the card. Arrange and adhere self-adhesive botanical stickers to the card. Simple to make!

CANDIED VIOLETS

These delicate, edible confections can be used as decorations on cakes or simply put out for nibblers on a glass plate. Both scent and flavor are exotic. You can also candy fresh mint leaves and other edible flowers. We used violas to match our party invitations.

16-oz. pkg. pasteurized egg whites
perfect, pesticide-free violets and leaves
sugar

Whip egg whites until they're frothy but do not stand in peaks. Wash violets and leaves gently and quickly in cold water and let water drip off. While damp, dip each violet or leaf in the egg white and roll it quickly in sugar to coat evenly, taking care not to get the sugar too thick. Lay on wax paper, without overlapping, to dry. After several hours or a day, the blossoms will be quite crisp and can keep for several months without losing fragrance or flavor. Store in airtight container, layered between wax paper. Makes dozens.

Juanita Williams
Jacksonville, OR

PRETTY LITTLE CAKES

These pretty little cakes make every party a special one.

Cake:
18¼-oz. pkg. white cake mix
1⅓ c. water
2 T. vegetable oil
3 egg whites
2 t. almond extract

Icing:
10 c. sifted powdered sugar
1 c. water
3 T. light corn syrup
1 t. vanilla or almond extract
Garnish: candied violets

For cake, line bottom of a greased 15½"x10½" jelly-roll pan with wax paper; grease wax paper. In a large bowl, combine cake mix, water, oil, egg whites and almond extract. Prepare according to package directions. Pour batter into prepared pan. Bake at 350 degrees for 18 to 22 minutes or until a wooden pick inserted in center of cake comes out clean and top is golden. Cool in pan 10 minutes. Invert cake onto a wire rack and cool completely. Transfer cake to baking sheet covered with wax paper. Freeze cake 2 hours or until firm. Using a serrated knife, cut away sides of cake to straighten. Cut cake into 2-inch squares. Place cake squares 2 inches apart on wire racks with wax paper underneath.

For icing, combine powdered sugar and remaining ingredients except garnish in a large saucepan; cook over low heat, stirring constantly, until smooth. Quickly pour warm icing over cake squares, completely covering top and sides. Spoon all excess icing into saucepan; reheat until smooth. (If necessary, add a small amount of water to maintain icing's original consistency.) Continue pouring and reheating icing until all cakes have been iced twice. Garnish each cake with candied violets. Let icing harden completely. Trim any excess icing from bottom edges of each cake square. Store cakes in an airtight container. Makes about 40 cakes.

REFRESHING MINT PUNCH

I love this! It's such a nice change from traditional punch.

2 c. mint leaves, packed
2 c. water
12-oz. can frozen lemonade
1 qt. ginger ale

Bring mint and water to boil; bruise leaves with potato masher. Set aside overnight. Strain and discard solids. Add lemonade, 3 lemonade cans of water and ginger ale to mint mixture; mix well and serve. Makes 10 to 12 servings.

Mary Murray
Gooseberry Patch

Delightful indulgences…Pretty Little Cakes garnished with Candied Violets, accompanied by Refreshing Mint Punch.

A smiling face is half the meal.
-LATVIAN PROVERB-

Of all nature's gifts to the human race, what is sweeter to a man than his children? ~ CICERO (106-43 BC)

FLORAL SCRAPBOOK

Turn a plain and simple photo album into a sweet memory album. Use decorative-edge craft scissors to cut a piece of handmade paper the size you want for the front of your album; glue it in place. Use a permanent marker to write your family name on a shipping tag; tie a piece of ribbon through the hole in the tag, then glue the tag to the paper. Overlapping as desired, adhere self-adhesive botanical stickers around the edges of the paper and tag.

MEMORY PAGES

Using acid-free papers and adhesives, arrange your photographs on the album pages. To preserve your photos, do like we did and use photo-mount corners to hold them in place. Use small shipping tags to identify the photographs...add ribbons and floral self-adhesive botanical stickers to the pages as desired. Make the pages extra-special by attaching pieces of lace or doilies that belonged to the cherished people in the photos.

Make a scrapbook of family photos to preserve the joys of ordinary days! You'll love recalling a day in the life of your family. Snap candid photos of sleepyheads in their beds at 6 a.m., the 7 a.m. toothbrush brigade, schoolwork, chores…all through the day! Make notes in your book beside each photo in your own handwriting…a lasting memory of a regular, wonderful day!

WHAT An iDeA !

A DAY IN THE LIFE of YOUR FAMILY

Fall

Autumn arrives in a vibrant blaze of color, with bright blue skies and brilliant foliage in shades of red and gold. It's time to unpack your cozy sweaters and light a fire in the hearth…time to send the children off to school and get set to cheer for the local football team! To celebrate the bountiful harvest, adorn your entryway with pots of colorful chrysanthemums and basketfuls of pumpkins, squash and fragrant apples. Swirl bittersweet along the porch railing and treat the front door to a handsome arrangement of dried flowers and grasses.

Who could forget the excitement of the first day of school? Riding the school bus, a fresh box of crayons, a shiny lunchbox and making new friends. It's all those little things that stir up the fondest memories.

CHEWY GRANOLA BARS

These are great for snacks or dessert served warm with ice cream. I sometimes substitute 1/2 cup of cocoa for half of the flour for an extra chocolate delight!

1/2 c. margarine, softened
1 c. brown sugar, packed
1/4 c. sugar
2 T. honey
1/2 t. vanilla extract
1 egg
1 c. all-purpose flour
1 T. cinnamon
1/2 t. baking powder
1/4 t. salt
1 c. quick-cooking oats, uncooked
1 1/4 c. puffed rice cereal
1 c. chopped pecans
1 c. raisins
1 c. chocolate chips

Beat margarine, sugars, honey, vanilla and egg, mixing well. Combine all dry ingredients and add to margarine mixture. Press into a greased 13"x9" baking pan and bake at 350 degrees for 22 to 28 minutes. Let cool; cut into bars. You can substitute peanut butter chips or butterscotch chips for the chocolate if you like. Makes 16 bars.

Laura Flournoy
Columbus, NC

Remember your lunchbox from grade school? Give it a fresh look with autumn motifs and pack it full of naturally delicious Chewy Granola Bars! See page 127 for the instructions.

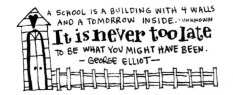

A SCHOOL IS A BUILDING WITH 4 WALLS AND A TOMORROW INSIDE. - UNKNOWN
It is never too late TO BE WHAT YOU MIGHT HAVE BEEN. — GEORGE ELLIOT —

PAINTED NAMEPLATE

The only rules here are to let the primer, paint and sealer dry after each application and to use hot glue for all gluing.

Apply primer, then white paint to a wooden plaque. Paint checkerboards, a few stars and stems for cherries on the plaque. Use a fine-point marker to outline the stars and draw dots around them. Use a black paint pen to write your name really big on the sign, then apply 2 to 3 coats of sealer. Sharpen a wooden pencil and glue it to the plaque. Glue 2 big red buttons on the sign for cherries and a knotted strip of homespun at the top of the stems for leaves.

Show your appreciation for a special teacher with a personalized nameplate for the classroom or a colorfully decorated denim vest; the vest instructions are on page 127.

END ZONE BROWNIES

So easy...add chocolate chips for even more rich flavor.

1/2 c. butter
1 c. sugar
4 eggs
16-oz. can chocolate
   syrup
1 c. plus 1 T. all-purpose
   flour
1 t. vanilla extract
1 c. chopped walnuts
Garnish: powdered sugar

Mix together all ingredients except powdered sugar and pour into a 15"x10" greased jelly-roll pan. Bake at 350 degrees for 20 to 22 minutes. Cool 10 minutes; remove from pan and dust with powdered sugar. Makes 2 1/2 dozen.

★ GOALS ★

are dreams with deadlines.
- Diana Scharf Hunt -

MARY E.

PACK·A·SACK

PERFECT PACKAGING FOR PICNICS, TAILGATE LUNCHES OR KIDS' PARTIES!

HOLLY

STEP ONE: PUT EVERYTHING YOUR GUEST WILL NEED INSIDE A LUNCH-SIZE BAG... (CHOOSE SCHOOL-COLORS FOR TAILGATE LUNCHES, OR TEAM HUES) SANDWICH, COOKIES, WHATEVER!

STEP TWO: FOLD OVER TOP OF BAG AND PUNCH 2 HOLES NEAR TOP.

STEP THREE: SLIDE PENNANT STICK, PENCIL OR STRAW THROUGH HOLES TO KEEP BAG SHUT.

STEP FOUR: GIVE ONE BAG LUNCH TO EACH GUEST AND EAT UP!

During autumn, the high school grandstand is always full for the Friday night football game, so cheer on your team! Pack a basket of goodies to enjoy while the marching band performs at halftime...crunchy apples, spicy molasses cookies and a thermos filled with warm cider would be just right.

Support your local football team at the big game! Stitch up a cozy blanket and hot water bottle cover in school colors and carry along a basketful of chocolatey End Zone Brownies for munching. To make the blanket and bottle cover, see page 127.

Make your house "eerie-sistible" to little ghosts and goblins this Halloween. Our crew of felt-face Jack-'O-Lanterns and glowing luminaries are sure to do the trick!

FELT-FACE PUMPKINS

These faces-of-the-season are safe & easy for children to create…no knives or carving involved! Use a copy machine to size your favorite face pattern from page 146 to fit your pumpkin. Cut out the pattern…child safety scissors will work. Draw around the shapes on the paper side of self-adhesive felt, then cut out the shapes. Peel the paper from the cutouts and adhere the face to your pumpkin. For Jill-'O-Lanterns, tie a strip of Halloween-motif fabric into a big bow around the stem, and you're done. These are quick enough to do even on a school night!

SIDEWALK LUMINARY

For each luminary, fill a plastic zipping bag with water and put into a small tin pail and freeze overnight…this will keep the pail from bending when you punch the holes.

Draw a face on your pail. Use a hammer and awl to punch holes inside the drawn lines and one hole on each side of the pail for the handle. Remove the bag of ice.

Allowing the paint to dry after each application, place the pail upside-down and apply orange stained glass spray paint to the outside.

Paint the face shapes with black.

Trace the leaf pattern from page 147 onto tracing paper and cut out. Use the pattern to cut one leaf from craft tin; punch a hole in the leaf. Paint the leaf green.

For the handle, thread the ends of a length of green craft wire through the holes on each side of the pail; place the leaf on one end of handle, then curl and twist the wire ends to secure. Place a candle in the pail, then hang the luminary on a short garden hook.

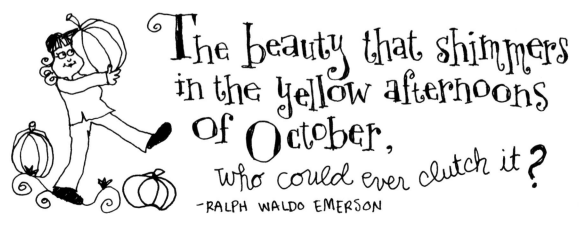

The beauty that shimmers in the yellow afternoons of October, who could ever clutch it?
—RALPH WALDO EMERSON

An autumn welcome...a basket of gourds and pumpkins by the mailbox and corn shocks tied around the post. Top bunches of Indian corn with raffia bows and drape on either side of the basket.

CREEPY CRAWLY SPIDERS

This is a super-simple creepy project for the kids to make. Use a craft stick to hold two foam balls together for the body...we used a 2½" and a 4" diameter ball. Paper maché over the spider body using craft glue and small pieces of tissue paper. After the spider is dry, paint it black. Cut 4 bumpy pipe cleaners in half for legs; stick four legs into each side of the body. Cut 2 bumps from another pipe cleaner and stick into the head for antennae. For each eye, thread one bead onto a large-head straight pin...stick eyes into spider.

OCTOBER is good for A SCARE!

Enjoy a Halloween bonfire...roast hot dogs and marshmallows, drink cocoa and tell ghost stories!

Jack-'O-Lantern Patch instructions on page 128.

"BOO" WELCOME MAT

A simple painted mat is a "boo-tiful" idea to welcome friends into your home. Use a copy machine to enlarge the patterns on page 149 to fit a sisal mat...ours came with the black fabric binding. Cut out the letters and arrange them on the mat. Use a marker to lightly draw around each letter; repeat for the candy corn pattern. Paint the designs. After the paint is good and dry, use a black paint pen to outline the candy corn sections. Finish off with a strip of green grosgrain ribbon glued along the inside edges of the binding.

Enjoy the tastes of autumn with a loaf of Harvest Pumpkin Bread and a jar of Roasted Pumpkin Seeds. The homespun pumpkin pins are so easy to make that you'll have a whole pumpkin patch in no time!

Things that go BUMP IN THE Night.
— CORNISH PRAYER

HARVEST PUMPKIN BREAD
Dress up this bread with raisins or walnuts if you like.

2 c. all-purpose flour
1 c. brown sugar, packed
1 t. cinnamon
¼ t. nutmeg
⅛ t. ground cloves
1 T. baking powder
¼ t. baking soda
¼ t. salt
1 c. canned pumpkin
½ c. milk
⅓ c. butter or margarine, softened
2 eggs

Grease a 9"x5" loaf pan. Combine one cup of flour, brown sugar, cinnamon, nutmeg, cloves, baking powder, baking soda and salt in mixing bowl. Add pumpkin, milk, butter and eggs and beat on low until blended; increase speed to high and beat for 2 minutes. Gradually add remaining flour and beat until well mixed. Pour batter into loaf pan and bake at 350 degrees for 60 to 65 minutes. Makes one loaf.

PUMPKIN PINS

For each pin, layer cotton batting between the wrong sides of two 4" squares of pumpkin-colored homespun. Trace the desired pumpkin shape from page 147 onto tracing paper and pin to the squares. Leaving an opening at the top of the pumpkin to fit a small twig for the stem, sew along the lines of the pattern, then carefully tear away the paper. Use pinking shears to cut out the shape just outside the outer sewn lines. Hot glue the stem between the fabric layers, then glue a jewelry pin back to the back of the pumpkin. For the leaves, cut a 1/2"x4" strip from green fabric; knot strip around the stem.

ROASTED PUMPKIN SEEDS

2 c. seeds
1 T. oil
½ t. salt
....

Rinse pumpkin seeds — dry on paper towels. Toss with oil. Place on baking sheet and bake at 350° for 20 minutes. Toss every 5 to 7 minutes. Remove from oven when golden brown. Salt ∴ eat up!

PUMPKIN SEED JAR

This jar is oh-so quick to make and perfect to hold a batch of roasted pumpkin seeds from your carved Jack-'O-Lantern. Spray paint the outside of the lid from a wide-mouth glass jar. Tie several strands of raffia into a bow around the neck of the jar.

BLACK CATS and GOBLINS and GHOSTIES... OH·MY!

Here's a spooky idea for a children's Halloween party game! First, select objects that are "creepy" to touch...try olives in a glass of water for eyeballs, a leaf for a bat's wing, scraps of torn cotton balls for spiderwebs, a pickle for a witch's nose and rawhide sticks for a skeleton. Place each object in a separate box, then drape with black fabric and label as "Dead-Man's Eyes," "Sleeping Bat's Wings," etc. Let one child at a time reach into the boxes and try to guess what the objects REALLY are!

TOMATO COSTUME

As easily as the Fairy Godmother changed the pumpkin into a coach, you can change your wee one into a too-cute tomato! First, you'll need two pieces of red felt...when folded in half, each piece needs to reach from elbow to elbow and hang from the shoulder to 3" below the knees on the child. Open the felt pieces, place them together and refold. At the center of the fold, use a dinner plate to mark a half-circle for the head opening; cut out the circle. Place the felt pieces over the child's head. Tie a piece of ribbon around each shoulder to gather the felt...it's okay to tie the ribbon at the top of the shoulders because it will be on the inside when you're finished. Now, mark the armholes on each side of the costume, then take it off the child. Time to sew up the sides...only sew up to the marks and sew through all four layers of felt! Sew the felt layers together around the bottom edge. For the elastic casing, fold the bottom edge up 1 1/2" and pin in place. Leaving an opening to insert the elastic, sew along the casing edge. Turn the costume right-side out and place it back on the child. Insert 3/4"w elastic in the casing and adjust to desired tightness and height around the legs. Trim the elastic and secure with a safety pin. Working through the armholes, stuff the tomato to desired plumpness...you can use fiberfill, plastic bags or foam peanuts.

(continued on page 128)

Even if you're short on time, you can "treat" your child to a unique Halloween costume. Choose from a funny bug, a plump tomato, a fancy fairy or a ferociously friendly lion. Instructions for the bug, fairy and lion costumes are on page 128.

"Everything is black and gold, black and gold, tonight: Yellow pumpkins, yellow moon, yellow candlelight: Jet-black cat with golden eyes, shadows black as ink, firelight blinking in the dark with a yellow blink. Black and gold, black and bold, nothing in between. When the world turns black and gold, then it's Halloween!"

— Nancy Byrd Turner

GIMME CANDY.

HALLOWEEN POPCORN BALLS
A fun Halloween treat for all ages.

1 c. light corn syrup
¼ c. margarine
2 T. water
1⅓ c. powdered sugar
1 t. salt
24 large marshmallows
½ t. vanilla extract
5 qts. popped corn, no salt
12-oz. pkg. candy corn pieces

In a heavy saucepan, combine corn syrup, margarine, water, powdered sugar, salt and marshmallows over medium-high heat. Stir until smooth and mixture just comes to a boil. Remove from heat; stir in vanilla. Place popcorn in a large roasting pan. Pour hot mixture over popcorn; toss to coat. Let mixture cool a few minutes before handling. Stir candy corn pieces into popcorn mixture. Wet hands with a very small amount of water and form popcorn balls. Press very firmly with hands when forming balls or they will fall apart! Place on wax paper to cool. Wrap each popcorn ball in cellophane and tie closed with a piece of raffia. Makes one dozen.

Great goodies for kids: candy corn and popcorn are a yummy combination. Place wrapped Halloween Popcorn Balls in a "witch's cauldron" by your front door. Youngsters will also love biting into Marshmallow Cookie Spiders.

MARSHMALLOW COOKIE SPIDERS
Spooky but sweet, these spiders are easy to fix for school parties.

black licorice rope for legs
4¼-oz. tube white icing
9-oz. pkg. chocolate-
   covered marshmallow
   cookies
assorted candies for eyes

For each spider, cut 4 pieces of licorice measuring from 2" to 3" in length. Using a knife, cut each licorice piece in half lengthwise. Place each pair of legs opposite each other, flat side down, on lightly greased wax paper. Cover inside ends of licorice with icing. Gently press cookie onto icing and legs. Use icing to "glue" the candies onto cookie for eyes. Allow icing to set up and carefully transfer cookie spiders to serving plates. Makes 8 spiders.

PAINTED TREAT POTS

Make your treats extra-special by giving in one of these handpainted clay pots. Trace the pumpkin pattern on page 149 onto tracing paper; use transfer paper to transfer several pumpkins around a 4" diameter pot (ours was already painted white). Allowing the paint to dry after each application, paint the pumpkins, then a checkerboard around the bottom of the pot. Use a black permanent marker to outline and add details to the pumpkins and draw dots and tiny stars around them. Apply 2 to 3 coats of clear acrylic sealer to the pot, give it plenty of time to dry, then fill with goodies and treats!

STAMPED TREAT BAGS

These bags are so easy...the kids can make them for school treats. Trace the leaf pattern on page 149 onto tracing paper. For each bag, use the pattern to cut one leaf from green corrugated craft cardboard; punch a hole in the leaf. Stamp pumpkins on a brown lunch-size paper bag; use colored pencils to color them. Fill the bag with treats and surprises, then gather the top of the bag; secure with a green pipe cleaner. Thread the leaf onto one end of the pipe cleaner, then curl the ends.

Autumn Lights

Light up an autumn evening with glowing candles and pumpkin lanterns...they're a snap to make with these quick & easy ideas!

CANDLE JARS

It just wouldn't be fall without the enchanting glow of dancing shadows produced by flickering candlelight. For each of these candles, follow the manufacturer's instructions to melt and fill a clean glass jar with candle wax and a purchased wick. For the label, use a copy machine to size and reproduce a nostalgic seasonal clipping or postcard to fit on the jar. Cut out the label and glue it to card stock, then trim the card stock just a bit larger than the label...glue it to the jar. (You may need to use rubber bands to hold the label in place until dry.) Cut a tag from card stock; punch a hole in one end. Stamp a message on the tag, then use raffia to attach the tag to the jar.

CARVED FAUX PUMPKINS

All that work...and something to show for it year after year! Try carving faux pumpkins for creations that last. You can use premade carving kits and patterns, or come up with your own ideas, then carve them just like real pumpkins. Be creative! Try filling holes with flat accent marbles or painting the carved areas yellow for a fun glow. If your pumpkin didn't come with a light, simply add a clip-on light kit through the back of the pumpkin.

Pumpkins weren't grown in Europe many years ago, so children used to carve turnips for Halloween. When colonists in America planted their crops, pumpkins were more plentiful than turnips, and our modern Jack-'O-Lantern was born!

For me, autumn is a time to really make my house cozy. I like to buy several pumpkins, placing some on my front porch along with the potted plants, and also on the tabletops throughout my house. I also fill baskets with pretty fall leaves and small, colorful gourds and hang Indian corn, tied with raffia, on my front door and over the fireplace, giving a real "harvest" feel to the house. Candles in the holders and lamps change from pastels to dark, rich, autumn colors. Bowls are filled with fragrant potpourri, and place mats and runners are changed to heavier weaves.

— Nancie Gensler

All-cheering plenty,
with her flowing horn,
led yellow autumn,
wreath'd with nodding corn.
— BURNS

Dress pillar candles to coordinate with your autumn décor…turn to page 129 for creative ideas!

There is
no season
when such
PLEASANT
and sunny spots
can be lighted on,
and
produce so pleasant
an effect on the feelings,
as now in
OCTOBER.
- HAWTHORNE -

FLORAL PLACE CARD

Make any place setting special with this beautifully personalized place card. Cut a 4¾"x5½" card from corrugated craft cardboard; match short edges and fold in half. Use decorative-edge craft scissors to cut a 2½"x4½" piece from card stock. Cut a 2¼"x4¼" piece from decorative paper. Glue the card stock piece, then the decorative paper piece on the folded card. Stamp your guest's name on the place card. For the finishing touch, cover the name with a length of sheer ribbon; glue the ribbon ends to the inside of the place card to secure.

LEAF LIGHT-CATCHER

Quick to make, yet elegant to display…that's what this sun-catcher is! Arrange silk or preserved leaves between two 4"x6" panes of glass. Apply a strip of ½" wide self-adhesive copper foil across the top edge of the panes. Cut another length of copper for the handle; trim the paper from the ends and attach to the light-catcher. Starting at the top of one side, cover the remaining edges with copper.

Use the vibrant colors of autumn…crimson, gold, copper and russet to make this beautiful wreath to greet family & friends. Gather a variety of dried flowers (bittersweet, globe amaranth, cockscomb, statice, sunflower heads and preserved leaves work really well), and then carefully hot glue them on a grapevine wreath. You can also tuck in a few silk blooms for added color. Add a loop of wire to the back of your wreath and it's ready to hang in no time!

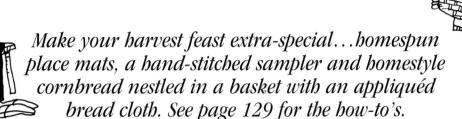

Make your harvest feast extra-special…homespun place mats, a hand-stitched sampler and homestyle cornbread nestled in a basket with an appliquéd bread cloth. See page 129 for the how-to's.

COUNTRY CORNBREAD

You can leave out the jalapeño and still have a terrific country-style cornbread, but you really should try it with the pepper. Either way, it's great served with a bowl of homemade soup.

1 1/4 c. cornmeal
3/4 c. all-purpose flour
5 T. sugar
2 t. baking powder
1/2 t. salt
1 c. buttermilk
1/3 c. vegetable oil
1 egg, lightly beaten
1 c. sharp Cheddar cheese, finely
   shredded
1 c. whole kernel corn
1 T. fresh jalapeño, seeded and
   minced

In a large bowl, mix together cornmeal, flour, sugar, baking powder and salt. Make a well in the center of the mix and pour in the buttermilk, oil and egg. Stir until ingredients are lightly moistened. Fold in cheese, corn and jalapeño. Pour mixture into lightly oiled 8"x8" baking dish. Bake at 375 degrees for 25 to 30 minutes, or until a tester inserted in the center comes out clean. Let cool slightly; cut into 2-inch squares. Makes 16 servings.

Missy Collier
Buellton, CA

TURKEY-VEGETABLE CHOWDER

This is a terrific, hearty chowder made using your leftover turkey!

1/4 c. butter
2 onions, chopped
2 T. all-purpose flour
1 t. curry powder
3 c. chicken broth
1 potato, chopped
1 c. carrots, thinly sliced
1 c. celery, thinly sliced
2 T. fresh parsley, minced
1/2 t. dried sage or poultry
    seasoning
3 c. cooked turkey, chopped
1 1/2 c. half-and-half

10-oz. pkg. frozen chopped
    spinach
Garnish: parsley leaves

Melt butter in a small Dutch oven. Add onions and sauté for 10 minutes. Stir in flour and curry powder. Cook for 2 minutes. Add broth, potato, carrots, celery, parsley and sage. Reduce heat to low. Cover and simmer 10 to 15 minutes. Add turkey, half-and-half and frozen spinach. Cover and simmer, stirring occasionally until heated through, about 10 minutes. Makes 8 cups.

Robyn Fiedler
Tacoma, WA

Happy Thanksgiving!

"Hurrah for the fun!
Is the turkey done?
Hurrah for the pumpkin pie!"
— Lydia Maria Childs

 I could be READING ...

 I could be LOOKIN' ...

 But I'm GIVIN' THANKS...

 'CAUSE I AIN'T COOKIN!

Fabric leaves serve as napkin holders on our checked placemats...add button-on nametags just for fun! See page 129.

HOLIDAY JAM

Easy-to-make jam…make some to give and some for your family to enjoy.

1 c. fresh cranberries
10-oz. pkg. frozen strawberries, thawed
2 c. sugar

Put cranberries into a blender, cover and chop by turning on and off, on and off, etc. Empty into saucepan; add strawberries and bring to a boil. Add sugar and boil until thickened. (It doesn't thicken a lot.) Pour into jelly glasses. Jam may be stored in refrigerator for 2 to 4 weeks. Makes about 2 cups.

Judy Norris

MULLED CIDER

Try cider instead of coffee once in a while…cut down on caffeine and enjoy the pure taste of fall!

2 qts. apple juice or sweet cider
1/2 c. brown sugar, packed
2" cinnamon stick
1 t. whole allspice
1 t. whole cloves
Garnish: long cinnamon sticks

Mix apple juice or cider and sugar in large saucepan. Add spices. Heat mixture slowly to simmering. Cover pan, simmer 20 minutes and strain. Serve hot, with a cinnamon stick in each mug. Makes 8 cups.

Harvest Fruit and Nut Pie

COMBINE THE FRUITS OF THE HARVEST IN THIS DELICIOUS PIE!

4 9-inch FROZEN DEEP-DISH PIE CRUSTS

4 GRANNY SMITH APPLES, PEELED & SLICED

1 C. CRANBERRIES
1/2 C. PINEAPPLE TIDBITS, DRAINED
1/2 C. CHOPPED WALNUTS
1 C. SUGAR
2/3 C. BROWN SUGAR, PACKED
4 T. ALL-PURPOSE FLOUR
1 t. CINNAMON
1/4 t. NUTMEG
3 T. BUTTER
… …

THAW 2 PIE CRUSTS AND FLATTEN FOR TOP CRUSTS. STIR TOGETHER APPLES, CRANBERRIES, PINEAPPLE, WALNUTS & SUGAR. SIFT TOGETHER BROWN SUGAR, FLOUR, CINNAMON & NUTMEG; ADD TO APPLE MIXTURE. DIVIDE EQUALLY BETWEEN 2 PIE CRUSTS; DOT EACH WITH BUTTER AND COVER WITH TOP PIE CRUSTS. BAKE AT 400 DEGREES FOR 45 MINUTES. MAKES 2 PIES.

Top jars of Holiday Jam with batting and homespun and decorate with buttons…great for sharing with friends & neighbors!

What would Thanksgiving dinner be without Spicy Pumpkin Pie topped with dollops of whipped cream? And instead of the traditional mincemeat, try the delicious mixture of apples, cranberries and walnuts in our Harvest Fruit and Nut Pie...it's heavenly!

SPICY PUMPKIN PIES

Makes 2 large pies for a family gathering or 4 small pies for sharing.

29-oz. can of solid-pack pumpkin
2 c. brown sugar, packed
3 T. pumpkin pie spice
1 t. salt
5 eggs, lightly beaten
2 12-oz. cans evaporated milk
2 10" deep-dish pie crusts or
   4 9" pie crusts, unbaked
Garnish: fresh whipped cream

In a large bowl, whisk pumpkin, brown sugar, spice and salt until well blended. Whisk in the eggs. Slowly whisk in the evaporated milk until completely blended. Pour the filling into the pie crusts. Bake at 375 degrees for 40 to 50 minutes or until the pies move very slightly in one mass when lightly jiggled. Transfer pies to a wire rack for cooling. Serve with plenty of fresh whipped cream.

Be Thee
Thankful
for your happy family.
Tell them so.

Winter

W hen the brisk autumn breezes become cold and blustery, we know that winter's on its way, and with it comes the festive holiday season! The short days and long nights provide wonderful opportunities to enjoy the warmth of a crackling fire, a mug of chocolatey cocoa and the company of family & friends. You'll want to extend a cheery greeting at the door...crimson ribbons and pots filled with winter-blooming amaryllis add merry touches to the traditional evergreen and holly decorations on the front porch.

Snow Friends

Our motto is "the more the merrier" when it comes to collecting snowfolk! Just like us, they come in all shapes, sizes and styles. If you're just starting out, a set of three or four will grow into an extended snow family in no time! We've got some friendly fellows to add to your collection, plus a whimsical display shelf; instructions for the shelf begin on page 129.

GOURD SNOWMAN

Use a craft stick to spread textured snow medium on a gourd. Drill arm holes and a nose hole in the gourd. Find a twig "nose" and two twig "arms" in the yard…glue them in the holes. Paint the nose orange; paint small pebbles for eyes, mouth and buttons black. Glue the pebbles in place.

For the scarf, sew buttons on a strip of fleece; work *Straight Stitches*, page 133, for snowflakes on the scarf. Cut narrow strips in the ends of the scarf for fringe.

For the hat, turn a child-size sock wrong-side out, then sew from heel-side bottom of cuff to toe to shape the hat; trim seam allowance and turn right-side out. For the tassel, cut four 1"x3" pieces from fleece, stack together and tie around the center…cut narrow strips in the ends for fringe. Sew the tassel on the hat. Fold the cuff of the hat up for a brim and sew buttons on it.

SNOWMAN PIN

Stack 2 pieces of felt together. Use pinking shears to cut a snowman shape from the felt pieces. Leaving small openings for arms and an opening for stuffing, sew shapes together close to the edge. Lightly stuff, then sew the opening closed. Cut the end from an orange wooden pick for the nose. Glue the stick arms in the armholes, the nose on the face and a pin clasp to the snowman. Use a colored pencil to add the cheeks and a black permanent marker for the eyes and mouth. Knot a torn strip of homespun around the snowman for the scarf.

SNOWMAN CUPS

For each cup, paint a gourd bell cup white, then lightly Sponge Paint, page 134, with thinned light blue. Paint pink cheeks on the cup…add a white highlight on each cheek. Use black dimensional paint to paint a face on the cup and orange dimensional paint to sculpt a nose. Use white dimensional paint to paint a squiggly line along the top front of the cup; while paint is still wet, apply iridescent glitter.

Drill a small hole on each side of the cup at the top. For the handle, curl the ends of a length of craft wire around a pencil, then thread the ends through the holes.

Winter Warmers

When the cold winds blow, there's nothing better than coming home to a hearty meal and a cup of hot chocolate! Share the warmth with a friend…decorate fleecy mittens with snowflakes and fill with goodies.

MIKE'S GRANDMA'S CHILI
Add more chili powder to make it as hot as you like!

1 lb. ground beef
1 c. onions, chopped
1 clove garlic, minced
15-oz. can kidney beans, undrained
1 qt. tomato juice
½ t. cumin
1 t. chili powder
1 t. salt
½ t. pepper
1 t. oregano
½ c. brown sugar, packed

In a large soup pot, cook ground beef, onions and garlic until meat is browned and crumbly. Add remaining ingredients and simmer on low for 30 minutes or longer. Makes 6½ cups.

For a quick and tasty treat, try adding a little extra flavor to your favorite packaged cocoa…cinnamon, chocolate syrup or sweetened condensed milk. Adults will love a splash of amaretto or butterscotch schnapps, and whipped cream with sprinkles will bring out the kid in anyone!

FLEECE MITTENS

Fleece mittens for frosty fingers…add a button and embroidered snowflake and you have a quick & cozy gift! To make the snowflake, sew on several different-sizes of white buttons to form a cross shape, then add white *Running Stitches* and *French Knots,* page 133, to make a star. To trim the cuff, sew the edges of a length of ribbon over the elastic on the mitten; remember to stretch the elastic as you sew…this will ensure that the cuff will still stretch when it's put on. Fill the mittens with goodies for extra fun.

CANDY CANE HOT CHOCOLATE MIX

Yummy cocoa mix with a taste of peppermint…a cozy gift!

1 1/2 c. powdered sugar
1 c. plus 2 T. baking cocoa
1 1/2 c. powdered non-dairy creamer
20 peppermint candies, broken into pieces
mini marshmallows

In a one-quart wide-mouth jar, layer powdered sugar, then cocoa, packing each layer as tightly as possible. Wipe the inside of the jar with a paper towel to remove any excess cocoa before adding the next layer. Add non-dairy creamer to jar, packing tightly. Add peppermint pieces. Fill any remaining space in top of jar with a layer of mini marshmallows; secure lid. Give with the following instructions: Empty jar into a large mixing bowl; blend well. Spoon mixture back into jar. To serve, add 3/4 cup boiling water to 1/4 cup cocoa mixture; stir to blend. Makes 16 servings.

Mary Deaile
Fresno, CA

Yum! Top the Country Friends® Casserole with crispy noodles and serve Pistachio Whip for a light dessert.

SPAGHETTI PIE

A great family meal; just add a salad and some garlic bread!

1/2 lb. spaghetti, cooked
2 eggs
1/4 c. grated Parmesan cheese
1/2 t. salt
1/4 lb. sliced pepperoni, divided
2 c. mozzarella cheese, divided
2 c. spaghetti sauce

Combine spaghetti, eggs, Parmesan cheese and salt. Mix thoroughly. Grease 13"x9" baking dish and place half of mixture in bottom. Layer top with half of pepperoni and mozzarella cheese, then layer with remaining spaghetti mixture. Add remaining pepperoni and mozzarella cheese. Bake at 350 degrees for 15 to 20 minutes. Cut into squares and serve topped with sauce.

Eleanor Bierly
Miamisburg, OH

Country Friends® Casserole

a recipe from Holly

2 T. butter
1 c. celery, chopped
1/4 c. onion, chopped
2 10-3/4-oz. cans cream of mushroom soup
2/3 c. chicken broth
4 c. chicken, cooked & diced
4 T. soy sauce
2 c. rice, cooked
1 c. chow mein noodles
1 c. cashews

In large saucepan, sauté celery & onion in butter 'til tender. Stir in soup & broth~simmer 5 minutes. Add chicken & soy sauce. Cook over low heat 5 minutes. Stir in rice. Pour into 13"x9" baking dish and bake at 375 degrees for 20 minutes, or 'til liquid is bubbling. Sprinkle noodles & nuts on top. Brown in oven. Serves 8 to 10.

PISTACHIO WHIP

Keep these ingredients on hand for a light and fruity dessert.

2 12-oz. cartons frozen whipped topping
2 16-oz. cans pineapple tidbits and juice
2 3.4-oz. pkgs. instant pistachio pudding mix

Combine whipped topping and juice from pineapple. Add pistachio pudding and mix well. Add pineapple and mix well.

LaVerne Biunno

Slow-Cooker Beef Stroganoff

START IT IN THE MORNING ~
ENJOY IT IN THE EVENING!

1 LB. LEAN ROUND STEAK CUBES
1 ENVELOPE DRY BEEFY ONION SOUP MIX
10 3/4-oz. CAN CREAM OF CELERY SOUP
10 3/4-oz. CAN CREAM OF MUSHROOM SOUP

PLACE ALL ITEMS IN SLOW-COOKER. COOK ON LOW FOR 6 TO 8 HOURS, STIRRING OCCASIONALLY. SERVE OVER COOKED NOODLES OR RICE. (FOR A DELICIOUS VARIATION, STIR IN 1/2 C. SOUR CREAM.)

Hearty fare: Cheesy Bread, Slow-Cooker Beef Stroganoff and Red and Green Slaw.

Freeze summer vegetables to enjoy year 'round. Create a "soup mix" by combining corn, carrots, celery, onion, broccoli, tomatoes and potatoes for hearty winter soups and stews.

RED AND GREEN SLAW
Yes, sweet red peppers are costly, but they are so good…you deserve one!

1 1/2 c. green cabbage, chopped or
   very thinly sliced
1/2 c. red cabbage, chopped or
   very thinly sliced
1/2 red pepper, very thinly sliced
   in long strips

Dressing:
1/4 c. mayonnaise
1 t. lime juice
1/4 t. sugar
1/4 t. garlic salt

Combine cabbages and pepper. Combine dressing ingredients; stir into cabbage mixture. Serves 8 to 10.
Karyl Bannister

CHEESY BREAD
Wonderful with soup on a cold, snowy, winter day.

1 loaf bakery French bread
8-oz. pkg. sliced Swiss cheese
2 T. onion, chopped
1 T. dry mustard
1 T. poppy seed
1 t. seasoned salt
1 cup margarine, melted

Using a serrated bread knife, cut diagonal slits in the bread, going almost all the way through. Put the bread on a large piece of foil on a baking sheet. Place pieces of the Swiss cheese in the slits. Combine the last 5 ingredients and pour over the bread. Wrap the foil around the bread. Bake at 350 degrees for 35 to 40 minutes. Serve warm.
Tammy McCartney
Oxford, OH

Hope is one of those things in life you cannot do without. ~ LeRoy Douglas

Cookies, cookies,

Moist and chewy, thin and crispy, iced and decorated…you can never have too many holiday cookies! This year, why not invite your fellow cookie-lovers over for an old-fashioned cookie swap? Everyone bakes one kind of cookie, but goes home with a delicious variety. You'll find the tastiest refreshments among the yummy recipes on the following pages.

Here are a few ideas to get you started (clockwise from top left): Raspberry-Almond Squares, Pecan Munchies, Christmas Wreaths, Cherry Bonbon Cookies, Candy Cane Cookies, and Grandma's Soft Sugar Cookies. The recipes are on pages 100-103.

COOKIES!

During the second week in December, before things get too hectic, I hold my annual cookie swap. I invite 25 friends, who each bake 10 dozen holiday cookies. We vote on the nicest-looking cookie…and even the saddest cookie! The winners get awards and we all have lots of laughs. All the women go home with a cookie cookbook that I have put together with all the recipes for the cookies. My family eats a lot of the cookies, but we also save some to put in pretty holiday tins that are given to people as little holiday remembrances.

— Barbara Leclair

These cookies are all winners (clockwise from top left): Gingerbread Men (in basket and on plate), Yummy Marshmallow Bars, White Velvet Cutouts iced with tinted Good and Glossy Cookie Frosting, and German Chocolate Cake Mix Cookies. The recipes are on pages 100-102.

CHRISTMAS WREATHS

The next time your kids enjoy a "snow day," spend part of it making these quick and easy cookies.

3½ c. corn flake cereal
30 regular-size marshmallows
½ c. margarine
1 t. vanilla extract
2 t. green food coloring
Garnish: red cinnamon candies or
   maraschino cherries

Spread corn flake cereal on a baking sheet. Heat marshmallows, margarine, vanilla and food coloring in a double boiler until marshmallows melt. Carefully pour marshmallow mixture over cereal. Blend well and, as mixture cools, spoon 2 tablespoons of mixture onto wax paper. Form cereal mixture into a wreath shape. Arrange candies on top of each wreath to resemble holly berries. Allow wreaths to set up. Makes about 2 dozen.

Roxanne Bixby
West Franklin, NH

RASPBERRY-ALMOND SQUARES

These cookies are light and buttery. I especially enjoy them during the holidays because of the different flavor the raspberry jam gives them. Best of all, they are quick and easy to make.

1 c. butter, softened
1 c. sugar
1 egg
½ t. almond extract
2½ c. all-purpose flour
½ t. baking powder
¼ t. salt
⅔ c. raspberry jam, melted
½ c. slivered almonds, toasted

Beat butter and sugar with an electric mixer until light and fluffy. Beat in egg and almond extract. Add flour, baking powder and salt; beat until blended. Spread in an ungreased 9"x9" pan; smooth the surface. Spread jam on surface. Sprinkle almonds over jam. Bake at 350 degrees for 20 minutes or just until edges are golden. Cool, then cut into 1½-inch squares. Makes 3 dozen.

Theresa Smith

WHITE VELVET CUTOUTS

We tinted Good and Glossy Cookie Frosting instead of the glaze to ice green, red and yellow Christmas balls.

Cookies:
1 c. butter, softened
3 oz. cream cheese, softened
1 c. sugar
1 egg yolk
½ t. vanilla extract
2½ c. all-purpose flour
sprinkles or colored sugar

Glaze:
1 c. powdered sugar
1 T. water
½ t. lemon juice

For cookies, beat butter and cream cheese together. Beat in sugar. Add egg yolk and vanilla, stir in flour. Shape dough into a ball. Wrap in plastic and chill overnight. On a lightly floured surface, roll out dough to ¼-inch thickness. Cut into 2½-inch circles or desired shapes. Place cookies on ungreased baking sheets. Bake at 350 degrees for 12 minutes or until edges are golden. Cool on wire racks. Ice with glaze or with tinted Good and Glossy Cookie Frosting. For glaze, mix ingredients together and spread a thin coat on top of each cookie. Decorate cookies with colorful sprinkles or sugar. When glaze is dry, store cookies in an airtight container. Makes about 3 dozen.

Sharon Hill

Grandma's Soft Sugar Cookies

...sweet memories of Grandmother's kitchen.

1½ c. sugar
1½ c. butter or margarine
1 c. flaked coconut
1 t. vanilla extract
1 egg
3 c. all-purpose flour
1 t. baking powder
½ t. salt

Mix sugar, butter, coconut, vanilla & egg together. Stir in remaining ingredients. Shape dough by rounded teaspoonfuls into balls. Place on ungreased baking sheet 3" apart. Flatten cookies to 2" in diameter with a glass dipped in sugar. Bake at 350° 'til cookies are set ~ about 7 to 9 minutes. Cookies will be pale in color. Cool slightly. Remove from baking sheet and store tightly covered. Makes 6 dozen.

The best way to clean metal cookie cutters is to carefully brush the crumbs away with a toothbrush. If you must use water, dry the cutters thoroughly to prevent rusting. Never wash them in the dishwasher!

The smiling gingerbread man on our sweet invitation provides a clue to the holiday fun to come! See page 130 for the surprisingly simple how-to's.

GINGERBREAD MEN

These fun fellows are always invited to cookie parties. Let the kids help dress them!

1 c. shortening
1/2 t. salt
3 t. baking soda
2 t. ground ginger
2 t. cinnamon
1 t. ground allspice
1 c. sugar
1 c. dark molasses
2 eggs, beaten
1 t. instant coffee granules, moistened with tap water
5 c. all-purpose flour
raisins, chocolate chips, sprinkles, colored sugar and candies

Cream together first 6 ingredients. Add sugar and molasses and continue to beat. Add beaten eggs, coffee and 3 or 4 cups of flour and continue to beat. Add remaining flour and mix by hand. (Dough will be very stiff.) Cover with plastic wrap and refrigerate for several hours or overnight. Flatten the dough on a floured board and cut out large and small gingerbread men with cookie cutters. Transfer to a baking sheet and use diced raisins, chocolate chips, sprinkles, sugar and candies to dress your gingerbread men. Bake at 325 degrees 10 to 13 minutes for small cookies and 15 to 20 minutes for large cookies. Makes 2 dozen small and 2 dozen large.

Good and Glossy Cookie Frosting

...SETS UP LIKE ROYAL ICING BUT WITH A GOOD & GLOSSY FINISH.

1/4 c. WATER
1 T. LIGHT CORN SYRUP
3 C. PLUS 3 T. POWDERED SUGAR
1/2 t. CLEAR VANILLA EXTRACT

Combine water & corn syrup in heavy saucepan. Add sugar & blend well. Using a candy thermometer, cook over medium-low heat until temperature reaches 100° ~ stir constantly! Remove from heat & stir in vanilla. Cool for 5 to 8 minutes. Ice cookies. Stir icing occasionally. You can sprinkle on candy decorations, nonpareils & colored sugars before the icing hardens. (★ Replace vanilla extract with almond or lemon extract just for fun ⌣ and yumminess!)

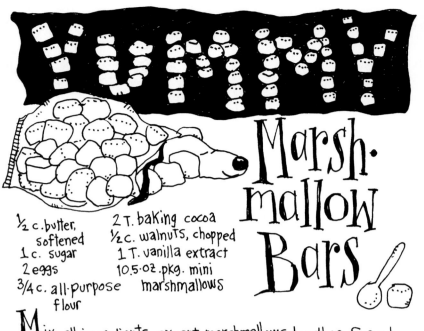

YUMMY

Marshmallow Bars

½ c. butter, softened
1 c. sugar
2 eggs
¾ c. all-purpose flour
2 T. baking cocoa
½ c. walnuts, chopped
1 T. vanilla extract
10.5-oz. pkg. mini marshmallows

Mix all ingredients except marshmallows together. Spread cookie mixture evenly in bottom of ungreased 13"x 9" pan. Bake at 350° for 15 to 20 minutes. Remove from oven ~ top with mini marshmallows. Return pan to oven ~ bake an additional 5 minutes or until marshmallows begin to melt. Cool in pan, then ice with...

CHOCOLATE FROSTING

1 c. sugar
½ c. milk
¾ c. butter
½ c. chocolate chips

Mix sugar, milk & butter in a saucepan. Bring to a boil. Let boil for 1 minute. Reduce heat ~ stir in chocolate chips. Keep stirring 'til well blended & chocolate has melted. Cool, then spread on bars.

"Hang the merry garlands over all the town.
Smell the spicy odors of cookies turning brown!
The mice have come to nibble, they're feeling mighty gay —
But only little children shall have my sweets today!"

— Unknown

PECAN MUNCHIES

Every year before Thanksgiving, my mother managed to have at least 40 dozen cookies baked and in the freezer for the holidays! Of all her recipes, this is the one I like most.

1 c. pecans, chopped
1 c. butter, softened
½ c. powdered sugar
2 t. vanilla extract
1 T. water
2 c. all-purpose flour
6-oz. pkg. chocolate chips
Garnish: powdered sugar

Spread pecans in a single layer on a baking sheet and toast at 375 degrees for 5 minutes; watch carefully to avoid burning pecans. Set aside to cool. Beat together the butter and powdered sugar until light and fluffy. Add vanilla and beat again. Thoroughly mix in the water and flour, then add chocolate chips and pecans. Shape into small balls, approximately 2 teaspoons of dough each. Place on ungreased baking sheets and bake at 300 degrees for about 20 minutes. While still warm, roll cookies in powdered sugar and place on cookie rack to cool. Makes 4 dozen.

Randi Daeger
Rockford, IL

GERMAN CHOCOLATE CAKE MIX COOKIES

These one-bowl cookies are quick and easy!

18¼-oz. German chocolate cake mix
1 c. semi-sweet chocolate chips
½ c. long-cooking oats, uncooked
½ c. raisins
½ c. oil
2 eggs, slightly beaten

Combine ingredients in a large bowl. Drop rounded teaspoonfuls of dough 2 inches apart onto ungreased baking sheets. Bake at 350 degrees 7 to 9 minutes or until cookie is set. Cool for one minute and remove from baking sheets. Makes 5½ dozen.

Ann Fehr
Collegeville, PA

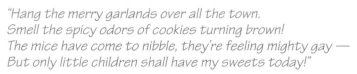

CHERRY BONBON COOKIES

A family recipe that's over 30 years old.

24 maraschino cherries
1/2 c. margarine, softened
3/4 c. powdered sugar, sifted
1 1/2 c. all-purpose flour
1/8 t. salt
2 T. milk
1 t. vanilla extract
Powdered sugar

Drain cherries, reserving 1/4 cup of juice for glaze; set aside. Beat margarine until creamy. Gradually add powdered sugar, beating well. Stir in flour and salt. Add milk and vanilla; mix well. Shape into 24 balls. Press each ball around a cherry, covering it completely. Place on ungreased baking sheets. Bake at 350 degrees for 16 to 18 minutes. Transfer to wire racks and cool completely. Sprinkle with powdered sugar.

Cherry Glaze:
2 T. margarine, melted
2 c. powdered sugar, sifted
1/4 c. reserved cherry juice
1 to 2 drops red food coloring

Mix margarine, powdered sugar, cherry juice and food coloring. Place in a small plastic zipping bag and seal. To drizzle, snip a tiny hole at one corner of bag and gently squeeze over cookies.

Flo Burtnett
Gage, OK

CANDY CANE COOKIES

This brings back the old-fashioned fun of baking Christmas cookies.

1 c. butter, softened
1/2 c. brown sugar, packed
1/4 c. sugar
2 egg yolks
1 t. vanilla extract
1/2 t. peppermint extract
1/4 t. salt
2 1/2 c. all-purpose flour
red food coloring

Beat butter and sugars together; add egg yolks. Stir in extracts and set aside. Combine salt and flour; stir into sugar mixture. Divide dough in 2 equal portions and tint one portion red. Remove one tablespoon of dough from each bowl. On a very lightly floured surface, shape each tablespoon of dough by rolling under both hands to form a rope. Place the 2 ropes side-by-side and gently twist together. Carefully bend the top to form a candy cane; continue with remaining dough in each bowl. Place candy canes on an ungreased baking sheet, about one inch apart; bake at 350 degrees for 8 minutes. Do not brown. Let cool on baking sheet. Makes 2 dozen.

Candy Hannigan
Monument, CO

Remind each guest to bring copies of her cookie recipe to share...everyone can tuck their favorite recipes in the handy pocket on the take-home cookie sacks that they'll fill at your party. Instructions are on page 130.

WRAP IT UP!

Don't wrap your country gifts in just any old Christmas paper! Check out these clever packaging ideas…snippets of festive homespun make great bags, or use scraps of fabric, decorative paper or pieces cut from brown paper sacks to wrap packages…dress them up with torn-fabric "ribbon," colorful raffia or rick-rack. Finish your wrapping with one-of-a-kind tags, and you're all set!

Keep wrapping materials handy. Put paper, ribbon, tags, scissors and tape in a large basket next to the fireplace or under an end table. You'll be ready to lend a hand for last-minute wrapping projects.

For quick-and-easy gift tags: Use decorative-edge craft scissors to cut pictures from old greeting cards, then cut colored paper a little larger than the pictures and glue them together.

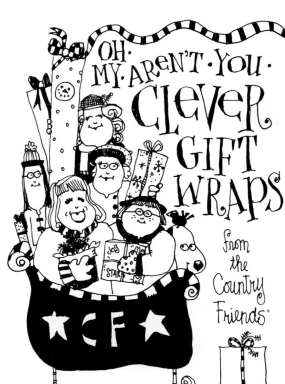

OH.
MY·AREN'T·YOU·
CLeVeR
GIFT
WRAPS

from
the
Country
Friends®

GIFT WRAP & TAG IDEAS

If it can be taped, sewn or glued, consider it for gift wrap...a piece of homespun, folded in half and sewn along the sides to make a bag, is an extra "gift" in itself! Use brown paper bags, scraps of fabrics, decorative paper, cellophane or whatever you have on hand to wrap the gift, then tie with raffia, ribbons or strips torn from fabric. Top off your presentation with small glass balls or a one-of-a-kind name tag tied onto the gift. You can use a photocopy of one of our tags from page 135, glue it onto card stock and cut it out. Color it with markers, crayons or colored pencils (don't forget to add small craft stick arms to the snowman). Mailing tags make quick gift tags! Handletter or use rubber stamps to add names and Christmas greetings.

You can transform plain brown or white paper into one-of-a-kind gift wrap! Use precut holiday stencils or simple sponge shapes to paint on festive borders or scenes.

Christmas Customs

One of the things we love best about the holidays is keeping traditions, like placing candles in the windows and trimming an evergreen with ornaments and lights. You can create an updated version of the Yule log to use as a candleholder (turn to page 130), or have a "family craft night" to make colorful decorations from paper and felt…they're sure to bring back favorite childhood memories!

Did you know that the tradition of the Yule log goes back to a ritual practiced by the Vikings? As the winter solstice approached, they would burn a large log in the hopes of not only bringing light and warmth to the dark winter days, but also to ensure the return of summer by pleasing their sun god. Europeans who later adopted this custom would venture out on Christmas Eve in search of the perfect log from an apple or oak tree to bring home. It would then be blessed and placed in the fireplace to burn during the 12 days of Christmas. Today, few people burn Yule logs, but the tradition has been passed on in a symbolic form as we enjoy a Bûche de Nöel, or Christmas log cake. This delicious cream-filled cake, covered in chocolate frosting, is a sweet reminder of the very beginnings of this ancient tradition.

Yarn Wreath

Cut a ring from cardboard. Wrap the ring with yarn, gluing the ends to secure. Add buttons, a yarn bow and a hanger to finish your festive adornment.

Felt Mitten Clip

Trace the pattern on page 153 onto tracing paper. Using the pattern, cut 4 mittens from felt. For each side of the clip, glue two mitten pieces together. Add rick-rack, sequins or other trims and sparkles to one mitten. Glue a mitten to each side of a spring-type hair clip or a clothespin. Use these cute clips on packages, the tree or to hang cards on the garland over the fireplace.

OLD-FASHIONED ORNAMENTS

Take a night out from your hectic holiday schedule to make holiday memories with your family...make one or all of these fun-for-kids ornaments to adorn your tree.

Paper Chain

Put some new twists on an old favorite...use decorative-edge scissors to cut out the strips, layer a narrow strip cut from decorative paper on top of the base strip and use rubber stamps to decorate some of the strips before you assemble your chain.

Paper Ball Ornaments

Cut 20 circles from paper (we used a huge circle cutter for scrapbooking and it went really fast). You can stamp some of the circles with Christmas stamps if you'd like. Fold in the edges of each circle to form a triangle. Now, start gluing! Glue the flaps of the circles together...pretty soon your ball will start to take shape. Don't forget to add a hanger before you glue the last piece in place.

We have all got our "good old days" tucked away inside our hearts, and we return to them in dreams like cats to favorite armchairs.
—BRIAN CARTER—

Yummy Little ♥ Gifts ♥

Need a bunch of little gifts for your friends, neighbors or teachers? Dress up plain mugs with simple hand-drawn designs and tuck in candy-coated pretzels for snacking, or share pretty little boxes filled with butter fudge. Our yummy beverage mixes and flavorful vanilla sugar are sure to warm hearts…and tickle tummies, too! See page 130 to paint the candy box.

PRETZEL WANDS
Delight your friends with this magical combination of sweet and salty flavors.

10 oz. white melting chocolate
9-oz. pkg. large stick pretzels
   (about 8½" long)
red and green mint candies,
   crushed

Melt chocolate in a microwave-safe 2-cup measuring cup on high power (100%) one to 2 minutes, stirring every 30 seconds, until smooth. Dip each pretzel into chocolate to cover half of pretzel. Sprinkle with crushed candies. Stand each pretzel, coated side up, in a glass until chocolate hardens. Makes about 2 dozen.

The Manner of giving is worth More than the gift.
— Pierre Corneille

DESIGNER MUGS
Use a paint pen to draw "peppermint" swirls or a name and dots on a plain mug…add stripes around the handle if you wish. Fill the mug with goodies or treats and you have the perfect gift for your favorite snacker!

CHRISTMAS BUTTER FUDGE

An old-fashioned recipe that's perfect to share with your neighbors.

4 c. sugar
2 c. milk
1/2 c. butter
1/4 t. salt
1 t. vanilla extract
1/4 c. candied cherries, finely chopped
1/4 c. pistachios, blanched

Combine sugar, milk, butter and salt in large saucepan. Bring to a boil, stirring constantly until sugar is dissolved. Cook over medium heat, stirring occasionally, until candy thermometer reads 236 degrees. Remove from heat immediately; set pan in cold water. Do not stir or beat until cooled to lukewarm. Add vanilla; beat until candy becomes thick and creamy and loses its shine. When candy begins to set, add cherries and nuts; fold in quickly. Pour into buttered 8"x8" pan. Let stand at room temperature until firm. Cut into squares. Makes 2 1/2 pounds.

Juanita Williams
Jacksonville, OR

Vanilla Sugar
SO GOOD YOU'LL WANT TO SNEAK A PINCH

PLACE ONE OR TWO WHOLE VANILLA BEANS WITH TWO CUPS OF SUGAR IN AN AIRTIGHT JAR. STORE IN A COOL PLACE FOR ABOUT TWO WEEKS BEFORE USING. USE IN PLACE OF REGULAR SUGAR IN RECIPES, BEVERAGES OR CEREAL.

Fix a jar full and tie on a pretty ribbon for someone with a sweet tooth.

FIRESIDE COFFEE MIX

Give this mix as part of a gift bag with some chocolate-covered spoons or cinnamon sticks, freshly grated nutmeg and a can of whipped cream!

2 c. hot chocolate mix
2 c. powdered non-dairy creamer
1 1/2 c. sugar
1 c. instant coffee granules
2 t. cinnamon
2 t. nutmeg

Blend together all ingredients and place in an airtight container. Include these instructions with your gift: For a single serving, place 2 tablespoons of mix in a mug, add one cup hot water and stir. Garnish with whipped cream and a sprinkling of nutmeg or cinnamon.

Lori Anderson
Eau Claire, WI

MULLING SPICE BAGS

Friends will think of you when they drink a mug of this spiced cider.

cheesecloth and butcher's twine
4 cinnamon sticks
8 whole allspice
8 whole cloves
4 T. dried orange peel

Cut a double thickness of cheesecloth into 4"x6" squares. Onto each square, place one cinnamon stick, 2 cloves, 2 allspice and one tablespoon orange peel; bundle up and tie with twine. To serve, place a spice bag in one gallon of cider. Simmer 30 minutes. Makes 4 bags.

Jacqueline Lash-Idler
Rockaway, NJ

PUPPY CHOW SNACK MIX ...FOR PEOPLE!

For a tasty variation, use butterscotch chips in place of chocolate chips.

8 oz. bite-size crispy rice cereal
    squares
½ c. margarine
6-oz. pkg. chocolate chips
½ c. peanut butter
2 c. powdered sugar

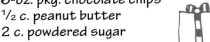

Put cereal squares in a large bowl. Melt margarine, chocolate chips and peanut butter together. Pour over cereal squares and mix well. Put sugar in a paper bag; pour cereal mixture into bag and shake. Put finished snack into a plastic zipping bag.

Barb Agne
Deleware, OH

A yummy blend of chocolate and peanut butter, our Puppy Chow Snack Mix is meant for people! Instructions for the peek-a-boo gift bag are on page 130.

DECORATED JAR LABELS

Make a gift of your family favorite recipe extra-special this gift-giving season. Use one of our designs from page 135 (or create your own), then refer to *Making A Tag Or Label*, page 132, to make your labels. Glue or use double-stick tape to secure each label to a jar filled with a sampling of the tasty treat.

For a family gift, pack a variety of homemade snacks in a big ribbon-tied basket or colorful plastic pail...add a tag that says "Emergency Rations."

An old Yugoslavian custom is to bake bread on Christmas Eve for family and friends. What is so special about this bread? Before it's baked, a large gold coin is inserted inside, and when it's served, it's anyone's guess who will receive that special piece. Children especially enjoy this old-fashioned tradition!

SAVORY CHEESE COINS

These make good prizes for children when playing dreidel.

2 c. shredded sharp Cheddar
    cheese
1/2 c. butter, softened
1 c. all-purpose unbleached flour
2 T. dried, minced onion
1 t. Worcestershire sauce
1/8 t. cayenne pepper
Optional: sesame seeds

Combine all ingredients except sesame seeds in a medium bowl; mix well by hand or with a heavy-duty mixer until a dough is formed. Divide the dough in half; shape each half into a log about one inch in diameter and 12 inches long. If desired, roll in sesame seeds to coat. Wrap the logs in plastic and chill 3 to 4 hours or overnight. When logs are completely chilled, cut each log into 1/4-inch slices. Place on greased or coated baking sheets; bake at 375 degrees for 10 minutes. Remove coins from baking sheets to cool. Store in an airtight container. Makes about 8 dozen.

CHOCOLATE ANIMAL CRACKERS

An easy-to-make treat during the busy holiday season.

12-oz. pkg. chocolate chips
2 T. shortening
1 large box animal crackers
colored sugar sprinkles

Melt chocolate and shortening in pan. Stir until smooth. Dip animal crackers into chocolate, covering both sides. Lift out with fork. Place on wax paper. While still hot, top with sugar sprinkles. Allow to harden. Store in an airtight tin.

Judy Norris

For munchers on the go, pack Savory Cheese Coins in peppermint-striped tubes or fill little pails with Spiced Pecans. How-to's for the packaging are on page 130.

SPICED PECANS

Keep extras of these sweet-and-spicy snacks on hand…they go fast!

1/4 c. margarine
4 c. pecans
1 1/2 c. sugar
1 T. cinnamon
1 T. ground cloves
1 T. nutmeg

Melt margarine and add pecans. Cook and stir 20 minutes. Drain on paper towels. Mix remaining ingredients in plastic container. Add warm pecans and shake to coat. Spread on a baking sheet to cool completely. Store in an airtight container.

Kathy Bolyea
Naples, FL

PITA CRISPS

Easy to prepare ahead of time. Just store in an airtight container for snacking.

3 T. virgin olive oil
1 t. dried basil
1/2 t. sea salt (or coarse salt)
12-oz. pkg. pita pockets (about 5),
    cut into eighths

In mixing bowl, whisk together olive oil, basil and salt. Add pita pieces and toss to coat well. Spread the pita triangles in a single layer on baking sheets. Bake at 450 degrees for 4 to 5 minutes or until crisp.

There's nothing nicer than giving (or receiving!) a handmade gift from the heart. Crafted from felt cutouts, our frosty wall hanging and personalized stockings are quick & easy to assemble using simple embroidery stitches…no real sewing involved! Instructions for the wall hanging and stocking start on page 130.

The custom of hanging stockings from the mantel comes from a legend that tells of St. Nicholas tossing gold coins down the chimney of three sisters who needed dowries. The money fell into the sisters' stockings that happened to be hanging beside the fireplace to dry!

...thinks the mistletoe tradition is a fabulous idea.

...has at least one Christmas tree in every room.

...has her picture taken with Santa every single year.

Preserve "special" artwork from your preschooler with contact paper and hot glue a magnet on back for smaller projects. For larger masterpieces...buy your own mat and frame and give grandparents an "original." Your child will be very proud to give something he made and you know how excited grandparents will be!

— Denise Turner

Kids still get pleasure from the simple things...a box of crayons, colorful marbles, a jigsaw puzzle, stuffed animals, Raggedy Ann or Andy, classic adventure books or a train set. These never go out of style.

FROST FAMILY

"Christmas, my child, is love in action. Every time we love, every time we give, it's Christmas."

— Dale Evans

PAINT CAN CANDLEHOLDER

Create custom candleholders out of something unique...like a paint can! Be sure to use a brand new paint can to avoid a fire hazard. Paint the can your desired base coat color, then follow the manufacturer's instructions to add a crackle finish. Knot a length of coordinating ribbon around the can, then glue a miniature, framed Christmas charm over the knot of the ribbon.

Instructions for the Quilt Piece Angel are on page 131.

May Peace
and Plenty
be the first
To lift the latch
on your door,
and
Happiness
be guided to
your house
by the
Candle
of
Christmas.
— old blessing —

ADVENT BOX

Paint this brightly colored box to hold small treasures to be opened one drawer at a time from December 1st through Christmas…perfect for little ones anxiously waiting for the big day!

Remove the drawers from a 25-drawer organizer, then paint the organizer blue. Use a white paint pen to draw snowflakes and dots on the organizer. Tape colored paper to the inside front of each drawer, then use a paint pen to number the outside of the drawer. For each drawer pull, fold a 2" length of ribbon in half and glue the ends inside the drawer.

GOING HOME FOR THE HOLIDAYS IS GOOD FOR THE HEART ★ SURPRISE SOMEBODY SPECIAL!

HAPPY NEW YEAR!

Resolve to make your New Year's party the best ever! Pack a merrymaking kit for each guest and add colorful charms to help folks keep track of their glasses. For a sweet treat, we vote for ice-cream sundaes…you can tuck bottles of yummy chocolate and caramel sauce in fancy bags. How-to's are on page 131.

HOT FUDGE SAUCE
Keep an extra jar in the fridge for late-night snacks!

1/2 c. baking cocoa
1 c. sour cream
1 1/2 c. sugar
1 t. vanilla extract

Using a double boiler, stir all ingredients together and cook over simmering water for about an hour, stirring occasionally. Drizzle warm sauce over vanilla or coffee ice cream. Makes one pint.

CARAMEL SAUCE
Tastes great on pound cake, shortbread and ice cream.

1 c. brown sugar, packed
1/2 c. whipping cream
1/4 c. light corn syrup
1 T. butter
2 t. cinnamon

In a large saucepan, heat all ingredients to boiling, stirring constantly. Reduce heat and simmer, uncovered, for about 5 minutes. Makes 1 1/2 cups sauce.

Sarina Quaderer
Friendship, WI

NEW YEAR'S EVE KIT

3, 2, 1…Hats off to the New Year! Make sure everyone at your party is ready to celebrate with their own party kit. Start with a glitter-covered hat…wrap it with some star garland for extra pizzazz. Throw in a loud noisemaker, a streamer-popping cracker and lots of glittery confetti wrapped in colorful cellophane. Wrap it all in clear cellophane and tie it up with shiny ribbons, sparkling wired garland and shiny trims. Add a copy of the tag from page 135, trimmed in sequins, to finish it off.

celebrate!
WITH HAT & HORN
THE OLD YEAR'S DONE
A NEW YEAR'S BORN!

YUMMY BREAKFAST ROLLS

Quick to assemble and bake...so delicious to eat.

2 8-oz. tubes crescent rolls
2 8-oz. pkgs. cream cheese, softened
1¼ c. sugar, divided
1 t. vanilla extract
½ c. margarine, melted
1 t. cinnamon

Unroll one can of crescent rolls into the bottom of a 13"x9" pan. Don't press seams together! Mix cream cheese with one cup of sugar and vanilla; spread over rolls. Place second can of rolls over top. Pour on melted margarine and top with mixture of ¼ cup sugar and cinnamon. Bake at 350 degrees for 30 minutes. Cut into triangles to serve. Makes 2 dozen.

Hazel Hayden

CHILE RELLENO PUFF

This recipe is excellent as a brunch dish. Serve with warmed flour tortillas or tortilla chips and salsa, crisp salad or a vegetable.

7-oz. can whole green chiles, drained and split
1 c. shredded Monterey Jack cheese
6 eggs, slightly beaten
¾ c. milk
1 T. all-purpose flour
1 t. baking powder
½ t. salt
1 c. shredded Cheddar cheese
2 T. fresh cilantro, chopped
4 green onions, chopped

Sauce:
8-oz. can tomato sauce
¼ c. salsa
1 t. dried oregano

In a lightly oiled 11"x7" baking dish, layer split chilies and Monterey Jack cheese. Combine eggs, milk, flour, baking powder and salt. Pour over chilies; top with Cheddar cheese. Bake at 350 degrees for 30 minutes or until puffed and browned. Heat combined tomato sauce, salsa and oregano 5 minutes. Spoon warm sauce over each serving of chile relleno puff. Sprinkle with cilantro and chopped green onions. Serves 6.

Nancie Gensler

Fun party favors: bundle gold-wrapped chocolate coins in squares of white tulle and tie closed with silver ribbon...a symbol for prosperity in the coming year!

Mild green chiles form a flavorful base for this cheesy Chile Relleno Puff. Top servings with warm, tomatoey salsa and serve for a midnight breakfast. Cut wedges of Yummy Breakfast Rolls...a creamy filling makes them especially good!

HOPPIN' JOHN

Hoppin' John is a traditional good luck dish popular in the South. Eating it on New Year's Day promises a prosperous and healthy New Year.

1 c. dried black-eyed peas
10 c. water, divided
6 slices bacon, cut up
3/4 c. onion, chopped
1 stalk celery, chopped
1 1/2 t. salt
3/4 t. ground red pepper
1 c. long-grain rice, uncooked

Rinse peas and put in a large saucepan with 6 cups water. Bring to a boil and reduce heat to simmer for 2 minutes. Remove from heat, cover and let stand one hour. Drain and rinse. In same pan, cook bacon until crisp. Remove bacon. Drain fat, reserving 3 tablespoons in pan. Add peas, 4 cups water, onion, celery, salt and red pepper. Bring to a boil, cover and reduce heat. Simmer 30 minutes. Add rice; cover and simmer 20 minutes longer until peas and rice are tender. Stir in bacon.

A good book is the best of friends, the same today and forever.
– Martin E. Tupper –

A GOOD BEGINNING MAKES A GOOD ENDING.
~old English Proverb

If you're short on time, you can use canned or frozen instead of dried black-eyed peas in Hoppin' John. It's a hearty side dish or main course!

Create a festive scene…decorate your New Year's table with clocks of every size and shape, candles and a sprinkling of confetti.

For a glittering centerpiece, fill a large, round glass bowl (such as a salad, punch or trifle bowl) with shiny gold and silver ornaments; wind little white fairy lights around and through the arrangement.

On New Year's Eve, I serve my family roast pork. A pig always roots forward, symbolizing going into the New Year, as opposed to a chicken, which scratches backwards. On New Year's Day, if the first person to enter our home is a male, we will have good luck throughout the coming year. Our "good-luck man" is then rewarded with a silver coin.

— Anne Legan

For Your Valentines

Send sweet sentiments to your valentines with handmade greetings. It's easy to decorate your own cards with stickers and ribbon…you can hand-write your message or use rubber stamps and colorful ink. Surprise a special someone with a heart-shaped brownie, or for quick little gifts, share candies in tiny decorated jars.

CHOCOLATE-RASPBERRY BROWNIES

The raspberry filling makes these brownies really special. Bake in a pan that has 6 individual heart-shaped molds.

1 c. unsalted butter
5 sqs. unsweetened baking chocolate, chopped
2 c. sugar
4 eggs
2 t. vanilla extract
1 1/4 c. all-purpose flour
1 t. baking powder
1/2 t. salt
1 c. chopped walnuts, toasted
1/2 c. seedless raspberry jam

Melt butter and chocolate in heavy saucepan over low heat, stirring constantly until smooth. Remove from heat. Whisk in sugar, eggs and vanilla. Mix flour, baking powder and salt in a small bowl. Add to chocolate mixture; whisk to blend. Stir in nuts. For each brownie, spoon 3 tablespoons of batter into a greased 1/2-cup heart-shaped mold; smooth batter forming an indentation in center. Fill with 1 teaspoon jam. Spoon 2 tablespoons batter over jam; smooth batter. Bake brownies at 350 degrees for approximately 20 minutes, or until tester comes out clean. Cool in pan 5 minutes; transfer to a wire rack to cool completely. Makes about 14 brownies.

Susan Brzozowski
Ellicott City, MD

WINDOW TO MY HEART CARD

A handmade Valentine for that special person! Trace the patterns, page 157, onto tracing paper. Using the medium heart, cut one heart each from red card stock, clear cellophane and decorative paper. For the window, draw around the small heart on the red heart and cut out with decorative-edge scissors. Glue the cellophane heart to the back of red heart. Leaving an opening for filling, glue the decorative paper heart to the back of the red heart. Glue Valentine stickers to card stock, then trim close to the stickers. Fill the heart with the stickers and some paper confetti; glue the opening closed. Draw around the large heart on white card stock and cut out using craft scissors with large scallop blades; glue the filled heart to the white heart. Punch a 1/8" diameter hole in each scallop, then glue on a pretty bow.

CANDY JARS

Great for the kids to take to school…these are fast and fun! Fill small food jars with pink, white and red Valentine candies. Top the jars with several squares of tissue paper tied with cotton string, then apply a sticker. Add a tag made from card stock that has been stamped or stickered with a Valentine greeting…see page 132 for helpful hints on *Making Tags and Labels*.

VALENTINE CARDS

Create custom cards! Start with a folded piece of card stock, then glue on a piece of decorative paper for the background. You can create a frosted overlay by attaching a piece of vellum with ribbon tied through holes in the top of the card. Add purchased tags with crimped ribbons (you can use a paper crimper to crimp satin ribbon), paper cutouts, stickers and your Valentine message. Don't forget rubber stamps…they're perfect for quick & easy lettering.

INSTRUCTIONS

EGG TREE
(shown on page 10)

Begin by removing the contents from the eggs. For each egg, use a long needle to punch a hole in each end of an egg (slightly enlarge the hole in the pointed end) and to break the yolk. Holding the egg over a bowl and gently blowing into the smaller hole, blow the contents from the shell. Wash out the shells and allow to dry thoroughly.

Now to the fun part…dyeing the eggs! Apply self-adhesive hole reinforcements or use a craft glue stick to adhere silk leaves or flowers (with hard centers removed) randomly to the eggs; cover each egg with a piece cut from nylon stockings and tie to secure.

Make a dye bath for your eggs following the directions on an Easter egg dye kit. Immerse the eggs in the dye…you'll need to use a spoon to keep them from floating. Remove the eggs and allow them to dry thoroughly; remove the stocking covering and adhered shapes. Use paint or markers to add details to eggs as desired.

For each egg, tie a length of wired ribbon into a bow; glue the knot of the bow over the hole in the top of the egg. For the hanger, use a needle to thread clear nylon thread through the top of the bow; tie the ends of the thread together to form a hanging loop.

Glue jumbo rick-rack around the base of a wired tree. Hang the eggs on the tree…fill in empty spaces by gluing ribbon daisies to the tree here and there. Thread brightly colored buttons onto the branches as desired.

CHENILLE BUNNY
(shown on page 14)

Spring is just not Spring without rabbits to deliver Easter eggs. This rabbit will help with that job and he promises to not nibble on seedlings beginning to grow in the garden!

Use a 1/4" seam allowance and match right sides unless otherwise indicated. Refer to Embroidery Stitches, page 133 before beginning project.

Trace the patterns, pages 136 and 137, onto tracing paper. Use the patterns to cut 2 heads, 2 ears and one carrot from white chenille. Cut 2 more ears from heavyweight fusible interfacing and 2 inner ears from striped chenille.

Pin the face pattern to the right side of one head piece. Using 6 strands of floss and working through the paper, work *Backstitches* for the mouth and *Satin Stitches* for the nose. Sew black shank buttons on the head for the eyes. Carefully tear away the pattern. For the whiskers, thread three 6-strand lengths of floss under the nose stitching; knot together to secure.

For each ear, fuse one piece of interfacing to the wrong side of one ear. Matching right sides and leaving the bottom of the ear open for turning, sew ear and inner ear together. Turn ear right-side out. Gather the bottom of ear, then sew to secure. Referring to Fig. 1, pin the ears at the top of the wrong side of the stitched head. Fold up the ears to keep them from getting caught in the stitching. Matching right sides and leaving an opening for turning, sew the head pieces together. Turn the head right-side out, stuff with fiberfill and sew the opening closed.

Fig. 1

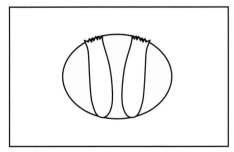

Matching right sides and leaving an opening for turning, sew the body pieces together. Turn the body right-side out, stuff with fiberfill and sew the opening closed. Sew the head and body together. Tack the feet to the head so the rabbit will stand.

Glue on a big, fluffy pom-pom tail; glue some silk flowers between the ears.

For the carrot, mix orange acrylic paint with water for a dye. Soak the carrot piece until it is orange; rinse and let dry. Matching right sides and leaving the top open for turning, fold the carrot piece in half and sew the edges together. Turn right-side out and stuff with fiberfill. Work *Running Stitches* along the top of the carrot; pull threads to gather, then knot thread ends together to secure. For the stem, cut a 2" square from green felt. Cutting to within 1/4" from one edge and at 1/8" intervals, cut strips across the square. Roll the uncut edge and glue to secure; glue in end of carrot.

INDOOR BIRDHOUSES
(shown on page 16)

Embellish purchased wooden birdhouses into a home any bird would be pleased to live in…except these are for decorative purposes only!

To make the birdhouse with the "front door," apply primer, then ivory paint to a wooden birdhouse. Glue a rusted door plate to the front of the house, then glue a rusted skeleton key in the keyhole for a perch. Trimming to fit and wrapping over the edges of the roof, glue embossed wallpaper to the roof. Paint the roof brown…when the paint is dry, *Dry Brush*, page 134, the roof with ivory. Very lightly *Dry Brush* the raised pattern on the roof black. For a "balcony," glue an ornate drawer pull to the front edges of the roof.

For the green birdhouse, glue wooden drawer pulls to the bottom of the house for "feet." Paint the feet and roof ivory; paint the rest of the house green. Apply a light coat of wood-tone spray to the house and roof. Glue a decorative drawer pull plate above the door and a drawer pull below the door. Use a screw to attach a clear glass drawer pull in the hole in the plate. Paint a tree-shaped wooden finial brown, then glue it to the top of the roof.

GARDEN TOOL RACK AND FLOWER BOUQUET

(shown on page 20)

Turn a wrought-iron window unit into a handy collect-all for your gardening items.

For the rack, apply green paint to a wrought-iron window unit…use a piece of natural sponge to add rust-colored highlights while it's still wet. Paint metal buckets and wire baskets the desired colors, then rust them as above…we even found and painted a metal envelope-style container to hang. Apply clear spray sealer to the containers. Use jute to tie the painted items to the rack, then fill with gardening hand tools, gloves, seed packets or other small items…you can even fill one bucket with a bouquet of flowers you make yourself.

For the flowers, we gathered wooden star and snowflake cutouts, candle cups, flowerpots and axle pegs. For each flower, place a pot or cup at the center of a star or snowflake, then drill a small hole through the center of each piece. Sand each piece and wipe with a tack cloth.

Use pliers to shape one end of a length of craft wire into a loop large enough to not slip through the holes. Thread the unlooped end of the wire through the inside of the pot or cup and through the star or snowflake (leave the end long for a stem); apply hot glue to the loop and, while glue is still melted, press a peg into the glue for a flower center.

Paint the flowers "springy" colors, and when the paint is dry, apply a coat of clear spray sealer. Wrap floral tape around the flower stems.

PAINTED POTS

(shown on page 20)

No garden is complete without flowerpots, and nothing perks up a patio better than one-of-a-kind pots!

Spray each clay pot and saucer with a coat of primer, then paint them with bright springtime colors. Use sponge brushes or spouncers to paint stripes, dots or flowers on some of the pots. Paint wavy lines, leaves, designs or sayings as desired. Apply 2 or 3 coats of clear acrylic spray sealer to the pots and saucers.

PAINTED BENCH

(shown on page 20)

When all is done, this bench will be a good resting place to admire your hard work in the garden.

Apply white primer to a wooden bench…maybe one you found at the flea market…then paint it with green exterior paint. After the bench is good and dry, refer to Dry Brush, page 134, to add a brown weathered look to the bench.

Apply 2 to 3 coats of clear sealer to the bench.

MOTHER'S DAY CARD

(shown on page 22)

What Mom wouldn't love something made especially for her? With this handmade card, you're bound to receive lots of smiles and maybe a hug or two!

Use a craft glue stick or spray adhesive to adhere coordinating decorative paper to the inside and outside of a blank card…you could use a 7"x10" piece of card stock for the card and just fold it in half.

Adhere a scalloped border sticker across the front of the card 1" from the bottom edge. Trim the card just below the border.

Glue petals from small white silk flowers to the front of the card…do not glue the edges of the petals down. Glue a button at the center of each flower. Cut leaves from decorative paper and glue them under the edges of the flowers.

For a message inside the card, use decorative-edge craft scissors to cut a rectangle from decorative paper. Use rubber stamps to stamp your message on the paper, then glue it inside the card.

Knot an 8" length of ribbon at the center. Notch the ends and glue the ribbon to the card.

MOTHER'S DAY PIN

(shown on page 23)

Have a fresh flower lapel pin ready to show off the sweet sentiment of flowers picked just for you from the yard. Simply attach a pin clasp to the back of a tiny perfume bottle using double-stick foam tape or household cement, then tie a ribbon around the neck. Now you're ready for unexpected gifts…you can also set it on the counter.

For a presentation card, use decorative-edge craft scissors to cut a rectangle from card stock large enough to accommodate the lapel pin and a message at the top. Use a permanent marker to draw a border around the card and write a message at the top of the card. Attach the pin to the card.

FLOWERING FIREPLACE SCREEN

(shown on page 26)

Use this planter to disguise the "black hole" in the fireplace during the warm-weather months.

Purchase a wooden window flower box to fit your fireplace opening; nail a length of picket fence to the back. (If you can't find a box to fit your fireplace, cut and nail 1"x8" lumber pieces together to form a box 8" deep.)

Paint the box and fence; when dry, Dry Brush, page 134, brown. Lightly sand the fence and box for an aged look.

Paint flowers, leaves, stems and scroll designs on the box. Apply clear acrylic sealer to the planter.

GET WELL BOOKMARK

(shown on page 29)

Layering colors of card stock and pieces of fabric, refer to Making a Tag or Label, page 132, to make a bookmark the desired size. (Ours measures 2³/₄"x7⁵/₈".) Punch a hole at the top of the bookmark, then adhere a colorful hole reinforcement. Use rubber stamps to stamp a message on the bookmark. Thread raffia through the hole and buttons onto the raffia, knotting raffia after each button. Place bookmark in a good book and present to an ailing friend.

FRIEND'S EMERGENCY KIT

(shown on page 30)

When a friend is sick, you want to do something nice for her. Why not fancy up a small suitcase and fill it with things to make her feel better? Note cards, a craft kit, puzzle books, hand lotion or a candle are all good things to include.

Allow paint and sealer to dry after each application.

(continued on page 124)

Apply masking tape to any hardware on the suitcase you do not want painted. Spray paint the suitcase…2 or more coats may be necessary for complete coverage. Paint the corners, then apply clear sealer to the suitcase.

Glue cute paper cutouts, paper lace and silk flowers with pony bead centers on the suitcase as desired. Stamp catchy sayings and words of encouragement on the suitcase.

Gluing as you go, wrap the handle with ribbon.

CROSS-STITCHED BOUQUET

(shown on page 33)

Refer to Cross Stitch, page 132, before beginning project. Use the color key on page 142 for embroidery floss colors.

Using 3 strands of embroidery floss for the *Cross Stitches*, 2 strands of floss for the *Quarter Stitches* and 1 strand of floss for the *Backstitches*, work the design from page 142 at the center of a 7"x9" piece of 14-count white Aida. When your piece is stitched, frame it as desired.

FRIENDSHIP CALLING CARDS

(shown on page 33)

Whether meeting new friends or finding old ones, what better way to exchange phone numbers than with these fun and personal calling cards? With scrapbooking and rubber stamping so popular these days, you probably have most of the supplies already on hand! Refer to Making a Tag or Label, page 132, for general instructions and use pretty papers or fabric scraps, rubber stamps, markers or paint pens to help you create unique cards to fit your personality.

UNIQUE UTENSIL CATCHALL

(shown on page 35)

Sand the mailbox, if necessary, and wipe with a tack cloth. Apply primer, then white spray paint to the entire box, allowing it to dry after each application.

Make a color photocopy of a vintage tablecloth large enough to cover the mailbox. Using a thin layer of craft glue, adhere the photocopy to the mailbox; trim to fit. Apply clear acrylic sealer to the mailbox.

RECYCLED BENCHES

(shown on page 35)

No room in the house anymore for those old benches? Turn them into a shelf unit for the porch or sunroom.

Refer to Painting Techniques, page 134, before beginning project. Allow primer, paint and sealer to dry after each application.

Apply 2 to 3 coats of white primer to 2 wooden benches.

Enlarge the patterns on page 140 to fit your benches. Cut out all but the word patterns.

Apply repositional spray adhesive to the wrong side of the sun and cloud patterns, then adhere them to the bottom bench. Mix one part water with one part light blue paint. Using a stiff brush and randomly crisscrossing brushstrokes, apply paint mixture to benches…before the paint dries completely, use a paper towel to wipe some of the blue paint off until the desired amount of white shows.

Remove the patterns. Lightly *Dry Brush* the clouds blue.

Using the enlarged sun pattern and referring to Stenciling, page 134, make a sun stencil. Tape the stencil over the sun shape on the bench, then *Sponge Paint* the sun yellow. Use transfer paper to transfer the detail lines from the pattern to the painted sun and the words pattern to the front of the top bench. *Sponge Paint* orange cheeks on the sun; paint the words yellow. Use a black permanent fine-point marker to draw over the transferred lines and to randomly outline the words.

Apply 2 to 3 coats of matte clear acrylic sealer to the benches, then stack them for shelves.

SHUTTER BULLETIN BOARD

(shown on page 37)

- spray primer
- yellow, green and white acrylic paint
- paintbrushes
- wooden window frame
- 2 short wooden shutters
- leaf-shaped rubber stamp
- hardboard
- roll cork
- craft glue
- small nails
- 6 mending braces
- picture hanging kit

Allow primer, paint and sealer to dry after each application unless otherwise indicated.

1. Apply primer, then yellow paint to the frame and shutters. Using slightly thinned paint, stamp green leaves around the frame facing.

2. For a yellow wash, mix one part water with 2 parts yellow paint. Working in small sections, apply yellow wash to the frame and shutters; wipe immediately with a soft cloth. Repeat to make a white wash; apply to frame and shutters.

3. Cut a piece of hardboard to fit opening in frame. Cut 2 pieces of cork the same size as the hardboard piece. Glue one piece of cork to hardboard, then glue remaining cork piece to first cork piece. Secure hardboard in frame and nail in place.

4. With pieces right-side down on a flat surface, arrange shutters on each side of frame; use 3 mending braces on each side of frame to secure pieces together.

5. Follow manufacturer's instructions to attach hanging kit to back of frame.

MUNCHIE BOWLS

(shown on page 41)

Nothing could be better than a piping-hot bowl of popcorn…unless maybe the popcorn is served in a personalized bowl!

For each bowl, wash and dry an enamelware bowl thoroughly, then wipe with rubbing alcohol and allow to dry. Using alphabet rubber stamps and permanent enamel craft paint, stamp the desired name or message on the bowl. Paint sprinkles, swirls, dots, stars or hearts randomly on the bowl for an extra personal touch. Follow the paint manufacturer's instructions for drying and washing the bowl.

PATRIOTIC PORCH SWAG

(shown on page 42)

Show your American pride with this patriotic bunting for your front porch!

Press 5 yards of 45" wide patriotic fabric in half lengthwise; cut along the fold. (This will make 2 panels…each panel will make an 8-foot swag…sew one short end of each panel together for a really long panel.) Press each raw edge ½" to the wrong side and sew in place…press the top long edge of the panel 2" more to the wrong side and sew in place for a casing.

Using heavy-duty thread and leaving long thread ends at tops, work loose *Running Stitches*, page 133, across the panel every 36". Thread a hanging rod through the casing. To shape the swags, pull the long threads to gather the fabric; knot the threads to secure.

For each star accent, paint a wooden star cut-out white. Cut a 3" long piece of 16-gauge wire and staple one end to the back of the star. Shape the remaining end into a hook. Hang a star on the rod over each gather.

FLAG PIN
(shown on page 44)

Cut three 2¼"x3½" pieces from white fabric and one from batting. Fuse a piece of paper-backed fusible web to the wrong side of a scrap of blue fabric; cut out a 1¼"x2" blue field. Cut four 1¾" long and three 3½" long pieces of red rick-rack.

Place the batting piece between 2 of the fabric pieces and baste together ½" from the edges for the pin front. Aligning the top and bottom pieces just inside the basting lines and spacing evenly, sew the rick-rack pieces across the pin front; fuse the field to the top left corner inside basting. Using 6 strands of white embroidery floss, work Cross Stitch, page 132, stars on the field.

Matching edges and leaving an opening for turning, place remaining fabric piece on pin front and sew the pieces together just outside the basting lines. Turn the pin right-side out and remove basting stitches. Sew the opening closed; sew a pin clasp to the back.

STAR-SPANGLED TABLECLOTH AND FLOWERPOTS
(shown on page 44)

Tablecloth
Use the patterns on page 141 to cut star shapes from household sponges, then red and blue paint to *Sponge Paint*, page 134, stars onto a white tablecloth.

Flowerpots
For each pot, apply primer, then white paint to clay pot. Paint the rim of the pot

blue…when the blue is dry, use a small star-shaped sponge to *Sponge Paint* white stars around the rim. Paint red stripes down the pot below the rim…paint a thin yellow line on each side of each stripe and dots on the rim. Lightly sand the pot for an aged look, then wipe with a tack cloth. Apply 2 to 3 coats of clear acrylic sealer to the pot.

FRAMED STITCHED PIECES
(shown on page 50)

For each framed piece, trace the desired pattern from pages 142 or 143 onto tissue paper. Pin the pattern to broadcloth. Referring to the *Stitching Key* on page 142, work the indicated *Embroidery Stitches*, page 133, through the pattern. Carefully tear away the pattern. Refer to the photograph to add buttons to the stitched piece.

Mount the stitched piece in the opening of a precut 8"x10" covered mat board with a 4"x6" opening. Mount the mat board in a wooden frame.

EMBROIDERED PILLOWS
(shown on page 50)

Match right sides and use a ¼" seam allowance for all sewing.

For each pillow, cut two 4½"x6½" strips, two 4½"x14½" strips and one 14½" square (back) piece from heavyweight fabric. Cut a 6½" square from hand-dyed muslin.

Trace the desired flower pattern from page 144 onto tissue paper. Pin the pattern at the center of the muslin piece. Working through the pattern and using 3 strands of embroidery floss, work *Backstitches*, page 133, along the pattern lines. Carefully tear away the pattern. Arrange and sew assorted white buttons to the flowers.

To make the front piece, sew the short strips at the top and bottom of the stitched muslin piece; sew the remaining strips to each side.

Place the front and back pieces together. Matching edges, pin jumbo rick-rack along the edges between the layers. Leaving one side open for turning, sew front and back together; turn right-side out. Place a 14" square pillow form in the pillow, then sew the opening closed.

CHEERY CHERRY APRON
(shown on page 53)

- 1⅔ yds. fabric for apron
- paper-backed fusible web
- red, green and brown fabric scraps
- black embroidery floss
- 4½ yds. jumbo rick-rack
- five ⅝" dia. buttons
- 14" of ⅝" wide ribbon
- safety pin

Use a ¼" seam allowance for all sewing and do all topstitching ⅛" from edge unless otherwise indicated.

1. Cut two 12"x13" bib pieces, two 4"x20" neck straps, a 4"x50" waistband and a 26"x45" skirt from fabric for apron.

2. Using the patterns on page 145 and referring to *Making Appliqués*, page 133, make one large and 2 small cherry appliqués from red fabric, 2 leaves from green fabric and one stem from brown fabric. Arranging stem, then cherries, then leaves, fuse appliqués to the right side of one bib piece. Referring to *Embroidery Stitches*, page 133, and using 3 strands of floss, work *Blanket Stitches* along the edges of the cherries and leaves and *Running Stitches* along the edges of the stem. Matching the edge of the rick-rack to the edge of the fabric, baste down the center of rick-rack along edges on the right side of the bib piece.

3. For each neck strap, matching right sides and long edges, fold strap in half, then sew long edges together; sew across one end and clip corner. Turn the straps right-side out and press. Refer to Fig. 1 to baste raw ends of straps to the bib piece.

Fig. 1

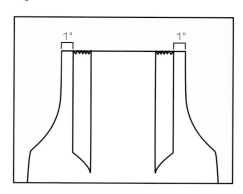

(continued on page 126)

4. Matching right sides and raw edges and leaving an opening for turning, sew remaining bib piece to appliquéd bib piece; turn right side out and sew opening closed.

5. Press the long edges of the waistband 1/4" to the wrong side. Matching right sides, fold the waistband in half lengthwise; sew across each end. Clip corners, then turn waistband right-side out. For apron placement, match ends, fold waistband in half and mark the center; unfold and mark 13" on each side of center mark.

6. For the skirt, cut gently rounded bottom corners on the skirt piece. Press the bottom and side edges of the skirt 1/4" to the wrong side. Leaving half the width of the rick-rack extending past the fabric, pin rick-rack along pressed edges on wrong side of skirt; topstitch in place. Baste 1/8" and 1/4" from the top edge of the skirt; pull the threads to gather the skirt to 26" wide. Placing the skirt between the folds, pin the top of the skirt between the marks on the waistband. Topstitch along long edges of waistband.

7. Working on the front side of the bib, sew one button to each top corner of the bib. Centering the bottom of the bib on the waistband and matching bottom edges, sew 3 buttons, evenly spaced, across the bib to secure it to the waistband. Tie ribbon into a bow; pin between the leaves.

Pot Holder
- tracing paper
- quilted fabric
- red and green fabrics
- button

1. Trace the pot holder pattern from page 145 onto tracing paper. Use the pattern to cut one cherry each from quilted fabric and red fabric. Layer the pieces, wrong sides together.

2. Cut a 1 1/2"x23" bias strip from green fabric, piecing as necessary. Press one long edge, then one end of the strip 1/4" to the wrong side. Beginning with pressed end and matching raw edges, pin the strip to the red side of the pot holder; use a 1/4" seam allowance to sew strip to pot holder. Fold the pressed edge of the strip to the back of the pot holder and stitch in place.

3. For the hanging loop, cut a 1 1/2"x7" strip from green fabric. Matching wrong sides, press strip in half lengthwise and unfold, then press long edges to center; refold and topstitch along edges. Match short edges and sew together at an angle; trim seam. Sew the ends of the loop to the top front of the pot holder; sew a button over the ends.

Towel
Sew the ends of a 6" length of ribbon together to form a hanging loop. Sew the ends of the loop to the center of a dish towel...hang the towel by the ribbon loop from one button on the apron.

CHERRY CHAIR BACK COVER
(shown on page 54)

Large kitchen towels are the starters for this project...they'll fit the back of a standard kitchen chair. If your chair is wider, use 2 towels hemmed together along the long edges.

For the chair back design, cut an 8" square of print fabric. Working on the right side of the square and matching the edge of a length of rick-rack to the edge of the fabric, sew down the center of the rick-rack along all edges. Press the fabric edge to the wrong side so rick-rack extends along edges of square. Position the square on the bottom half on the right side of the towel; sew a button at each corner of the square to tack it to the towel.

Cut 2 strips from fabric 5" wide and 2 times the width of the towel. For each ruffle, matching right sides and long edges, fold one strip in half lengthwise, then sew across each end of the strip; clip the corners, turn right-side out and press. Baste along the raw edges of the strip, then pull the threads to gather the ruffle to fit the end of the towel. Pin the ruffle to the wrong side of one end of the towel, then sew in place. Repeat to sew remaining ruffle to opposite end of towel.

Matching wrong sides and short edges, fold the towel in half. With rick-rack extending along edges, pin jumbo rick-rack between towel side layers, then sew the side edges together, catching the rick-rack in the stitching.

CHERRY CHAIR CUSHION
(shown on page 54)

For all those long hours spent at the table crafting or just chatting, why not add a comfy seat cushion to make the time pass more comfortably?

To make a pattern for the cushion cover, draw around the chair seat on a piece of newsprint, then cut it out. Use the pattern to cut 2 cover pieces, 1" larger on all sides than the pattern, from fabric.

For each chair tie, cut a 3"x10" strip from a dish towel (we used one that matched our chair back cover). Matching right sides, fold tie in half lengthwise; using a 1/4" seam allowance, sew the long edges together. Turn the tie right-side out, then sew across each end.

Layer cover pieces, matching right sides and raw edges. Fold each chair tie in half; place one tie at each back corner between cover pieces, matching fold in tie with raw edges of cover pieces. Leaving a small opening for turning, sew the cover pieces together. Turn the cover right-side out, stuff with fiberfill and sew closed.

Sew hook and loop fasteners on opposite sides of the tie. Place the cushion on the chair and fasten the ties around the uprights to secure in place. Stack and glue 2 buttons together at the top end of each chair tie.

CASSEROLE COZY
(shown on page 60)

Deliver that special home-cooked dish in this super-soft dish cozy...a perfect housewarming or hostess gift!

For the cover, measure the length and width of your pan and add 4" to each measurement. Using the determined measurements, cut a piece of batting, a piece of fabric for the lining and a piece of fabric for the outside. Layer the fabric pieces, right sides together, then pin the batting piece on top of the fabric pieces; cut a 2" square from each corner.

Cut eight 4" lengths of ribbon. Pin one ribbon between the fabric layers at each outer corner...the long end of the ribbon should be inside the fabric stack, not sticking out the edges. Leaving an opening for turning and using a $1/4$" seam allowance, sew the pieces together; turn the cozy right-side out and sew the opening closed.

Glue a pretty trim or ribbon along the top edges of the cozy. Tie the ribbon together at each corner.

AUTUMN-PRINT LUNCHBOX
(shown on page 68)
- sandpaper
- metal lunchbox
- tack cloth
- masking tape
- spray primer
- light green spray paint
- natural sponges
- assorted acrylic paint in fall and metallic colors
- paintbrushes
- fall-motif rubber stamps
- wooden pick
- clear acrylic sealer

Allow primer and paint to dry after each application.

1. If necessary, sand any rusted areas on the lunchbox, then wipe with a tack cloth. Mask the handle of the box if it doesn't need painting. Apply primer, then 2 coats of spray paint to the outside of the box. *Sponge Paint*, page 134, the rims with metallic paint.

2. Using a paintbrush, apply paint to the rubber stamp...layer colors to get a variegated imprint; stamp designs on the box for a sponge-painted look.

3. Use the wooden pick to draw dotted tails from some of the leaves.

4. Apply 2 to 3 coats of clear acrylic sealer to the lunchbox.

5. Fill your newly crafted tote with goodies for a quick autumn picnic, a school ball game or just to be the envy of the lunch crowd!

TEACHER'S VEST
(shown on page 69)
Match right sides and use a $1/4$" seam allowance for all sewing unless otherwise indicated. Use 3 strands of floss and refer to Embroidery Stitches, page 133, for all stitching.

Start with a purchased denim vest with a straight bottom edge and a collar; remove the buttons from the vest. Measure the width of the bottom edge. Now, using the determined measurement as the length, cut two strips each from the following colors of fabric: $1 1/4$" wide green, 2" wide yellow, $1 1/4$" wide red and $5 1/2$" wide blue. Using the order above, sew the strips together along the long edges to make two fabric panels; press the seams to one side.

Working on the right side, sew a length of red jumbo rick-rack along the long raw edge of the green strip on each panel; press the seams to the wrong side.

Press the outer edge of each panel $1/4$" to the wrong side. If necessary, arrange and pin the panels on the vest to trim rounded corners to a $1/4$" seam allowance. Press the bottom and inner seam allowances $1/4$" to the wrong side. Arrange and pin the panels to the vest, then sew the outer, bottom and inner edges in place. Work *Running Stitches* along the top edges of the green and red strips and along both edges of the yellow strips. Work *Cross Stitches* over the red/blue seam, then work *Blanket Stitches* along the bottom and inner edges. Cut through the buttonholes that were covered and *Whip Stitch* fabric in place around the holes.

Trace the word patterns, page 141, onto tissue paper. Pin the patterns to the yellow strip, then work *Backstitches* over the words; carefully remove the paper. Work *French Knots* to dot each "i."

Using the star pattern, page 141, follow *Making Appliqués*, page 133, to make 2 stars. Fuse the stars to the vest. Work *Blanket Stitches* along the edges of the stars...stitch a *Running Stitch* tail from one point of each star.

Sew rick-rack to underside of collar along edges (half of rick-rack should extend past edge of collar), then work yellow *Running Stitches* along top edge of the collar. Replace buttons on vest with bright-colored buttons...sew buttons between the words.

HOT WATER BOTTLE COVER
(shown on page 70)
You can show your school pride (and stay warm) by using fleece in your team colors.

Cut eight $4 1/2$" squares from each color of fleece, two $8 1/2$"x$16 1/2$" pieces for the lining and one 3"x$8 1/2$" piece for the fringe.

Overlapping the edges $1/4$" and alternating colors, use a zigzag stitch to sew 4 squares together to form a row; make 4 rows. Repeat to sew 2 rows together to make 2 panels.

Matching right sides, sew a lining piece to each panel along one short edge; turn the panels right-side out.

Matching lining sides, place panels together. Pin $1/2$" of fringe piece between panels at bottom of cover. For a tie, fold a 24" length of $1/4$" diameter cotton cord in half. Pin fold of cord between panels, one square below the top at one edge of cover. Using a zigzag stitch, sew along side and bottom edges of cover. Make clips in fringe piece at $1/4$" intervals.

STADIUM BLANKET
(shown on page 71)
- $2 1/2$ yds. each of 2 colors of fleece
- rotary cutter and cutting mat

Sizes given in instructions will make a 50"x70" blanket. Overlap fleece $1/4$" and use a zigzag stitch for all sewing.

1. Cut seventeen $10 1/2$" squares from first color of fleece and eighteen $10 1/2$" squares from remaining fleece, then cut two 4"x50" and two 4"x70" borders from fleece.

2. Alternating colors, sew 7 squares together to make a strip. Alternating colors of first squares, make 4 more strips. Matching long edges, sew strips together.

3. Overlapping at corners, sew borders along edges of blanket. For fringe, clip borders at $1/4$" intervals.

JACK-'O-LANTERN PATCH

(shown on page 75)

Paint a wooden planter as desired and allow to dry; *Dry Brush, page 134*, with brown paint. Glue a miniature twig fence to the front of the planter. Trimming to fit, glue plastic foam blocks in the planter, then sheet moss over the foam.

For each Jack-'O-Lantern, cut a face from black paper and glue onto a miniature pumpkin. Glue the pumpkin to a stick from the yard. Tightly twist a long length of craft wire around the stem, pumpkin and stick several times to secure the pumpkin on the stick...curl the wire ends. "Plant" the pumpkin in the box.

Fill in around the pumpkins with more sticks and twigs. Cut some "leaves" from corrugated craft cardboard and glue randomly to the sticks and twigs.

For the sign, use a black paint pen to write "Happy Haunting!" on a small hanging wooden sign with a rusted tin plaque. Hang the sign from one of the twigs.

TOMATO COSTUME

(continued from page 79)

For the hat, trace the leaf pattern, page 147, onto tracing paper. Using pinking shears, cut 5 leaves and one 3½" diameter circle from green felt...you will also need to cut a 6"x12" rectangle for the stem and a 1"x30" strip for the ties. Glue the circle at the center of the tie strip. Glue a 6" length of pipe cleaner along one long edge of the stem felt piece. Tightly roll the felt around the pipe cleaner, then glue to secure. Glue one end of the stem to the center of the circle on the side with the tie strip. Pinching the leaf at the narrow section and gluing the pinched area to the circle, glue the leaves around the stem; bend the stem slightly.

BUG COSTUME

(shown on page 79)

- three colors of felt for wings and spots on romper, stripe down wings and spots on wings
- fabric glue
- knit romper
- fabric to match romper
- self-adhesive hook and loop fastener
- ½"w paper-backed fusible web tape
- three pairs of child-size socks
- polyester fiberfill
- safety pins
- heavy-duty thread and needle
- 2 pipe cleaners
- headband with spring antennae
- 2 pom-poms

1. Use a photocopier to enlarge wing pattern, page 148, to desired size... if necessary, cut the pattern apart and enlarge by sections, then tape enlarged copies together. Using enlarged pattern, cut wings, then 2 jumbo spots, 3 large spots, 2 medium spots and 5 small spots from felt for wings; cut 2 jumbo spots, 4 large spots, 4 medium spots and 10 small spots from felt for spots on wings. Cut stripe from remaining felt color.

2. Referring to the wing pattern for placement, glue the spots, stripe and hook and loop fastener on the wings. Referring to the front diagram, page 148, glue the spots on the front of the romper.

3. For each "extra" arm, measure length of romper sleeve from under arm to end of cuff; add 3½". Measure height of cuff; add 1". Cut a rectangle of fabric the determined measurements; use fusible tape to hem one short edge. Fuse a length of tape along one long edge on the right side of the fabric piece; remove the paper backing. Matching right sides, fuse long edges together; turn right-side out. Fold raw end up 1½" two times to make a cuff. Fill the toe of one sock with fiberfill. Insert the sock in the cuff end of the arm and glue to secure. Lightly stuff the arm and glue the opening closed.

4. Working from the inside of the romper, use safety pins to secure the arms to the romper...the arms should be close together. To make the arms move together, sew a length of heavy-duty thread between each arm...make sure it's long enough for the arms to hang slightly.

5. For each mitten, turn one sock wrong-side out. Cut a slit in the toe long and wide enough for the child's thumb. Use glue to "seam" the edges together, then allow to dry. Turn mitten right-side out.

6. For the antennae, insert a pipe cleaner in each spring of headband; trim even with end of spring. Wrap the remainder of pipe cleaners around springs. Glue a pom-pom to the end of each antenna.

LION COSTUME

(shown on page 78)

There's nothing cowardly about this lion! Turn a plain brown sweat suit into an adorable costume for a fall carnival...or just for playtime.

Trace the ear pattern from page 147 onto tracing paper; use the pattern to cut two ears from brown felt. Glue the ears to a plastic headband. Gluing as you go, make 8" long loops of yarn along the headband for the mane.

For the collar, measure around the child's neck and add 2". Cut a strip of felt 1" wide by the determined measurement. Apply self-adhesive hook and loop fasteners at opposite sides of the ends of the strips. Working on the same side of the strip with the rough piece of fastener, glue 8" long loops of yarn along the strip. Repeat to make wristbands.

For the tail, cut a 7"x23" piece of beige felt. Glue the long edges together to form a tube; turn right-side out. Wrap yarn around a 5" square piece of cardboard...wrap lots of yarn for a fuller tail. Tightly knot a length of yarn around the yarn at one end of the cardboard; cut the yarn at opposite end. Tie a length of yarn around tassel near top. Glue top of tassel inside one end of tail. Stuff tail with fiberfill and pin to pants.

Glue an oval of beige felt to the front of the shirt.

FAIRY COSTUME

(shown on page 78)

Use pinking shears for all cutting and allow paint to dry after each application.

- sheer fabric for capelet, collar and hat
- thumbtack
- string
- pinking shears
- assorted colors of dimensional paint
- small self-adhesive acrylic jewels
- ⅛" wide satin ribbon
- elastic thread
- 2 pipe cleaners
- hot glue gun
- plastic headband
- paintbrush
- gold glitter paint

1. For the capelet, measure the child from the back of the neck to the wrist; double the measurement. Cut a square of fabric the determined measurement.

2. To determine inside cutting line measurement, measure around child's head; divide measurement by 4. Using determined measurement for inside cutting line and original neck to wrist measurement for outside cutting line, follow *Making A Fabric Circle*, page 132, to cut out capelet.

3. Working 2½" from the outer edge and spacing evenly, pin desired number of photocopies of the circle design, page 148, to wrong side of the capelet…the design should show through to the right side. Using dimensional paint and working on the right side of the capelet, randomly draw stars in the upper area of the capelet; press an acrylic jewel in the center of each star. Make dots of paint over each circle design, then draw short, wavy lines along the outer edge.

4. For the collar, cut a 3"x24" strip of fabric. Use dimensional paint to draw wavy lines and stars along one long edge; attach one jewel to the center of each star. Using ribbon, work *Running Stitches*, page 133, along opposite edge.

5. Cut an 18" square from fabric. Using 9" as the outer cutting line and no inner cutting line, follow *Making A Fabric Circle* to cut out hat piece. Use dimensional paint to draw wavy lines along edge and random stars on hat. Using elastic thread, work *Running Stitches* 2" in from edge. Gather hat to fit head and knot ends on inside of hat.

6. For antennae, coil one end of each pipe cleaner and glue to headband; wrap ends around finger to curl. Brush headband and antenna with gold glitter paint.

DECORATED CANDLES
(shown on page 83)
Candles, candles everywhere…is there such a thing as too many candles?

For some of your candles, use corrugated craft cardboard (and decorative paper if you desire) to make a sleeve for the candle…tie it on with raffia or ribbon. You could even add a tag embellished with a metal charm.

For a vintage look, try covering pillar candles with grains and spices from the kitchen. First, cover a large work area with newspaper. Next, melt wax to coordinate with the color of your candle in a coffee can that has been placed in an electric skillet filled with water and heated to a boil. After the wax is melted, stir your favorite spices into the mixture. Use a 1" wide paintbrush to apply the wax mixture to the candle.

To add texture to the candle, spread a layer of uncooked oatmeal or bran on aluminum foil…apply wax mixture to the candle, then immediately roll the candle in the grain. Repeat, layering the wax mixture and rolling in grain until you achieve the desired results…it is not necessary to allow the mixture to dry between applications. Allow the wax to harden before lighting candle.

"THANKS" WALL HANGING
(shown on page 86)
- black, grey and coordinating colors of embroidery floss
- 15"x27" piece of 7-ct. Klostern
- paper-backed fusible web
- assorted felt

1. Using 6 strands of black floss and following the diagram on page 150, center and Cross Stitch, page 132, the words on the Klostern.

2. Using the patterns, pages 150 and 151, follow *Making Appliqués*, page 133, to make one appliqué of each shape from felt.

3. Referring to photograph, arrange and fuse appliqués on wall hanging. Using 2 strands of coordinating floss and referring to *Embroidery Stitches*, page 133, work desired stitches around, and detail stitches on, the appliqués. Use 6 strands of grey floss to work a Cross Stitch sidewalk.

4. Frame piece as desired.

STITCHED BREAD CLOTH
(shown on page 87)
This fall-motif bread cloth is the perfect complement to your baked goods.

Using the patterns, page 149, and following *Making Appliqués*, page 133, make pumpkin, stem and leaf appliqués from fabrics.

Arrange and fuse the appliqués on one corner of a muslin bread cloth. Using 3 strands of embroidery floss, work your favorite *Embroidery Stitches*, page 133, to embellish the appliqués. Work *Running Stitches* along the edges of the cloth.

LEAF PLACE MAT
(shown on page 87)
Refer to Embroidery Stitches, page 133, before beginning project.

For each place mat, cut two 13"x21" pieces of fabric. Matching right sides, leaving an opening for turning and using a ½" seam allowance, sew fabric pieces together; turn right-side out and press. Topstitch pieces ½" from the edges.

For the leaf napkin holder, fuse the wrong sides of two 7"x10" pieces of fabric together. Enlarge the leaf pattern on page 151 by 125%; use the pattern to cut a leaf from the fused fabric. Stitch "veins" on the leaf. Use 3 strands of embroidery floss to work *Blanket Stitches* along the edges of the leaf. Pin the leaf on the placemat…put a napkin in it to gauge spacing. Stitch a straight line on the leaf on each side of the napkin. Sew a large button to the leaf.

For the nametag, use pinking shears to cut a 2"x4" piece from felt. Use embroidery floss to work *Running Stitches* along the edges. Cut a buttonhole at one end to fit the button on the leaf. Lightly draw the name on the tag, then use floss to work *Backstitches* over the drawn lines. Button the tag on the leaf.

COLLECTOR'S SHELF
(shown on page 92)
If you can't find an antique-looking shelf already made, they're really easy to make. Start with a piece of 1"x4" lumber the desired length for your backboard. Nail a piece of 1" thick rounded molding along the bottom and a piece of crown molding along the top (we mitered and beveled the corners on some of our lumber). Cut a piece of 1"x6" lumber for the shelf and nail it on top of the crown molding. Stain the shelf, then add heavy-duty hangers to the back.

(continued on page 130)

Use a photocopier to enlarge the patterns on page 152 to fit your backboard. Use transfer paper to transfer the words to the backboard. Referring to *Painting Techniques*, page 134, paint the letters. Paint a thin outline around each letter, then randomly outline the outlines in a few places. *Shade* the left half of each letter outside of the outlines brown. Apply stain to the bottom half of the letters and immediately wipe away with a soft cloth.

COOKIE EXCHANGE INVITATIONS
(shown on page 101)

For each invitation, cut a 7"x10" card from card stock; matching short edges, fold card in half. Cut a 4¾"x6½" overlay from vellum; use decorative-edge craft scissors to cut a background from decorative paper the same size. Use a permanent marker to draw over the word pattern, page 153, on the vellum. Using a craft glue stick, adhere the edges of the background, then the overlay, to the front of the card.

Trace the gingerbread man and heart patterns, page 153, onto tracing paper. Use the patterns to cut 2 hearts from fabric and a gingerbread man from card stock. Use a fine-point marker to draw a face and a red colored pencil to draw cheeks on the gingerbread man. Glue the gingerbread man to the front of the card; layer the hearts and glue them to the gingerbread man.

GINGERBREAD MAN TREAT BAGS
(shown on page 103)

Make one of these adorable bags for each guest at your cookie exchange party to carry home samples from the party.

Cut a 3½"x5½" piece from card stock for a pocket; glue sides and bottom of the pocket to the front of a decorative lunch-size paper bag. Trace the gingerbread man and heart patterns, page 153, onto tracing paper. Use the patterns to cut one gingerbread man from card stock, 2 hearts from fabric and one heart from batting. Glue the gingerbread man to white card stock; leaving a ¼" border, use decorative-edge craft scissors to cut out gingerbread man.

Glue batting heart between 2 fabric hearts. Glue the heart to the gingerbread man. Use a fine-point marker to draw a face and a red colored pencil to draw cheeks on the gingerbread man...draw a black zigzag line along the edges of the pocket.

Cut a 3"x4½" card from red & white striped decorative paper. Matching bottom edges, glue it to a blank 3"x5" card; write desired recipe on the card, then tuck it into the pocket.

Fill the bag with treats. Fold the top of the bag 1" to the wrong side. Punch two holes at the top center of the bag through the fold...use a strand or 2 of raffia to tie the bag closed.

YULE LOG
(shown on page 106)

Making sure your log sits flat to avoid a fire hazard, drill holes in a log to fit your candles. Place the candles, then arrange fresh greenery around them.

PAINTED BOX
(shown on page 109)

Apply primer, then light blue paint to the outside of a small round paper maché box and lid; allow to dry. Apply self-adhesive snowflake-shaped stickers to the box.

For the knob, stack and glue several white buttons to the lid.

SNACK BAG
(shown on page 110)

Turn a plain colored lunch bag into a cute peek-a-boo bag for presenting a gift of snack mix to your friend.

Cut a square from the front of the bag. Cut a piece of clear cellophane and decorative paper 2" larger on all sides than the opening; glue cellophane inside the bag, covering the opening.

For the frame, cut an opening in the decorative paper slightly smaller than the opening in the bag...use decorative-edge craft scissors to trim the outside edges. Glue the frame to the front of the bag.

Glue a 1½" wide strip of decorative paper, trimmed with decorative-edge craft scissors, along the flap. Glue a length of grosgrain ribbon along the top of the strip.

Glue a large fabric-covered button to the flap. Hang a rubber-stamped tag from the button.

DECORATED BUCKET
(shown on page 111)

Cover a metal sap bucket with self-adhesive felt...trim the top and bottom edges even with the bucket.

Use decorative-edge craft scissors to cut a vintage Christmasy motif from a postcard or greeting card. Glue the motif to a piece of felt; use craft scissors to trim the felt ¼" larger on all sides than the motif. Glue the motif to the front of the bucket.

Place your gift in cellophane and tie it closed with ribbon. Tie on a tag embellished with decorative paper and a Christmas charm. Place gift in bucket.

CANDY-STRIPED POPPER
(shown on page 111)

Use this unique gift wrap to keep them guessing what's inside!

Wrap a paper towel tube with white paper...glue the seam to secure; tuck the extra paper inside the ends of the tube. Gluing the ribbon ends inside the ends of the tube, spiral lengths of ribbons around the tube. Place gift inside tube, then fill the ends with tissue paper. Wrap the tube in cellophane and tie the ends closed with raffia.

Cut a tag from card stock; glue to a piece of decorative paper, then trim the paper ⅛" larger than the tag. Punch a hole in the tag; apply a self-adhesive hole reinforcement to the hole. Write a message on the tag; attach the tag to the raffia.

SNOWMAN WALL HANGING
(shown on page 112)

- tracing paper
- polyester batting
- orange and black felt
- ¾"x3½" yellow fabric for hatband
- 15¼"x15½" piece of blue felt
- white, black and yellow embroidery floss
- 2 black snaps
- tissue paper
- 16¼"x19" piece of red felt
- fabric glue
- buttons for holly berries
- artificial holly leaves

Refer to Embroidery Stitches, page 133, before beginning project. Use 6 strands of floss for all stitching.

1. Trace the patterns on page 155 onto tracing paper. Using the patterns, cut head from batting, nose from orange felt, hat from black felt and hatband from fabric. Arrange and pin head, hat and hatband on blue felt; pin nose on head. Work *Running Stitches* around head, hat, hatband and nose.

2. Work *French Knots* for the snowman's mouth; sew on snaps for eyes.

3. Trace the letter patterns, pages 154 and 155, onto tissue paper; trace another E and R. Arrange and pin the letters on the blue felt; cut out the letters. Center and pin the blue felt 3" below the top edge of the red felt. Work *Running Stitches* along the edges of each letter and the outside edges of the blue felt.

4. Use white floss to work *French Knot* and *Straight Stitch* "snowflakes" on the blue felt.

5. For the hanging sleeve, press the top edge of the red felt piece 2½" to the back; glue edge to secure. Glue buttons and leaves to the hatband.

CHRISTMAS STOCKINGS
(shown on page 113)

Stockings are fun for everyone to make. Whether making easy felt stockings or fabric stockings, you can use the pattern on page 156 as your starting place.

Basic Felt Stocking

Trace the stocking pattern onto tracing paper. Using the pattern, cut 2 stocking pieces from felt…cut out one heel and one toe shape if desired. If you're adding a heel and toe, pin them on one stocking piece and work *Blanket Stitches*, page 133, along the inner edges. Pin the stocking pieces together and use *Blanket Stitches* or *Running Stitches*, page 133, to sew them together.

For the cuff, cut a 4"x11½" strip from contrasting felt. Overlapping ends at back, glue one long edge of the cuff around the top of the stocking; fold the cuff down.

Basic Fabric Stocking

Use a ½" seam allowance for all sewing.

Trace the stocking pattern onto tracing paper. Using the pattern, cut 2 stocking pieces from fabric and 2 stocking pieces from lining. Matching right sides and leaving the top open, sew the stocking pieces together; repeat for the lining.

Cut an 8"x12" piece of fabric for the cuff. Matching right sides, sew the short ends together. Matching wrong sides and raw edges, fold the cuff in half.

Turn the stocking only right-side out and place the lining in the stocking. Matching raw edges and the seam of the cuff to the heel-side seam of the stocking, pin the cuff in the lining. Sew all pieces together along the top edge, then turn the cuff out.

Embellishing the Stockings

Buttons, beads and sequins can be glued or sewn on; appliqués can be glued, fused or sewn. If you want professional-looking letters, try some of the fonts from your computer for your patterns. Computer clip art, picture books and coloring books are great places to find patterns for trees, snowflakes and other Christmas motifs. Once you've found your pattern, cut the shapes from fabric or felt (refer to *Making Appliqués*, page 133, to make fusible appliqués) and start decorating.

QUILT PIECE ANGEL
(shown on page 114)

Made from a well-loved quilt, this angel can keep watch over a special friend.

Refer to Embroidery Stitches, page 133, before beginning project.

Trace the patterns, page 157, onto tracing paper. Using the body patterns, cut 2 bodies from an old quilt, 2 wings from cotton batting and one head from muslin. Sew a button to one body piece…this will be the front. Leaving an opening for stuffing, work *Blanket Stitches* along the edges of the body pieces to sew them together; lightly stuff with polyester fiberfill and sew the opening closed. Work *Running Stitches* along the edges of the wings to sew them together.

For the head, make a *French Knot* for each eye and a *Straight Stitch* for the mouth at the center of the muslin circle. Using a 1⅛" diameter covered button kit, cover the button with the embroidered head. Gluing to secure, encircle the head with a "halo" of small, pliable twigs. Sew the head to the top of the body and the wings to the back. Glue a small piece of trim to the neck for a collar. Hang several charms from the button.

GLASS CHARMS
(shown on page 116)

Never mix up glasses at a large gathering again…these fun charms make each glass unique!

For each charm, cut a 6" length of craft wire…if your stemware is larger than standard, you will need to adjust the length of your wire. Use needle-nose pliers to shape a small loop in one end of the wire; wrap wire around itself to secure. Thread beads onto the wire to within 1" from the end of the wire; place the beaded wire around the stem to make sure it fits. Twist the end of the wire around itself above the last bead to form a loop; flatten the loop, then bend the opposite end to make a hook.

To make the dangle, hook a 3" length of wire around the wire between 2 beads on the beaded circle. Thread beads onto the wire, then coil the end to secure.

BOTTLE BAG
(shown on page 116)
- two 7"x16" pieces of fabric for outer bag
- two 7"x16" pieces of fabric for lining
- ruffle trim for top of bag
- satin ribbon

Use a ½" seam allowance for all sewing unless otherwise indicated.

1. Matching right sides, sew long edges of outer fabric pieces together to form a tube. Repeat using lining fabric pieces. Turn liner right-side out.

2. Matching raw edges, pin ruffled trim along top edge of liner; baste in place.

3. Matching top edges and side seams, place liner in outer tube; sew around top edge, joining liner and tube. Pull the liner out and fold it over the outer tube. Flatten the bag…the bag will be inside-out with the bottom edge open; sew across the bottom edge.

4. To make a flat bottom, match each side seam to bottom fold line; sew across each corner 1½" from point. Clip corners and turn the bag right-side out.

5. Place bottle in bag, tie with ribbon and fold top of bag down to show lining.

GENERAL INSTRUCTIONS

CROSS STITCH

Counted Cross Stitch (X): Work one Cross Stitch to correspond to each colored square in chart. For horizontal rows, work stitches in two journeys (Fig. 1).

Fig. 1

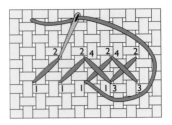

For vertical rows, complete stitch as shown in Fig. 2.

Fig. 2

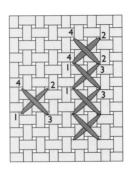

Backstitch (B'ST): For outline detail, Backstitch (shown in chart and color key by black or colored straight lines) should be worked after all Cross Stitch has been completed (Fig. 3).

Fig. 3

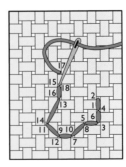

French Knot: Referring to Fig. 4, bring needle up at 1. Wrap floss once around needle and insert needle at 2, holding end of floss with non-stitching fingers.

Fig. 4

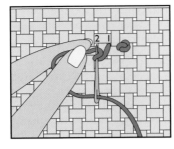

Quarter Stitch: Quarter Stitches are shown as triangular shapes of color in chart and color key. Come up at 1, then split fabric thread to take needle down at 2 (Fig. 5).

Fig. 5

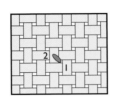

MAKING A FABRIC CIRCLE

1. Cut a square of fabric the size indicated in project instructions.

2. Matching right sides, fold fabric square in half from top to bottom and again from left to right.

3. Tie one end of string to a pencil or fabric marking pen. Measuring from pencil, insert a thumbtack through string at length indicated in project instructions. Insert thumbtack through folded corner of fabric. Holding tack in place and keeping string taut, mark cutting line (Fig. 1).

Fig. 1

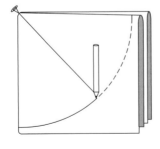

4. Cut along drawn line through all fabric layers.

MAKING PATTERNS

When the entire pattern is shown, place tracing paper over the pattern and draw over lines. For a more durable pattern, use a permanent marker to draw over pattern on stencil plastic.

When patterns are stacked or over-lapped, place tracing paper over the pattern and follow a single colored line to trace the pattern. Repeat to trace each pattern separately onto tracing paper.

When tracing a two-part pattern, draw over the first part of the pattern onto tracing paper, then match the dashed lines and arrows and draw over the second part of the pattern.

When only half of the pattern is shown (indicated by a solid blue line on pattern), fold tracing paper in half. Place the fold along the solid blue line and trace pattern half; turn folded paper over and draw over the traced lines on the remaining side. Unfold the pattern.

MAKING A TAG OR LABEL

For a quick and easy tag or label, photocopy or trace (use transfer paper to transfer design) a copyright-free design onto card stock...or just cut a shape from card stock.

Color tag with colored pencils, crayons or thinned acrylic paint; draw over transferred lines using permanent markers or paint pens. Use straight-edge or decorative-edge craft scissors to cut out tag; glue to colored or decorative paper or card stock, then cut tag out, leaving a border around it.

Use a pen or marker to write a message on the tag. You can also choose items from a wide variety of self-adhesive stickers, borders or frames; rubber stamps and inkpads; or gel pens in an assortment of colors, densities and point-widths, to further embellish your tags or labels.

EMBROIDERY STITCHES

Preparing floss: If your project will be laundered, soak floss in a mixture of one cup water and one tablespoon vinegar for a few minutes and allow to dry before using to prevent colors from bleeding or fading.

Backstitch: Referring to Fig. 1, bring needle up at 1; go down at 2; bring up at 3 and pull through. For next stitch, insert needle at 1; bring up at 4 and pull through.

Fig. 1

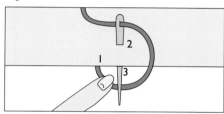

Blanket Stitch: Referring to Fig. 2a, bring needle up at 1. Keeping thread below point of needle, go down at 2 and come up at 3. Continue working as shown in Fig. 2b.

Fig. 2a

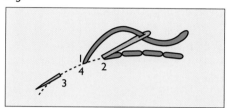

Fig. 2b

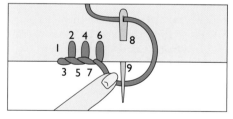

Cross Stitch: Bring needle up at 1 and go down at 2. Come up at 3 and go down at 4 (Fig. 3).

Fig. 3

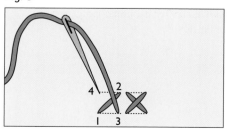

French Knot: Referring to Fig. 4, bring needle up at 1. Wrap floss once around needle and insert needle at 2, holding end of floss with non-stitching fingers.

Fig. 4

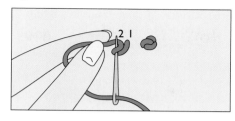

Outline Stitch: Come up at 1. Keeping thread below the stitching line, go down at 2 and come up at 3. Go down at 4 and come up at 5 (Fig. 5).

Fig.5

Running Stitch: Referring to Fig. 6, make a series of straight stitches with stitch length equal to the space between stitches.

Fig. 6

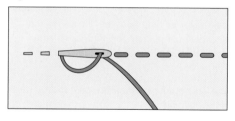

Satin Stitch: Referring to Fig. 7, come up at odd numbers and go down at even numbers with the stitches touching but not overlapping.

Fig. 7

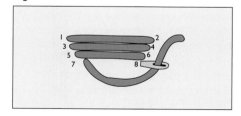

Straight Stitch: Referring to Fig. 8, come up at 1 and go down at 2.

Fig. 8

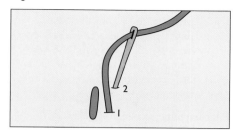

Whip Stitch: With right sides of folded fabric edges together, bring needle up at 1; take thread around edge of fabric and bring needle up at 2. Continue stitching along edge of fabric.

Fig. 9

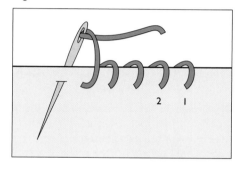

MAKING APPLIQUÉS

To prevent darker fabrics from showing through, white or light-colored fabrics may need to be lined with fusible interfacing before being fused.

To make reverse appliqués, trace the pattern onto tracing paper; turn traced paper over and continue to follow all steps using the reversed pattern.

1. Trace the pattern onto paper side of fusible web as many times as indicated in project instructions. When making more than one appliqué, leave at least 1" between shapes.

2. Cut out shape 1/2" outside of drawn lines. Fuse the shape to the wrong side of fabric, then cut out along drawn lines.

PAINTING TECHNIQUES

Transferring a pattern: Trace pattern onto tracing paper. Place transfer paper, coated side down, between project and traced pattern. Use removable tape to secure pattern to project. Use a pencil to draw over outlines of design (press lightly to avoid smudges and heavy lines that are difficult to cover). If necessary, use a soft eraser to remove any smudges.

Painting base coats: Use a medium round brush for large areas and a small round brush for small areas. Do not overload brush. Allowing to dry between coats, apply several thin coats of paint as needed for desired coverage.

Transferring details: To transfer detail lines to design, reposition pattern and transfer paper over painted base coats and use a pencil to lightly draw over detail lines of design.

Adding details: Use a permanent marker or paint pen to draw over transferred detail lines, or freehand details onto project.

Dry Brush: Do not dip brush in water. Dip a stipple brush or old paintbrush in paint; wipe most of the paint off onto a dry paper towel. Lightly rub the brush across the area to receive color. Repeat as needed for desired coverage of color.

Shading and highlighting: Dip one corner of a flat brush in water; blot on a paper towel. Dip dry corner of brush into paint. Stroke brush back and forth on palette until there is a gradual change from paint to water in each brush stroke. Stroke paint-loaded side of brush along detail line on project, pulling brush toward you and turning project if necessary. For shading, side load brush with a darker color of paint. For highlighting, side load brush with a lighter color of paint.

Spatter Painting: Dip the bristle tips of a dry toothbrush into paint, blot on a paper towel to remove excess, then pull thumb across bristles to spatter paint on project.

Sponge Painting: Use an assembly-line method when making several sponge-painted projects. Place project on a covered work surface. Practice sponge-painting technique on scrap paper until desired look is achieved. Paint projects with first color and allow to dry before moving to next color. Use a clean sponge for each additional color.

For allover designs, dab a dampened sponge piece (natural, compressed or household sponge) into paint; remove excess paint on a paper towel. Use a light stamping motion to paint item.

For painting with sponge shapes, dip a dampened sponge shape into paint; remove excess paint on a paper towel. Lightly press sponge shape onto project. Carefully lift sponge. For a reverse design, turn sponge shape over.

STENCILING

These instructions are written for multicolor stencils. For single-color stencils, make one stencil for entire design.

1. For first stencil, cut a piece from stencil plastic 1" larger than entire pattern. Center plastic over pattern and use a permanent pen to trace outlines of all areas of first color in stencil cutting key. For placement guidelines, outline remaining colored area using dashed lines. Using a new piece of plastic for each additional color in stencil cutting key, repeat for remaining stencils.

2. Place each plastic piece on cutting mat and use craft knife to cut out stencil along solid lines, making sure edges are smooth.

3. Hold or tape stencil in place. Using a clean, dry stencil brush or sponge piece, dip brush or sponge in paint. Remove excess paint on a paper towel. Brush or sponge should be almost dry to produce best results. Beginning at edge of cut-out area, apply paint in a stamping motion over stencil. If desired, highlight or shade design by stamping a lighter or darker shade of paint in cut-out area. Repeat until all of first stencil have been painted. Carefully remove stencil and allow paint to dry.

4. Using stencils in order indicated in color key and matching guidelines on stencils to previously stenciled area, repeat Step 3 for remaining stencils.

DECOUPAGE

1. Cut desired motifs from fabric or paper.

2. Apply decoupage glue to wrong sides of motifs.

3. Arrange motifs on project as desired; overlap as necessary for complete coverage. Smooth in place and allow to dry.

4. Allowing to dry after each application, apply 2 to 3 coats of clear acrylic sealer to project.

LETTERING

For unique and personal labels or lettering on your crafts, try using one of your favorite fonts from your computer...try the "bold" and "italic" buttons for different variations of the font. Size your words to fit your project, then print them out.

Using your printout as the pattern, use transfer paper to transfer the words to your project. If you're making appliqué letters, you'll need to trace the letters, in reverse, onto the paper side of the fusible web.

Don't forget about the old reliable lettering stencils...they're easy to use and come in a wide variety of styles and sizes. And, if you're already into memory page making, you probably have an alphabet set or 2 of rubber stamps...just select an inkpad type suitable for your project. Then, there are 100's of sizes, colors and shapes of sticker and rub-on letters...small, fat, shiny, flat, puffy, velvety, slick, smooth, rough...you get the idea! Only your imagination limits you.

DECORATED JAR LABELS
(shown on page 110)

GIFT WRAP & TAG IDEAS
(shown on page 105)

NUTS
about
You!

Home
Made
by

NEW YEAR'S EVE KIT
(shown on page 117)

Happy New Year!

body

head

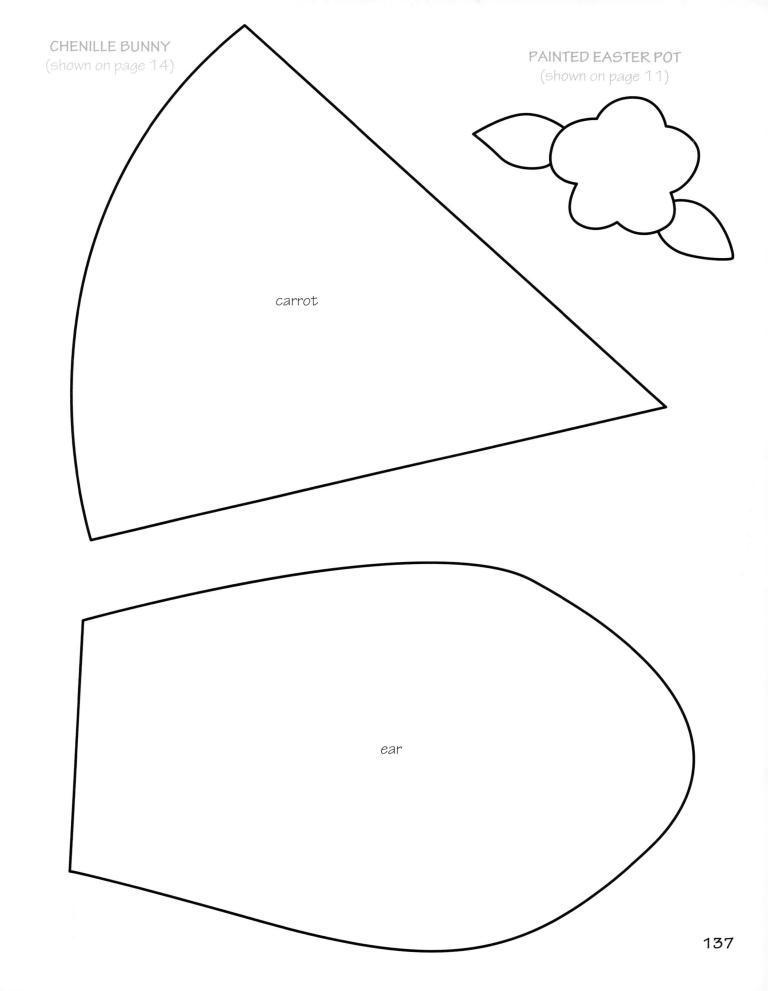

carrot

ear

EMBROIDERED PIN
(shown on page 14)

STITCHING KEY

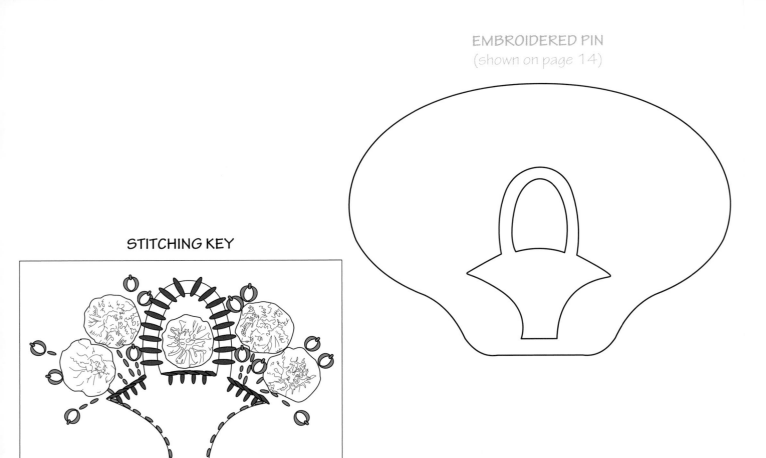

FRIENDSHIP FLOWERS
(shown on page 21)

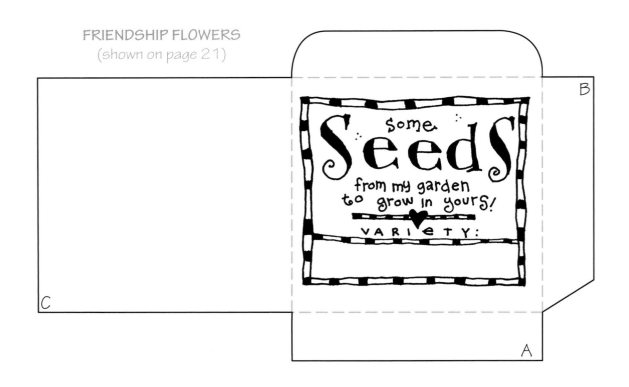

some
Seeds
from my garden
to grow in yours!

VARIETY:

B

C

A

138

SOOTHING TEA SET
(shown on page 29)

WASHTUB OF FLOWERS
(shown on page 25)

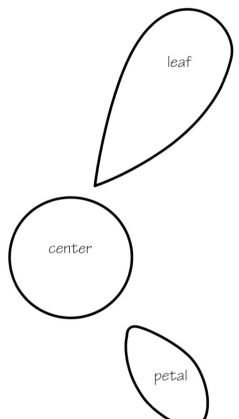

leaf

center

petal

More than anything,
I must have flowers,
always . . .

you are my sunshine!

SPONGE-PAINTED
TABLECLOTH & FLOWERPOTS
(shown on page 44)

TEACHER'S VEST
(shown on page 69)

APPLE PENCILS KIDS
CRAYONS GLUE STARS

64w x 43h

If friends
were flowers
I'd pick you

CROSS STITCHED BOUQUET

X	DMC	¼X	B'ST
♡	210		
⬯	309		
4	334	◩	◩
★	550		◩
‖	553		
▲	561	◩	
✔	562	◩	
▽	3325	◩	
⬍	3753		
○	3822		
⦿	550 French Knot		

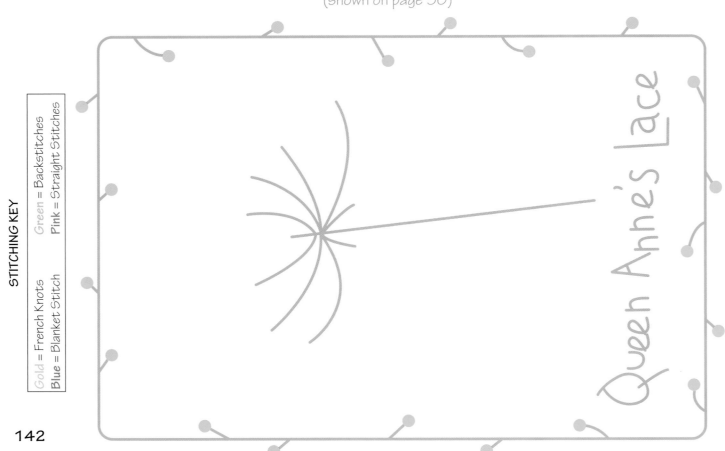

STITCHING KEY

Gold = French Knots   *Green* = Backstitches   Pink = Straight Stitches
Blue = Blanket Stitch

Queen Anne's Lace

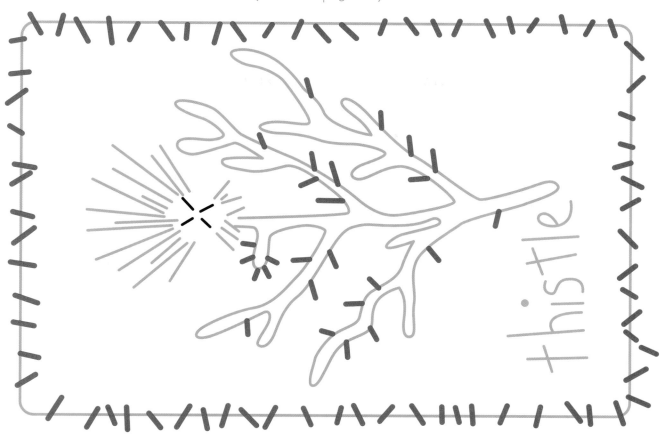

thistle

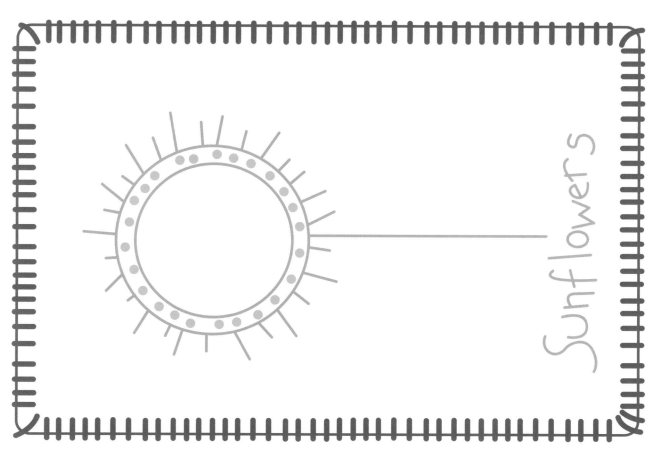

Sunflowers

X = button placement

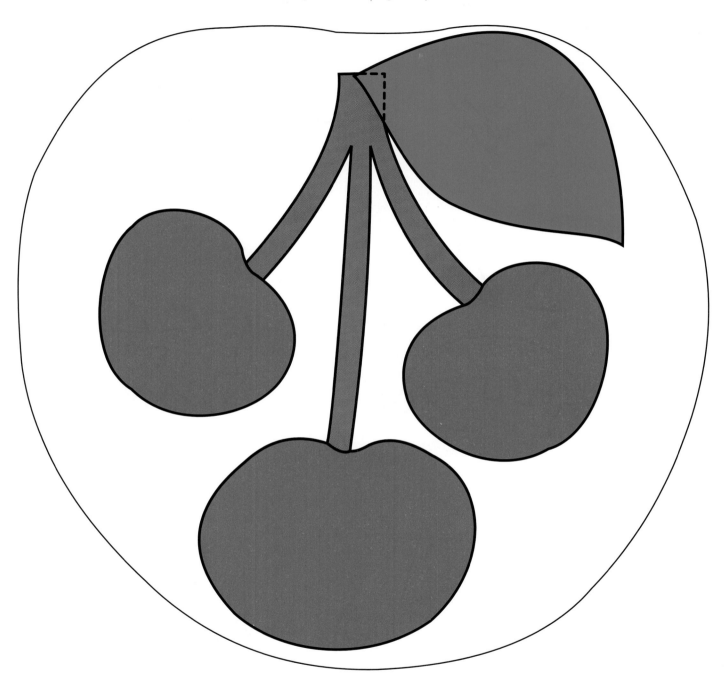

146

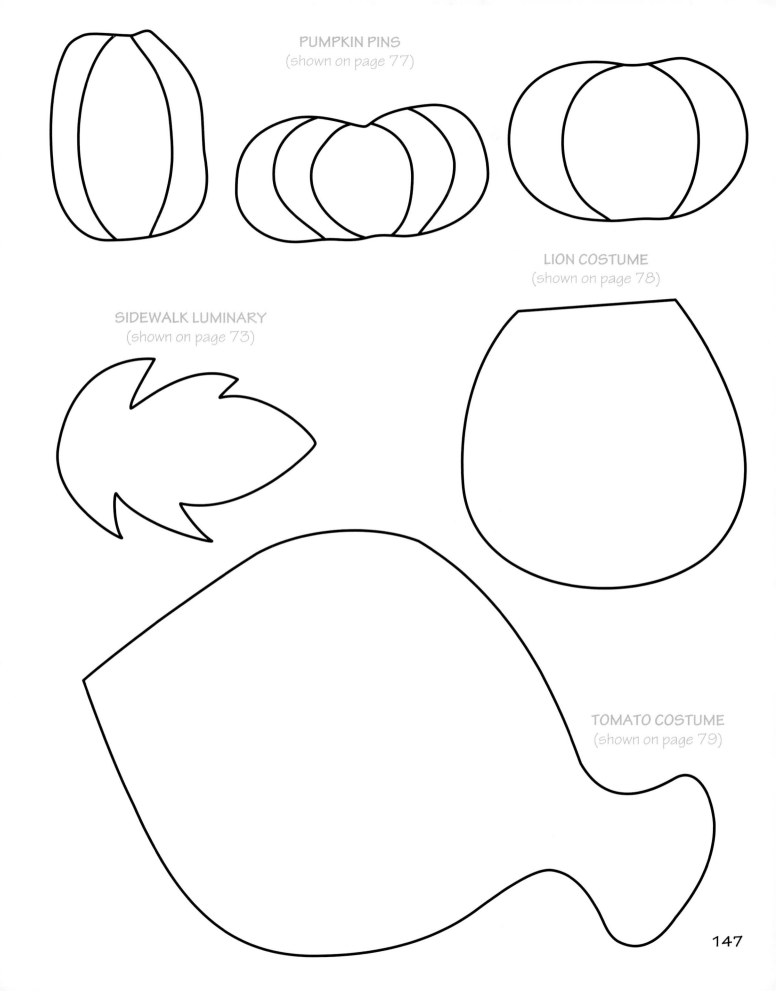

PUMPKIN PINS
(shown on page 77)

LION COSTUME
(shown on page 78)

SIDEWALK LUMINARY
(shown on page 73)

TOMATO COSTUME
(shown on page 79)

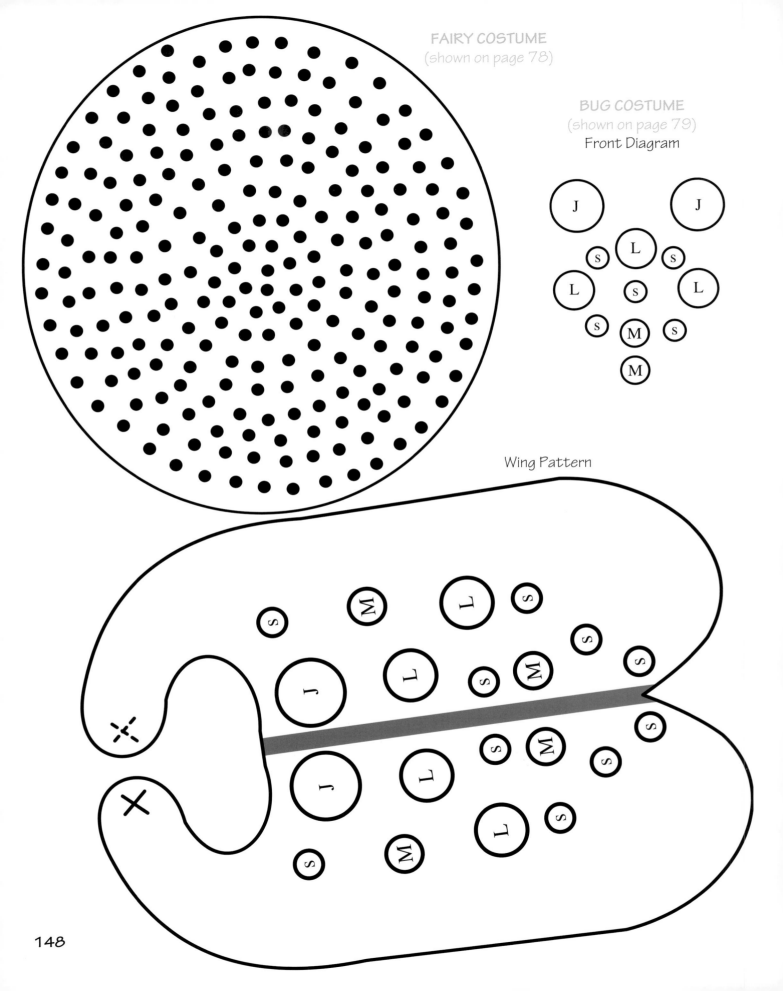

FAIRY COSTUME
(shown on page 78)

BUG COSTUME
(shown on page 79)
Front Diagram

Wing Pattern

148

STAMPED TREAT BAGS
(shown on page 81)

PAINTED TREAT POTS
(shown on page 81)

STITCHED BREAD CLOTH
(shown on page 87)

To give good thanks

"THANKS" WALL HANGING
(shown on page 86)

COLLECTOR'S SHELF
(shown on page 92)

THREE

anything

of

a

is

COLLECTION

COOKIE EXCHANGE INVITATIONS
(shown on page 101)
GINGERBREAD MAN TREAT BAGS
(shown on page 103)

COOKIE EXCHANGE

PARTY!

OLD-FASHIONED ORNAMENTS
(shown on page 107)

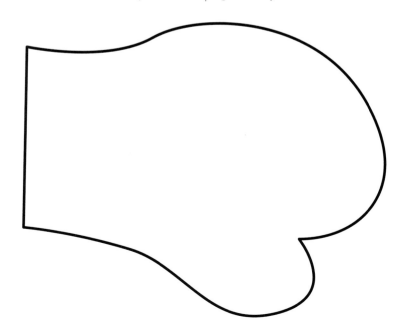

SNOWMAN WALL HANGING
(shown on page 112)

SNOWMAN WALL HANGING
(shown on page 112)

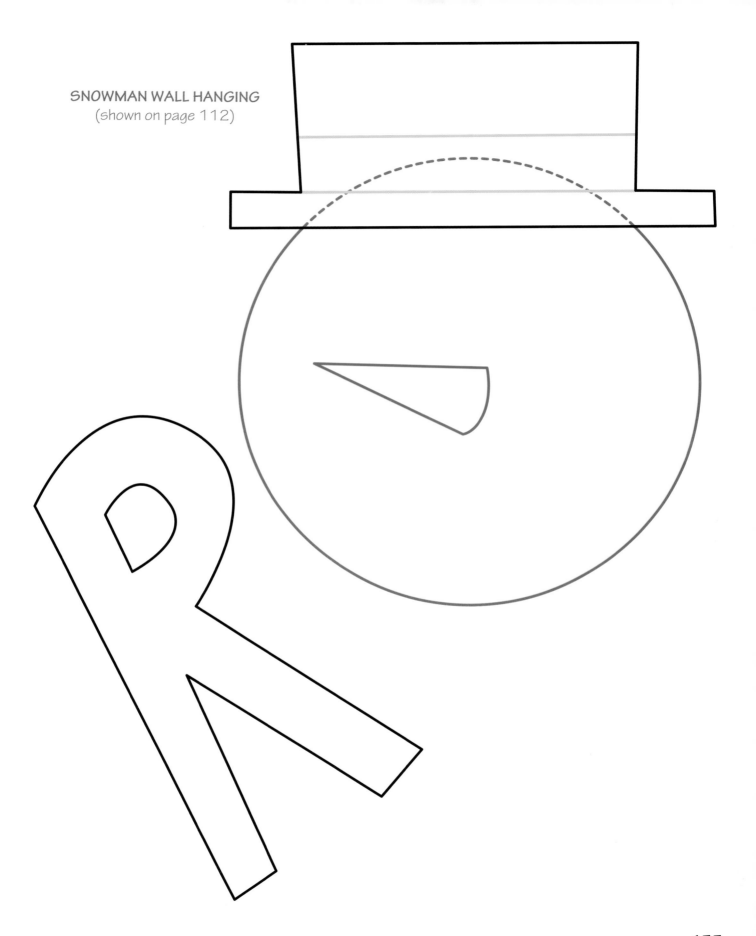

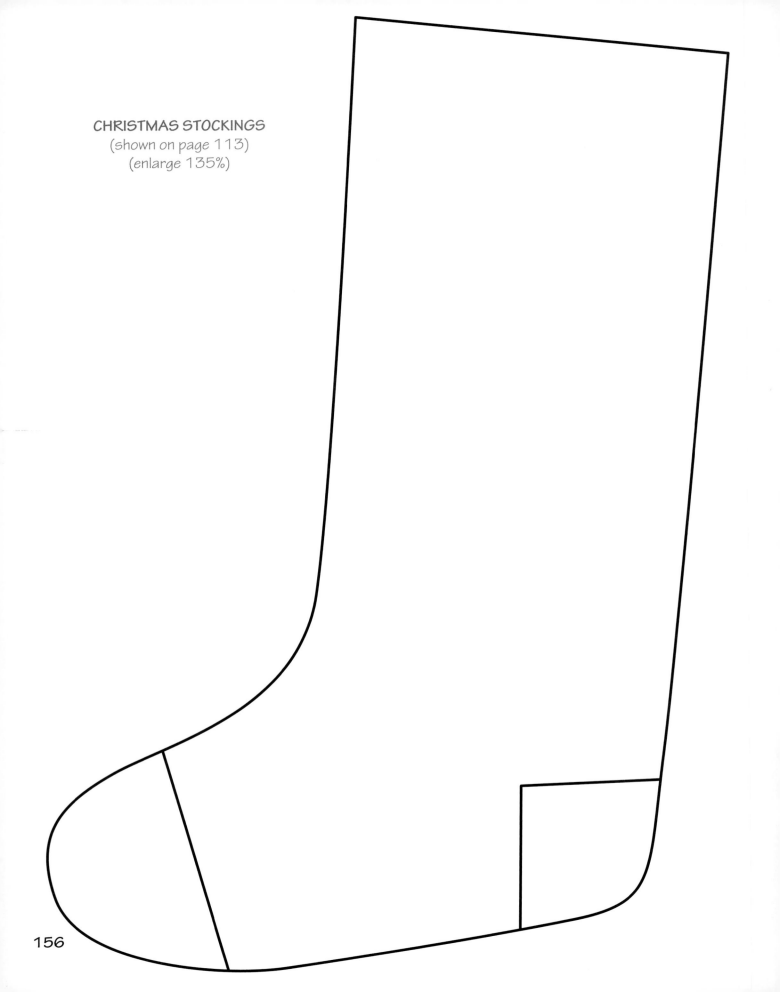

CHRISTMAS STOCKINGS
(shown on page 113)
(enlarge 135%)

156

WINDOW TO MY HEART CARD
(shown on page 120)

QUILT PIECE ANGEL
(shown on page 114)

family favorite recipes

...JUST A PINCH...

It seems our favorite foods bring back sweet memories of times spent with family & friends. And no matter what the season, we all have fond memories of Sunday dinners at Grandma's house, family-night treats and special birthday desserts. Flip through these pages to find dishes that will bring back heartfelt memories. And, you just might discover some new recipes to share with your own family...creating the sweetest memories of all!

Parmesan-Artichoke Crostini, page 186

munchies
& more

Appealing appetizers, kid-approved snacks and thirst-
quenching beverages fill the pages of this party-pleasing chapter.
Let Parmesan-Artichoke Crostini (page 186) be a part of your
next gathering...this popular spread gets an update as a savory
pickup. Keep a stash of Grab 'n' Go Gorp (page 167) handy for
a yummy and healthy snack. And for neighborly chats,
whip up cupfuls of Hot Chocolate Supreme (page 165).
Where these munchies are, you can bet you'll find
family & friends!

MEXICAN COFFEE

Stir up this single-serving beverage as dessert after an evening meal…it's sure to satisfy any sweet tooth. The chocolate and hint of cinnamon give the coffee its Mexican origin.

1 c. hot, strong brewed coffee
1 T. grated semi-sweet chocolate
3 T. coffee liqueur

Whipped cream
Garnish: cinnamon stick

Combine first 3 ingredients in a large cup or mug; stir until chocolate melts. Dollop with whipped cream; garnish, if desired. Makes about 1¼ cups.

cup of cheer

Each fall, close friends and I get together for what we call our "Cup of Cheer." Though busy schedules keep us from gathering during the year, this special time gives us the opportunity to renew our friendships. It's a delightful afternoon spent enjoying tea, chatting and making memories. As a special keepsake, we exchange a teacup and saucer we've found at tag sales or antique shops during the past year. After five years of this cherished tradition, we each have a lovely and unique collection of teacups that reminds us of a special time with dear friends.

Delinda Blakney
Bridgeview, IL

SPICY CITRUS CIDER

Keep this cider warm in a slow cooker…guests can help themselves.

8 c. apple juice
2¼ c. water
1½ c. orange juice
¼ c. molasses

1 T. whole cloves
3 (4-inch) cinnamon sticks
Garnish: apple slices

Combine all ingredients except apple slices in a large saucepan over medium heat. Simmer 10 minutes, stirring occasionally. Strain before serving. Garnish with apple slices, if desired. Makes about 3 quarts.

Ellen Folkman
Crystal Beach, FL

HOT BUTTERED CIDER

A spicy aroma that fills the air on a cool winter evening.

2 qts. apple cider
Optional: 2½ c. rum
juice of 2 oranges
juice of 2 lemons
15 whole cloves

6 cinnamon sticks
1 T. honey
1 T. allspice
1 t. cinnamon
3 T. butter

Simmer all ingredients, except butter, in a pot over medium heat for about 30 minutes. Strain, if you like; stir in butter and serve hot. Serves 10.

Hot Chocolate Supreme

HOT CHOCOLATE SUPREME

Curl up and enjoy a mug of this chocolatey cocoa on a frosty winter's day.

1 c. sugar
½ c. baking cocoa
¼ t. salt
5 c. water
2 c. milk

1 c. whipping cream
Garnishes: mini marshmallows or
 whipped topping, peppermint
 sticks

Combine sugar, cocoa and salt in a saucepan; whisk in water. Bring to a boil over high heat, stirring until sugar is completely dissolved. Reduce heat to medium; add milk and cream. Heat thoroughly and keep warm over low heat. If desired, serve topped with marshmallows or whipped topping and peppermint sticks. Makes 8¾ cups.

Lisa Allbright
Crockett, TX

WINTERTIME SPICE TEA

1¾ c. sugar
1 c. sweetened lemonade mix
1 c. powdered orange drink mix

½ c. instant tea
½ t. cinnamon
½ t. ground cloves

Mix together all ingredients and store in an airtight container. Include recipe instructions for serving. Makes enough for about 50 servings.

Instructions:

To serve, add 3 to 4 teaspoons to one cup of hot water; stir well.

Mary Beth Smith
St. Charles, MO

"This is quite a favorite at our home. It's always a nice gift for teachers, friends & neighbors."

Mary Beth

"This is a favorite snack Mom made every Christmas while I was growing up. She lost the recipe years ago and then found it and sent it to me right away. You can easily substitute walnuts or pecans, but no matter what you choose, you're sure to love it."

Kerry

CINNAMON-SUGAR NUTS

If you don't have a candy thermometer, try this simple test to know when your mixture has reached soft-ball stage: Drop a small amount of the candy mixture into cold water; the syrup will form a soft ball that flattens when removed from the water.

1 c. sugar	1/2 t. vanilla extract
1/4 c. evaporated milk	1/8 t. salt
1 T. water	2 1/4 c. cashews
1/2 t. cinnamon	

Combine sugar, evaporated milk, water, cinnamon, vanilla and salt in a saucepan. Bring to a boil over medium heat; boil until mixture reaches soft-ball stage, or 234 to 240 degrees on a candy thermometer.

Stir in cashews; turn out onto wax paper. Separate quickly using a fork. If nuts are stuck together after they cool, break them apart by hand. Store in an airtight container. Makes about 3 cups.

Kerry McNeil
Anacortes, WA

GRAB 'N' GO GORP

Go ahead and dig into this merry mix of dried berries, chocolate and nuts...a perfect after-school snack. Or package it up into gifts or into single-serving snacks for lunch boxes.

2 c. crispy wheat cereal squares
2 c. mixed nuts
1 c. dried cherries
1 c. sweetened dried cranberries

1 c. dried blueberries
1 c. semi-sweet chocolate
    chips

Combine all ingredients in a large bowl; store in an airtight container. Makes 8 cups.

for parties...

Fill different baskets with dippers and snacks like pretzels, bagel chips, veggies, bread cubes and potato chips. Use a small riser (a book works well) to set under one side of the bottom of each basket to create a tilt...looks so nice, and guests can grab the food easily!

HARVEST MOON CARAMEL CORN

Turn ordinary microwave popcorn into an extraordinary caramel snack. Not only is it good for movie night, but also it's a good treat for giving… especially since it makes an abundant amount!

10.5-oz. box microwave popcorn,
   popped
1 c. butter
2 c. brown sugar, packed

½ c. corn syrup
½ t. salt
1 t. vanilla extract
½ t. baking soda

Place popcorn in a lightly greased large roasting pan; set aside.

Combine butter, brown sugar, corn syrup and salt in a heavy saucepan. Bring to a boil over medium heat; cook 5 minutes. Remove from heat. Add vanilla and baking soda; stir well and pour over popcorn. Mix well.

Bake at 250 degrees for one hour, stirring occasionally. Let cool; break up and store in an airtight container. Makes 27 cups.

Kendra Guinn
Smithville, TN

> "This treat is a family favorite during movie night at our home."
>
> **Kendra**

snack containers

Use vintage canning jars to share snack mixes with friends & neighbors. Tie on bows and tags and you're all set…what could be easier?

CELEBRATION SNACK MIX

Hail your favorite team's game day or the end of a school day as you munch on this smoky-flavored cereal and nut mix.

4 c. bite-size crispy corn cereal
   squares
4 c. bite-size crispy rice cereal
   squares
1 c. dry-roasted peanuts
1 c. mini pretzels
2 t. paprika
1 t. sugar

½ t. garlic salt
½ t. onion powder
¼ t. dry mustard
⅛ t. Cajun seasoning
3 T. canola oil
1½ t. Worcestershire sauce
½ t. smoke-flavored cooking
   sauce

    Combine first 4 ingredients in a 2-gallon plastic zipping bag; set aside. Mix together paprika and next 5 ingredients in a small bowl; set aside. Combine oil and sauces; mix well and pour over cereal mixture. Close bag; shake gently until well coated. Gradually add spice mixture; close bag and shake until well coated. Store in an airtight container. Makes 8 cups.

Helen Woodard
Necedah, WI

GAME-DAY HUDDLE
menu on page 462

DONNA'S PARTY PUNCH

With only three ingredients, this recipe will prove to be a party pleaser time and time again. Its red color makes this punch the perfect accompaniment for a Valentine's Day or Christmas party.

46-oz. can red fruit punch
1 qt. raspberry sherbet, softened

1-ltr. bottle ginger ale, chilled

Mix together punch and sherbet; chill. Add ginger ale at serving time. Makes about 13 cups.

Linda Day
Wall, NJ

"This recipe is from a dear friend...it is so easy and tastes so good!"

Linda

WHITE CHRISTMAS PUNCH

Add a sprinkle of sliced almonds on top of each serving!

2 c. sugar
1 c. water
12-oz. can evaporated milk

1 T. almond extract
6 2-ltr. bottles lemon-lime soda
3 ½-gal. cartons vanilla ice cream

In a saucepan, combine sugar and water. Stir constantly over medium heat until sugar dissolves. Remove from heat. Add evaporated milk and almond extract; let cool. Chill until ready to serve. Combine milk mixture and lemon-lime drink in punch bowl just before serving. Add ice cream; stir to break ice cream into small pieces. Serves 50.

Rebecca Boone
Olathe, KS

CRANBERRY SLUSH

Create a festive garnish for each glass…just slip the cranberries and orange and lime slices onto wooden skewers.

¾ c. sugar
8 c. water, divided
2 c. white grape juice
12-oz. can frozen orange juice
   concentrate
12-oz. can frozen cranberry juice
   cocktail concentrate

6-oz. can frozen limeade
   concentrate
2-ltr. bottle lemon-lime soda, chilled
Garnishes: fresh cranberries, orange
   slices, lime slices

    Combine sugar and 2 cups water in a large saucepan over medium heat, stirring until sugar dissolves. Add grape juice, next 3 ingredients and remaining 6 cups water. Pour into 2 (one-gallon-size) heavy-duty plastic zipping bags; freeze until solid.

    To serve, place frozen mixture into a punch bowl; pour chilled lemon-lime soda over mixture. Stir to break up chunks until mixture is slushy. Garnish each serving, if desired. Makes 23½ cups.

Judy Borecky
Escondido, CA

"Frozen grapes, strawberries and raspberries make flavorful ice cubes in frosty beverages. Freeze washed and dried fruit in a plastic zipping bag for up to three months…perfect for summer gatherings."
Gooseberry Patch

ICED COFFEE

*If you prefer a stronger coffee flavor, increase the amount
of instant coffee granules to ¼ cup.*

½ c. sugar
2 c. half-and-half
1 c. cold water
3 T. instant coffee granules

4 c. milk
¼ c. chocolate syrup
1 t. vanilla extract

    Combine sugar and half-and-half in a large freezer-safe container.
Combine water and coffee granules, stirring until granules dissolve; add to
half-and-half mixture. Stir in milk, syrup and vanilla. Freeze 4 hours or until
slushy. Makes 7 cups.

FESTIVE EGGNOG PUNCH

A good punch for the holidays.

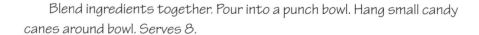

1 qt. eggnog, chilled
2 pts. peppermint ice cream,
   softened

1 c. ginger ale, chilled

    Blend ingredients together. Pour into a punch bowl. Hang small candy
canes around bowl. Serves 8.

Caren Schulze
Arlington Heights, IL

RAZZLEBERRY TEA

Sweet raspberries combine with tangy lemonade to make a fruity tea that's equally good served warm or chilled.

8 c. water, divided
5 regular-size tea bags
1¼ c. sugar
64-oz. bottle cranberry-raspberry
  juice, chilled

12-oz. pkg. frozen raspberries,
  thawed
12-oz. can frozen lemonade
  concentrate, thawed and divided

Bring 3 cups water to a boil in a saucepan. Remove from heat; add tea bags and let steep 8 minutes or until tea is desired strength. Discard tea bags.

While tea is warm, stir in sugar until dissolved; add enough of remaining water to equal 2 quarts. Pour tea into a large serving pitcher. Stir in juice, raspberries and half of the lemonade concentrate; save the remaining lemonade concentrate for another recipe. Serve warm or chilled. Makes 17¾ cups.

Susan deGraaff
Nicholasville, KY

a sweet gesture!

Sugar the rims of glasses before filling them with tea or punch. Just run a small lemon wedge around each rim and place the glass upside down on a small plate of sugar. Tap off any extra sugar before filling the glass.

GARDEN-FRESH SALSA

Fresh-picked veggies from your garden or your local farmers' market really add flavor to homemade salsa. Offer no substitute here…store-bought salsa simply won't do!

14½-oz. can diced tomatoes, drained
¾ c. green pepper, diced
⅓ c. black olives, sliced
⅓ c. Spanish onion, diced
⅓ c. red onion, diced
2 T. fresh parsley, finely chopped
2 T. garlic, minced

1 T. fresh cilantro, finely chopped
1½ T. lemon juice
1 T. lime juice
2 plum tomatoes, diced
2 green onions, sliced
1 jalapeño pepper, diced
salt and pepper to taste

Combine all ingredients in a large bowl; refrigerate until ready to serve. Makes 4 cups.

Staci Meyers
Cocoa, FL

homemade tortilla chips

Make your own tortilla chips to go with salsas and dips…you won't believe how easy it is. Just slice flour tortillas into wedges, spray with non-stick vegetable spray and bake at 350 degrees for 5 to 7 minutes.

RED PEPPER HUMMUS

Roasted red peppers add variety and a splash of color to this classic Mediterranean dip.

15-oz. can chickpeas (garbanzo beans), drained
7-oz. jar roasted red peppers, drained
1 clove garlic

1 t. ground coriander
½ t. ground red pepper
¼ t. salt
pita chips or fresh vegetables

Process all ingredients in a food processor until smooth. Store in an airtight container in the refrigerator up to one week. Serve with pita chips or fresh vegetables. Makes 1 ½ cups.

FRESH HERB & GARLIC DIP

Serve with fresh vegetables or chips.

1 c. low-fat sour cream
1 c. low-fat mayonnaise
2 T. fresh parsley, chopped
2 T. fresh chives, chopped

1 T. fresh thyme, chopped
1 T. fresh rosemary, chopped
2 T. garlic chives, chopped
1 clove garlic, pressed

Mix together sour cream, mayonnaise, herbs and garlic in a glass bowl. Cover and refrigerate overnight. Makes 2 cups.

DiAnn Voegele
Mascoutah, IL

GREEK SPREAD

Flavors of the Greek isles are found in this popular appetizer. Try preparing this spread in a shaped 2-quart mold for a bit of fun at your next get-together.

1 c. plus 1 T. almonds, chopped and divided
2 (8-oz.) pkgs. cream cheese, softened
10-oz. pkg. frozen spinach, thawed and drained

8-oz. pkg. feta cheese, crumbled
7-oz. jar roasted red peppers, drained and chopped
1 clove garlic, chopped
crackers or toasted pita wedges

Line a 2-quart bowl with plastic wrap; sprinkle with one tablespoon almonds. Mix together ½ cup almonds, cream cheese and next 4 ingredients in a separate mixing bowl; blend well. Press cream cheese mixture into prepared bowl over almonds. Cover and chill overnight.

Invert spread onto a serving dish. Remove plastic wrap; press remaining almonds onto the outside. Serve with crackers or pita wedges. Makes about 7 cups.

Stephanie Doyle
Lincoln University, PA

creative chip 'n' dip

Prepare quick chip-n-dip sets in no time. Spoon dips into pottery soup bowls and set the bowls on top of dinner plates that hold crackers, veggies, pretzels, chips and bread.

ANTIPASTO

Keep this recipe handy when you need something that's easy and can be made ahead. Serve with a slotted spoon or provide wooden picks for your guests.

16-oz. pkg. Cheddar cheese, cubed
16-oz. pkg. provolone cheese, cubed
16-oz. pkg. sliced mushrooms
1 lb. hard salami, cubed
½ lb. pepperoni, cubed
6-oz. can whole pitted ripe black
    olives, drained

1 onion, chopped
1 green pepper, chopped
1 jalapeño pepper, sliced
16-oz. bottle Italian salad dressing

Toss together all ingredients in a serving bowl. Cover and chill overnight. Makes 18 cups.

Doreen DeRosa
New Castle, PA

appealing skewers

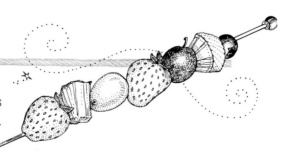

When appetizers need to be served with skewers, think beyond wooden picks...try sprigs of rosemary, bamboo picks or sugar cane spears.

SMOKY SALMON LOG

Keep this scrumptious spread on hand in the fridge…you'll be ready when surprise guests stop by!

2 c. canned salmon, drained and
   flaked
8-oz. pkg. cream cheese, softened
3 T. onion, chopped
1 T. lemon juice
1 t. prepared horseradish

¼ t. salt
¼ t. smoke-flavored cooking sauce
3 T. dried parsley
Optional: ½ c. pecans, chopped
Melba toast or assorted crackers

Combine first 7 ingredients in a large bowl; mix well. Shape into a log; wrap in plastic wrap and chill. At serving time, roll in parsley and, if desired, pecans. Serve with toast or crackers. Makes about 4 cups.

Remona Putman
Rockwood, PA

creative cutouts

Use mini cookie cutters to cut toasted bread into charming shapes to serve alongside savory dips and spreads.

THE CHEESY BOWL

Loaded with cheese and bacon, this appetizer is guaranteed to be a hands-down winner with your armchair quarterback! Light mayonnaise produces a creamier dip, so don't be tempted to substitute regular mayonnaise.

8-oz. block Colby-Jack cheese,
   shredded
1 c. shredded Parmesan cheese
2.8-oz. pkg. bacon bits

1½ c. light mayonnaise
½ c. onion, chopped
2 cloves garlic, minced
26-oz. round loaf bread

   Stir together all ingredients except bread; set aside.
   Hollow out bread, reserving torn pieces. Spoon dip into bread; place on an ungreased baking sheet. Bake at 350 degrees for one hour. Serve with torn bread or sliced apples. Makes 3½ cups.

Lisa Holdren
Wheeling, WV

"My relatives always ask me to bring this warm dip along to family gatherings. I like to serve it in a fragrant loaf of rosemary-olive oil bread from the bakery."

Lisa

GAME-DAY HUDDLE
menu on page 462

APPLE & BRIE TOASTS

A buttery mixture of brown sugar and chopped walnuts tops sweet apple slices and savory cheese for an elegant appetizer that will appeal to everyone. We used a combination of Granny Smith and Braeburn apples, but you can use your favorite. Fresh pears are a good option, too.

1 baguette, cut into ¼-inch-thick
   slices
½ c. brown sugar, packed
½ c. chopped walnuts
¼ c. butter, melted

13.2-oz. pkg. Brie cheese, thinly
   sliced
3 Granny Smith apples and/or
   Braeburn apples, cored and sliced

Arrange bread slices on an ungreased baking sheet; bake at 350 degrees until lightly toasted. Set aside.

Mix together sugar, walnuts and butter. Top each slice of bread with a cheese slice, an apple slice and one teaspoon of brown sugar mixture. Bake until cheese melts. Makes about 2½ dozen.

Jo Ann
Gooseberry Patch

PARMESAN-ARTICHOKE CROSTINI

We've taken the familiar (and popular) artichoke dip, jazzed it up with chopped green chiles and red peppers, then spread it over baguette slices. Save time by looking for toasted baguette slices in the supermarket bakery or substitute bagel chips or Melba toast rounds.

1 baguette
12-oz. jar marinated artichoke
   hearts, drained and chopped
4.5-oz. can chopped green chiles,
   drained

1 c. mayonnaise
1 c. shredded Parmesan
   cheese
¼ c. red pepper, finely chopped
2 cloves garlic, minced

Diagonally cut baguette into 42 (¼-inch-thick) slices. Reserve any remaining baguette for other uses. Arrange slices on large ungreased baking sheets. Broil slices one to 2 minutes or until toasted.

Stir together chopped artichoke hearts and next 5 ingredients.

Spread one tablespoon artichoke mixture on toasted side of each baguette slice.

Bake at 450 degrees for 6 to 7 minutes or until lightly browned and bubbly. Makes 3½ dozen.

TASTY WHITE SPINACH PIZZA

A prebaked crust gives you a jump start on this tasty pizza. With larger servings, this could be served as a main dish.

1 T. garlic, minced
2 T. olive oil
4 c. baby spinach, diced
12-inch prebaked Italian pizza crust
½ c. Alfredo sauce
8-oz. pkg. shredded mozzarella
   cheese, divided

1 c. grated Parmesan cheese,
   divided
Optional: sliced mushrooms, diced
   green olives with pimentos

"My own creation... a delicious change from tomato-based pizza."

Mike

Sauté garlic in oil in a large skillet over medium heat. Add spinach; cook until spinach wilts and absorbs oil. Remove from heat.

Place pizza crust on a lightly greased baking sheet; spread with Alfredo sauce. Sprinkle half the mozzarella and half the Parmesan over sauce. If desired, top with mushrooms and olives. Sprinkle remaining cheese over mushroom layer; top with spinach. Bake at 350 degrees for 15 to 20 minutes or until golden. Serves 6.

Mike Johnson
Columbus, OH

FRIED CHEESE STICKS

Just about everyone loves fried cheese sticks. Our version gets a punch of heat from cayenne pepper and cheese spiced with jalapeños. To tame the heat, use plain Monterey Jack (without the peppers), mozzarella or Swiss cheese, and either omit the cayenne pepper or use less of it.

2 (8-oz.) pkgs. Monterey Jack
   cheese with jalapeño peppers
1 c. all-purpose flour
1½ t. cayenne pepper
1 c. fine, dry bread crumbs

1 t. dried parsley
4 eggs, beaten
vegetable oil
Optional: marinara sauce

Cut cheese crosswise into ¾-inch slices. Lay slices flat and cut in half lengthwise.

Combine flour and cayenne pepper; stir well. Combine bread crumbs and parsley in another bowl; stir well. Dip cheese sticks in beaten eggs. Dredge in flour mixture. Dip coated cheese in egg again; dredge in bread crumb mixture, pressing firmly so that crumbs adhere. Place cheese sticks on a wax paper-lined baking sheet and freeze at least 30 minutes.

Fry cheese sticks in 375-degree deep oil until golden brown. Drain on paper towels. Serve immediately with marinara sauce, if desired. Makes 28 appetizers.

MAPLE-TOPPED SWEET POTATO SKINS

Sweet potato skins offer a tasty alternative to regular potato skins. These are loaded with spices and topped with sugary walnuts…a savory-sweet side dish for any dinner.

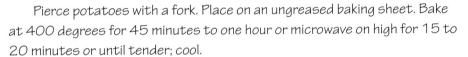

6 large sweet potatoes
1/2 c. cream cheese, softened
1/4 c. sour cream
2 t. cinnamon, divided
2 t. nutmeg, divided
2 t. ground ginger, divided

2 c. walnuts or pecans, chopped
1/4 c. brown sugar, packed
3 T. butter, softened
Garnishes: maple syrup, apple slices,
    additional nuts

Pierce potatoes with a fork. Place on an ungreased baking sheet. Bake at 400 degrees for 45 minutes to one hour or microwave on high for 15 to 20 minutes or until tender; cool.

Slice each potato in half lengthwise; scoop out pulp, keeping skins intact. Mash pulp in a mixing bowl until smooth; add cream cheese, sour cream and one teaspoon each of spices. Mix well and spoon into potato skins. Stir together nuts, brown sugar, butter and remaining spices; sprinkle over top. Place potato skins on an ungreased baking sheet; bake at 400 degrees for 15 minutes. If desired, drizzle with warm syrup and garnish with apple slices and additional nuts. Serves 12.

Linda Corcoran
Metuchen, NJ

TURKEY-CRANBERRY ROLLS

If you could put the taste of Thanksgiving in a sandwich, this would be it. Nothing could be easier than using prepackaged rolls that you slice, fill and then bake in the pan they came in. Since they freeze well, these rolls are good make-ahead sandwiches.

8-oz. pkg. cream cheese, softened
2 T. mayonnaise
2 T. sour cream
2 T. chutney
1 T. Dijon mustard
½ t. curry powder
½ t. cayenne pepper

1 c. whole-berry cranberry sauce
3 T. onion, minced
4 (7½-oz.) pkgs. party rolls in aluminum trays
1 lb. smoked turkey, thinly sliced

Combine first 7 ingredients in a medium bowl. Beat at medium speed with an electric mixer until blended. Stir together cranberry sauce and onion.

Remove rolls from aluminum tray. Slice rolls in half horizontally, using a serrated knife; do not separate rolls. Spread a thin layer of cream cheese mixture over top and bottom halves of each package of rolls.

Layer one-fourth of the turkey slices over bottom half of each package of rolls. Spread a thin layer of cranberry mixture over turkey. Cover with top halves of rolls. Cut rolls into individual sandwiches and return rolls to aluminum trays.

Cover and bake at 350 degrees for 25 minutes or until warm. Bake, uncovered, during last 10 minutes, if desired, for crisper rolls. Makes 80 appetizers.

GREEK OLIVE CUPS

These tasty cups can be made ahead and frozen. Fill the cups in their trays, then place the trays in heavy-duty plastic zipping bags and freeze them up to one month. When ready to bake, remove the cups from their trays and place them on an ungreased baking sheet. Let the cups stand 10 minutes before baking. Bake as directed in the recipe.

1 ½ c. shredded Cheddar
   cheese, divided
½ c. pimento-stuffed olives or other
   green olives, chopped
½ c. kalamata olives, pitted and
   chopped

⅓ c. pecans, chopped and toasted
⅓ c. pine nuts, toasted
2 ½ T. mayonnaise
2 (2.1-oz.) pkgs. frozen mini phyllo
   shells

Combine one cup cheese and next 5 ingredients in a medium bowl. Remove phyllo shells from packages, leaving them in trays.

Spoon one heaping teaspoon olive mixture into each phyllo shell; sprinkle evenly with the remaining ½ cup cheese. Remove from trays and place cups on an ungreased baking sheet.

Bake at 375 degrees for 12 to 15 minutes or until thoroughly heated. Serve immediately. Makes 30 appetizers.

stack it up

Use tiered cake stands for bite-size appetizers…so handy, and they take up less space on the buffet table than setting out several serving platters.

BLUE-RIBBON CHICKEN FINGERS

Don't keep these chicken fingers just as an appetizer option. You'll want to serve them as a dinner entrée as well…you'll definitely get the thumbs-up!

6 boneless, skinless chicken breasts
1 c. milk
2 T. white vinegar
1 egg, beaten
1 t. garlic powder

1 c. all-purpose flour
1 c. seasoned bread crumbs
1 t. salt
1 t. baking powder
vegetable oil

Cut chicken into ½-inch strips; place in a large plastic zipping bag. Combine milk and vinegar in a small bowl; add egg and garlic powder. Pour milk mixture over chicken in bag; seal and refrigerate 4 to 6 hours.

Combine flour and next 3 ingredients in a separate plastic zipping bag. Drain chicken, discarding milk mixture. Place chicken in flour mixture; seal bag and shake to coat. Fry coated chicken strips in 375-degree deep oil 4 to 5 minutes on each side or until golden. Place on paper towels to drain. Serves 6 to 8.

Jackie Balla
Walbridge, OH

GAME-DAY HUDDLE
menu on page 462

ASIAN GINGERED SHRIMP

Asian-style flavors make something special out of simple boiled shrimp. If you'd like to cook and peel your own shrimp, start with 3 pounds of raw shrimp in the shells.

1 ½ lbs. cooked, peeled and cleaned
   medium shrimp
¼ c. soy sauce
2 t. fresh ginger, peeled and finely
   chopped

¼ c. white vinegar
2 T. sugar
2 T. sweet sake or apple juice
1 ½ t. salt
2 to 3 T. green onions, thinly sliced

"Serve with steamed rice for a delicious main dish."

Lynn

Arrange shrimp in a single layer in a shallow glass container; set aside.

Bring soy sauce to a boil in a small saucepan; add ginger. Reduce heat and simmer 5 minutes or until most of liquid is absorbed. Stir in vinegar, sugar, sake or apple juice and salt; pour over shrimp. Cover with plastic wrap; refrigerate 2 hours to overnight.

Remove shrimp from marinade with a slotted spoon; arrange on a serving platter. Sprinkle with green onions. Serves 8 to 10.

Lynn Williams
Muncie, IN

BACON-WRAPPED SCALLOPS

Wrapped in bacon strips, these succulent scallops will be snapped up quickly! Be sure to buy sea scallops, which are larger in diameter than the smaller bay scallops.

"This is an elegant and tasty appetizer for a New Year's Eve gathering!"

Robyn

11 bacon slices, cut in half
½ c. all-purpose flour
1½ t. paprika
½ t. salt
½ t. ground white pepper
½ t. garlic powder

1 c. milk
1 egg
22 sea scallops
1 to 2 c. Japanese bread crumbs
   (panko)
Rémoulade Sauce

Cook bacon slices 3 to 4 minutes or until translucent.

Combine flour and next 4 ingredients in a shallow dish. Beat together milk and egg in a small bowl. Roll scallops in seasoned flour, shaking off excess. Dip scallops in egg mixture, then coat with bread crumbs.

Wrap each scallop with bacon and secure with a wooden pick. Place scallops on a lightly greased baking sheet. Bake at 400 degrees for about 30 minutes or until bacon is crisp and scallops are cooked. Serve hot with Rémoulade Sauce. Serves 11.

RÉMOULADE SAUCE:

½ c. celery, minced
½ c. green onions, minced
½ c. mayonnaise
½ c. cocktail sauce
¼ c. prepared mustard
¼ c. horseradish

¼ c. lemon juice
¼ c. red wine vinegar
2 t. paprika
1 t. salt
½ t. pepper
⅛ t. cayenne pepper

Mix together all ingredients in a quart jar; shake well and chill 45 minutes. Makes 2¼ cups.

Robyn Wright
Delaware, OH

Beef in Rosemary-Mushroom
Sauce, page 232

memorable
main dishes

If you're searching for that perfect dish for a birthday celebration, hearty servings of Italian 3-Cheese Stuffed Shells (page 227) are sure to satisfy partygoers, and for the big holiday feast, savory Roast Turkey with Sage Butter (page 215) will bring smiles to the faces of your guests. Check out these and other scrumptious recipes in this chapter to fit your special occasion.

SEAFOOD LASAGNA

Chock-full of shrimp, scallops and crab meat, this creamy lasagna is a dream come true for seafood lovers.

1 c. onion, chopped
5 large cloves garlic, divided
1/4 c. butter, divided
3 T. all-purpose flour
1/4 t. salt
1/2 t. pepper
3 c. milk
8-oz. pkg. cream cheese, cut into cubes
1 c. grated Parmesan cheese, divided

1/2 lb. medium shrimp, peeled, cleaned and cooked
8 oz. bay scallops, cooked
16-oz. bag frozen cut-leaf spinach
1 lb. mushrooms, chopped
1 T. olive oil
18 lasagna noodles, cooked in salted water
1 lb. crab meat
4 c. shredded mozzarella cheese

Sauté onion and 3 cloves garlic in 3 tablespoons butter in a 3-quart saucepan over medium heat until tender. Whisk in flour, salt and pepper until smooth. Gradually whisk in milk. Cook, whisking constantly, until thickened and smooth. Whisk in cream cheese and 1/2 cup Parmesan cheese until cream cheese melts and sauce is smooth. Reserve one cup sauce. Stir shrimp and scallops into remaining sauce; set aside.

Prepare spinach according to package directions. Sauté mushrooms and remaining 2 cloves garlic in remaining one tablespoon butter and olive oil until tender. Stir in spinach; drain.

Spread reserved one cup sauce in a thin layer on the bottom of a lightly greased 15"x10" lasagna dish. Layer 6 lasagna noodles over sauce. Spread one-third of seafood sauce over noodles; top with half of spinach mixture, half of crab and one cup mozzarella cheese. Repeat layers. Layer remaining 6 noodles and remaining one-third of seafood sauce over mozzarella cheese. Top with remaining 1/2 cup Parmesan cheese and remaining 2 cups mozzarella cheese. Bake, uncovered, at 350 degrees for 40 minutes or until bubbly. Let stand 10 minutes before serving. Serves 12.

Christi Miller
New Paris, PA

COCONUT SHRIMP

Coated with shredded coconut and then fried, these golden gems are good!
Garnish with fresh orange slices, if desired.

1½ c. canola oil
1 c. all-purpose flour
1 c. beer

1 lb. uncooked medium shrimp,
   peeled and cleaned
14-oz. pkg. shredded coconut

Pour oil into a large skillet and heat oil to 375 degrees. Stir together flour and beer. Coat shrimp with batter, then roll in coconut. Fry shrimp in small batches about 2 to 3 minutes until golden and curled. Drain on paper towels. Serves 4.

eye-catching arrangements

It's easy to make oh-so-pretty floral arrangements by using unexpected containers. Instead of vases, try standing flowers in jars of water, then tuck the jars into simple shopping bags, formal top hats or vintage purses.

SHRIMP & WILD RICE

Here's a great one-dish meal to serve with salad and bread.

6-oz. pkg. long-grain and wild rice
   mix, uncooked
1 yellow onion, chopped
1 green pepper, chopped
½ c. butter
8-oz. pkg. sliced mushrooms
1 t. hot pepper sauce

salt and pepper to taste
1 c. heavy cream
½ lb. cooked, peeled and
   cleaned medium shrimp
¼ c. slivered or sliced
   almonds

Prepare wild rice mix according to package directions.

Sauté onion and green pepper in butter in a large skillet until tender. Add mushrooms, hot pepper sauce and salt and pepper to taste; remove from heat. Add cream and rice; cool slightly. Add shrimp, mixing well, and pour into a buttered 11"x 7" baking dish; top with almonds. Bake, uncovered, at 350 degrees for 30 minutes. Serves 4.

Teresa Mulhern
Powell, OH

> "I've used this many times for potlucks and have never had to bring home leftovers!"
>
> **Teresa**

shrimp math

To save time, have the seafood department steam the shrimp for you. They'll need to start with 1 pound of unpeeled raw shrimp.

"Sometimes I add a teaspoon of red pepper flakes along with the oregano...my family likes a little kick!"

Kristie

LINGUINE & WHITE CLAM SAUCE

Canned clams are given a flavorful boost when combined with a creamy sauce and served over linguine.

2 (6¹/₂-oz.) cans minced clams,
   drained and juices reserved
milk
¹/₂ c. onion, finely chopped
1 clove garlic, minced
2 T. butter
¹/₄ c. all-purpose flour

¹/₂ t. dried oregano
¹/₂ t. salt
¹/₄ t. pepper
¹/₄ c. sherry or chicken broth
2 T. dried parsley
8-oz. pkg. linguine, cooked
¹/₂ c. grated Parmesan cheese

   Combine reserved clam juice with enough milk to equal 2 cups liquid; set aside.

   Cook onion and garlic in butter in a medium saucepan over medium heat until tender and golden; stir in flour. Add clam juice mixture to pan; stir over low heat until smooth. Add oregano, salt and pepper; cook until thick and bubbly, stirring frequently. Stir in clams and sherry or chicken broth; cook one more minute. Sprinkle with parsley and stir. Toss with cooked linguine; sprinkle with Parmesan cheese. Serves 4.

Kristie Rigo
Friedens, PA

a special touch

   When serving seafood, wrap lemon halves in cheesecloth, tie with colorful ribbon and set one on each plate. Guests can squeeze the lemon over their food...the cheesecloth prevents squirting and catches seeds!

LIME & GINGER GRILLED SALMON

This salmon not only tastes good…it's good for you as well. Eat up and enjoy!

2-lb. salmon fillet, cleaned and
   boned
2 T. fresh ginger, peeled and minced
2 T. lime zest

½ t. salt
½ t. pepper
2 T. butter, melted, or olive oil
½ t. lime juice

Preheat grill to medium-high heat (350 to 400 degrees). Sprinkle salmon with ginger, lime zest, salt and pepper. Combine butter or olive oil and lime juice in a small bowl; brush salmon with mixture. Grill about 5 minutes on each side or until salmon flakes easily with a fork. Serves 4.

SUMMERTIME CELEBRATION
menu on page 460

DIXIE FRIED CHICKEN

Fried chicken is comfort food at its best! And this crispy Southern-style chicken, complete with a creamy gravy, doesn't disappoint. See menu, page 461.

2½- to 3-lb. whole chicken, cut up, or	1 t. cayenne pepper
2½ lbs. assorted chicken pieces	1 egg, lightly beaten
½ t. salt	⅓ c. milk
½ t. freshly ground black pepper	vegetable oil
1½ c. all-purpose flour	Cream Gravy

Season chicken with salt and black pepper. Combine flour and cayenne pepper; set aside. Combine egg and milk; dip chicken in egg mixture and dredge in flour mixture, coating chicken well. Pour oil to a depth of one inch in a heavy 10" to 12" skillet; heat oil to 350 degrees. Fry chicken in hot oil over medium heat 15 to 20 minutes or until golden, turning occasionally. Remove small pieces earlier, if necessary, to prevent overbrowning. Drain chicken on paper towels, reserving ¼ cup drippings in skillet for Cream Gravy. Serve with gravy. Serves 4.

CREAM GRAVY:

¼ c. reserved pan drippings	½ t. salt
¼ c. all-purpose flour	¼ t. freshly ground black pepper
2½ to 3 c. hot milk	dash of cayenne pepper

Heat pan drippings in skillet over medium heat. Add flour, stirring until browned. Gradually add hot milk; cook, stirring constantly, until thick and bubbly. Add salt, black pepper and cayenne pepper. Serve hot. Makes 2¾ cups.

holiday traditions

Every 4th of July was an event for our family. Mother made fried chicken, salads and all the trimmings, and Dad was in charge of the fireworks. Grandpa brought everything needed for root beer floats, and we could have as many as our tummies could hold!

Sylvia Mathews
Vancouver, WA

GARLIC & LEMON ROASTED CHICKEN

Roasted potatoes and baby carrots make this chicken a satisfying one-dish meal...delicious!

4-lb. roasting chicken	¼ c. butter, softened
½ t. salt	1 lemon, halved
½ t. freshly ground black pepper	3 T. water
½ t. dried parsley	1 lb. potatoes, peeled and cubed
7 cloves garlic	2 c. baby carrots

Place chicken on a lightly greased rack in a 13"x9" roasting pan. Combine salt, pepper, parsley, 2 cloves pressed garlic and one tablespoon butter; rub over chicken. Squeeze lemon halves over chicken. Place lemon halves, remaining 5 cloves garlic, halved, and remaining 3 tablespoons butter inside chicken cavity. Tie ends of legs together with string.

Pour water into roasting pan. Cover pan tightly with aluminum foil, making sure foil doesn't touch top of chicken. Bake at 375 degrees for 20 minutes. Add potatoes and carrots to pan. Bake, uncovered, 40 to 60 more minutes or until a meat thermometer inserted into thigh registers 170 degrees, basting occasionally with pan juices. Serves 4 to 6.

Terry Esposito
Freehold, NJ

FROM THE GARDEN
menu on page 460

HONEYMOON CHICKEN & BISCUITS

Quick-cooking oats and maple syrup are the "secret" ingredients in the biscuits you'll find atop this chicken casserole.

1 c. red onion, chopped
1/2 c. butter, divided
10 1/2-oz. can condensed
   chicken broth
1/4 c. dry sherry or water
1 c. all-purpose flour, divided
1 t. poultry seasoning
2 1/2 c. chopped cooked chicken
   breast

10-oz. pkg. frozen vegetables
   (mushrooms, corn, carrots,
   peas, green beans)
3/4 c. quick-cooking oats
2 t. baking powder
1/2 c. fat-free milk
1 egg white
1 T. maple syrup

Cook onion in 2 tablespoons butter in a large skillet over medium-high heat 3 minutes or until tender. Stir together broth, sherry or water, 1/4 cup flour and seasoning; add to skillet. Cook 3 minutes or until thickened. Stir in chicken and vegetables; pour into a lightly greased 2-quart baking dish.

Combine remaining 3/4 cup flour, oats and baking powder. Cut in remaining 6 tablespoons butter until crumbly. Stir in milk, egg white and syrup until moistened. Drop by 1/4 cupfuls onto chicken. Bake at 425 degrees for 35 to 40 minutes. Serves 6.

Carol Blessing
Cropseyville, NY

tickled pink!

Many times our church had dinner outside. There were several tables loaded with made-from-scratch food. Granny would always bring the chicken & dumplings, which were the best in the world. Sometimes she would add just a drop of yellow food coloring to the dumplings for some color, but once she added red by mistake! Even though the chicken & dumplings were pink and there were lots of laughs, the wonderful taste was still the same!

Robin Wilson
Altamonte Springs, FL

"My husband's 80-year-old grandmother had lots of cooking advice for me and watched me like a hawk in the kitchen. One day I made this dish while she was out. That night Grandma ate with wild abandon! There wasn't a trace of food left on her plate! She's 88 now and never fails to request this dish whenever she visits."

Carol

GIFT-WRAPPED CHICKEN

Good things come in small packages…like these chicken breasts layered in the middle with cranberry sauce and wrapped in phyllo dough. These goodies turn an ordinary meal into something extraordinary.

4 boneless, skinless chicken breasts
¹/₂ t. salt
¹/₄ t. pepper
¹/₄ c. whole-berry cranberry
   sauce

¹/₄ c. butter
¹/₂ (16-oz.) pkg. phyllo dough,
   thawed
¹/₂ c. butter, melted

Cut each chicken breast in half the short way and pound each piece to flatten slightly; sprinkle with salt and pepper. Place one tablespoon cranberry sauce and one tablespoon unmelted butter on each of 4 pieces of chicken breast and place another breast piece on top.

Unroll dough and cut dough in half lengthwise. Working with 8 strips of dough at a time, stack 2 strips together for a total of 4 stacks. (Keep remaining phyllo covered with a damp towel to prevent drying out.) Brush each stack with melted butter. To make a package, layer 2 sets of stacks to make an "x," then layer remaining 2 sets of stacks on top to form a "t." Place filled chicken in center of dough stack and pull ends up together in the center, pinching ends closed at the top like a beggar's purse. Place on a greased baking sheet. Repeat procedure with remaining ingredients. Bake at 375 degrees for 30 minutes. Shield tops with aluminum foil during last 10 minutes of baking, if necessary. Serves 4.

The Governor's Inn
Ludlow, VT

"We think this makes a beautiful presentation...just like a package!"

Gooseberry Patch

"Everyone will think you spent all day in the kitchen!"

Kathy

ITALIAN STUFFED CHICKEN

This is good! Sautéed mushrooms and Italian bread crumbs combine with three types of cheese to make the flavorful stuffing for these chicken breasts. The mixture is equally tasty stuffed into pockets of thick pork chops.

8-oz. pkg. sliced mushrooms
2 T. butter
1 c. ricotta cheese
1 c. shredded mozzarella
   cheese
1/2 c. grated Parmesan cheese

1/4 c. dried parsley
1/4 c. Italian-seasoned dry bread
   crumbs
4 bone-in chicken breasts
paprika

    Sauté mushrooms in butter in a skillet over medium heat until tender; set aside. Combine cheeses, parsley and bread crumbs; mix well. Stir into mushroom mixture.

    Loosen skin from chicken breasts without detaching it. Spoon mixture underneath skin; sprinkle with paprika. Arrange chicken in a lightly greased 13"x9" baking dish. Bake at 350 degrees for one hour and 7 minutes or until chicken is done. Serves 4.

Kathy Solka
Ishpeming, MI

MAPLE-GLAZED TURKEY BREAST

Sprinkle in some sweetened dried cranberries for an extra burst of color and flavor.

6-oz. pkg. long-grain and wild rice
    mix, uncooked
1 1/4 c. water
1-lb. turkey breast

1/4 c. maple syrup
1/2 c. chopped walnuts
1/2 t. cinnamon

Mix together rice mix, seasoning packet from rice mix and water in a 4-quart slow cooker. Place turkey breast, skin-side up, on rice mixture. Drizzle with syrup; sprinkle with walnuts and cinnamon.

Cover and cook on low setting 4 to 5 hours or until a meat thermometer inserted into breast registers 165 degrees. Let stand 10 minutes before slicing. Serves 4.

Eleanor Paternoster
Bridgeport, CT

 *kitchen journal*

Jot down favorite recipes and family members' preferences in a kitchen journal. It'll make meal planning a snap!

ROAST TURKEY WITH SAGE BUTTER

Any meal is a special occasion when this roasted turkey is the centerpiece of your menu. A luscious sage butter is used for seasoning, basting and serving your turkey.

"An all-American dish that's perfect for your harvest table."

Kendall

1 c. butter, softened
3 T. fresh sage, chopped
8 slices bacon, crisply cooked and crumbled
salt and pepper to taste
16-lb. turkey, thawed if frozen

3 c. leeks, chopped
8 sprigs fresh sage
3 bay leaves, crumbled
4 c. chicken broth, divided
Garnishes: fresh sage sprigs, crabapples, pears

Combine butter, sage and bacon in a medium bowl; sprinkle lightly with salt and pepper. Set aside.

Remove giblets and neck from thawed turkey; reserve for another use. Rinse turkey and pat dry. Sprinkle inside of turkey with salt and pepper; add leeks, sage sprigs and bay leaves. Loosen skin and spread 1/3 cup butter mixture over breast meat under skin. Place turkey on the rack of a large broiler pan. Rub 2 tablespoons butter mixture on outside of turkey. Set aside 1/3 cup butter mixture for gravy; reserve remaining butter mixture for basting. Pour 1/3 cup broth over turkey.

Bake turkey at 350 degrees for about 2 1/2 hours or until a meat thermometer inserted into thigh registers at least 170 degrees, shielding if necessary to prevent overbrowning. Baste turkey every 30 minutes with 1/3 cup broth; brush occasionally with remaining butter mixture. Transfer turkey to a platter; keep warm. Let stand 30 minutes.

To make gravy, pour pan juices and golden bits from roasting pan into a large glass measuring cup. Spoon off fat and discard. Bring juices and 2 cups broth to a boil over high heat in a large saucepan; boil until liquid is reduced to 2 cups, about 6 minutes. Whisk in reserved 1/3 cup butter mixture. Season with pepper. Garnish with sage, crabapples and pears, if desired. Serve turkey with gravy. Serves 12.

Kendall Hale
Lynn, MA

SAVORY TURKEY LOAF

Not your ordinary meatloaf! Grated apple keeps it moist.

1 t. canola oil
1 c. onion, chopped
1 stalk celery, chopped
¾ t. dried thyme
½ t. dried sage
1½ lbs. ground turkey
1½ c. bread crumbs
1½ c. apple, peeled, cored and
   grated

1 egg, beaten
2 T. fresh parsley, chopped
1 T. mustard
¾ t. salt
½ t. pepper
Glaze

Heat oil in a skillet over medium-high heat. Add onion and celery; sauté about 3 minutes. Stir in thyme and sage. Cool slightly.

Combine ground turkey, onion mixture, bread crumbs and next 6 ingredients in a bowl; mix well. Shape into a loaf; place in a greased 8"x4" loaf pan.

Bake, uncovered, at 350 degrees for one hour. Drain drippings from pan; brush Glaze over top of loaf. Return to oven; bake about 10 to 15 more minutes until top is golden or until a meat thermometer inserted into thickest portion registers 160 degrees. Serves 6 to 8.

GLAZE:

2 T. brown sugar, packed
2 T. cider vinegar

2 t. mustard

Stir together all ingredients in a bowl until brown sugar dissolves. Makes about ¼ cup.

Kim Hill-DeGroot
Macomb Township, MI

MAPLE-CURRY PORK ROAST

Pure maple syrup in the pork marinade hints of the flavors of fall.

1½ lbs. pork tenderloin
½ c. maple syrup
2 T. soy sauce
2 T. catsup
1 T. Dijon mustard

1½ t. curry powder
1½ t. ground coriander
1 t. Worcestershire sauce
2 cloves garlic, minced

Place pork in a large, heavy-duty plastic zipping bag; set aside. Whisk together syrup and next 7 ingredients in a medium bowl. Pour over pork; refrigerate at least one hour.

Transfer pork with marinade to an ungreased 13"x9" baking pan. Bake, uncovered, at 350 degrees for 35 minutes or until a meat thermometer inserted into thickest portion registers 155 degrees. Let stand, covered, 10 minutes or until thermometer registers 160 degrees. Thinly slice and drizzle with sauce from pan. Serves 6.

Sharon Demers
Dolores, CO

"This is wonderful on a cool fall day served with oven-roasted root vegetables, homemade applesauce and sweet potato biscuits."

Sharon

COZY COMFORT FOOD
menu on page 462

SUNDAY PORK ROAST

Simple ingredients enhance the flavors of this roast for a meal special enough for Sunday dinner.

3 cloves garlic, minced
1 T. dried rosemary
salt and pepper to taste
2-lb. boneless pork loin roast

2 T. olive oil
½ c. white wine or chicken
   broth

Crush garlic with rosemary, salt and pepper. Pierce pork with a sharp knife tip in several places and press half the garlic mixture into openings. Rub pork with remaining garlic mixture and olive oil. Place pork in a lightly greased 13"x9" baking pan.

Bake, uncovered, at 350 degrees for one hour and 15 minutes or until a meat thermometer inserted into thickest portion registers 155 degrees. Let stand, covered, 10 minutes or until thermometer registers 160 degrees. Remove to a serving platter; slice and keep warm.

Add wine or broth to pan, stirring to loosen browned bits. Serve pan drippings over pork. Serves 6 to 8.

Tiffany Brinkley
Broomfield, CO

"Arrange pork slices over mashed potatoes for a farm-style meal that's so hearty and filling."

Tiffany

AUTUMN PORK WITH APPLE CHUTNEY

A bold dry rub coats these tenderloins as they bake. Then they're served with a chutney full of apples, raisins, ginger and pecans...perfect for an autumn evening meal.

1 clove garlic, minced
1 T. ground ginger
1 T. mustard seed
1 1/2 t. red pepper flakes
1 t. allspice

1 t. fennel seed
1 t. dried thyme
2 (1-lb.) pork tenderloins
Chutney

Process garlic and seasonings in a blender until ground to a powder. Coat pork with powder. Place pork in a lightly greased shallow roasting pan.

Bake at 450 degrees for 20 to 25 minutes or until a meat thermometer inserted into thickest portion registers 155 degrees. Let stand, covered, 10 minutes or until thermometer registers 160 degrees. To serve, slice pork into 1/2-inch medallions and top with Chutney. Serve remaining Chutney on the side. Serves 6.

CHUTNEY:

1 apple, peeled, cored and chopped
3/4 c. fennel, diced
3/4 c. brown sugar, packed
1/2 c. cider vinegar

1/3 c. raisins
1 T. crystallized ginger, chopped
1/2 t. salt
1/4 c. chopped pecans

Combine first 7 ingredients in a medium saucepan; mix well. Bring mixture to a boil. Reduce heat to low; cover and cook 15 minutes. Remove cover and cook 15 to 20 more minutes or until fruit is tender. Stir in pecans. Makes 2 cups.

Jo Ann
Gooseberry Patch

PORK CHOPS SUPREME

A creamy sauce tops these slow-cooked, tender chops to make them superior.

6 pork chops
paprika to taste
salt and pepper to taste
2 T. olive oil
1 c. water
½ c. celery, chopped

1½-oz. pkg. onion soup mix
2 T. all-purpose flour
1 T. fresh parsley, chopped
¼ c. cold water
5-oz. can evaporated milk

Sprinkle pork chops with paprika, salt and pepper. Brown chops slowly in hot oil in a large skillet over medium heat; drain off excess oil. Add water, celery and onion soup mix. Cover and cook over low heat 45 minutes or until chops are tender. Remove chops from pan and place on a platter.

In a small bowl, combine flour, parsley and cold water; mix until smooth. Whisk into pan drippings, adding evaporated milk. Cook and stir until sauce is thick and bubbly, about 2 to 3 minutes. Cover chops with sauce. Serves 6.

Sharon Pawlak
Castle Rock, CO

> "These pork chops are terrific served with rice, mashed potatoes or pasta."
>
> **Sharon**

handwritten menus

These lend a personal touch to any table. Cut colored papers to fit the front of old-fashioned milk bottles or Mason jars. Write the details on them and wrap them around the jars with a pretty ribbon...fill jars with water and flowers and arrange in the center of the table.

FARMHOUSE PORK & CABBAGE SAUTÉ

Coleslaw, apples and potatoes are cooked with these golden chops for a hearty, warming one-dish dinner.

4 bone-in pork loin chops
¾ t. salt, divided
¼ t. pepper, divided
6 slices bacon, crisply cooked,
   crumbled and drippings reserved
1 onion, thinly sliced
16-oz. pkg. shredded coleslaw mix

2 Golden Delicious apples, cored
   and sliced
¾ lb. redskin potatoes, cubed
¾ c. apple cider
¼ t. dried thyme
1 T. cider vinegar

Sprinkle pork chops with ¼ teaspoon salt and ⅛ teaspoon pepper; set aside. Heat reserved bacon drippings in a Dutch oven over medium-high heat. Cook chops about 8 minutes or until golden on both sides and nearly done. Remove chops to a plate; keep warm.

Add onion to pan. Cover and cook over medium heat 8 minutes or until tender and golden, stirring occasionally. Gradually stir in coleslaw mix; cook about 5 minutes or until wilted. Add apples, potatoes, cider, thyme and remaining salt and pepper; bring to a boil. Reduce heat; cover and simmer 15 to 20 minutes or until potatoes are tender. Stir in vinegar; return chops to pan and heat thoroughly. Sprinkle with bacon. Serves 4.

Jo Ann
Gooseberry Patch

PRALINE MUSTARD-GLAZED HAM

A savory raisin sauce with sliced apples glazes this spiral-cut ham.

7- to 8-lb. bone-in, smoked
   spiral-cut ham half
1 c. maple syrup
¾ c. brown sugar, packed
¾ c. Dijon mustard

⅓ c. apple juice
½ c. raisins
1 Granny Smith apple, cored,
   peeled and thinly sliced

Remove and discard skin and any excess fat from ham. Place in a lightly greased 13"x9" baking pan; insert a meat thermometer into thickest part of ham. Combine syrup, brown sugar, mustard and apple juice; pour over ham. Set pan on lowest oven rack. Bake at 350 degrees, basting with drippings every 20 minutes for 2½ hours or until a meat thermometer inserted into thickest portion of ham registers 140 degrees. Let ham stand for 10 minutes; remove from pan to a platter, reserving drippings.

To make sauce, heat drippings with raisins and apple slices in a small saucepan over low heat 5 minutes. Serve sliced ham with warm sauce. Serves 12.

Sheri Dulaney
Englewood, OH

CELEBRATE SPRING!
menu on page 459

VIRGINIA'S BAKED SPAGHETTI

A favorite like this cheesy spaghetti casserole is a perfect choice for a family dinner or to take along to a potluck.

16-oz. pkg. spaghetti noodles, cooked
2 (24-oz.) jars spaghetti sauce
2 lbs. ground beef, browned
¼ c. butter
¼ c. all-purpose flour
¼ c. grated Parmesan cheese
2 t. salt
½ t. garlic powder
12-oz. can evaporated milk
3 c. shredded sharp Cheddar cheese, divided

Combine spaghetti noodles, spaghetti sauce and ground beef in a large bowl; set aside. Melt butter in a saucepan over medium heat; add flour, Parmesan cheese, salt and garlic powder, stirring constantly until smooth and bubbly. Add evaporated milk and one cup Cheddar cheese; stir until thickened.

Pour half of spaghetti noodle mixture into a greased 13"x9" casserole dish and pour cheese mixture over top. Pour remaining noodle mixture into dish; top with remaining 2 cups Cheddar cheese. Bake at 350 degrees for 25 to 30 minutes. Serves 12.

Mindy Beard
Yorktown, IN

"This is my husband's grandma's recipe. She loved to bake and cook but rarely used a recipe...it came straight from her heart! I am so fortunate to have written this one down."

Mindy

kids' table

Make the kids' table fun! Use a sheet of butcher paper for the tablecloth; place a flowerpot filled with markers, crayons and stickers in the middle...they'll have a blast!

Draw Here!

ITALIAN 3-CHEESE STUFFED SHELLS

Stuffed pasta shells have never been as good as these, which are filled with three types of cheese and zesty Italian flavors. A side salad and garlic toast turn the pasta into a meal for family or friends.

"A super dish for any get-together, and it's so simple to whip up."

Melanie

1 lb. ground chuck
1 c. onion, chopped
1 clove garlic, minced
2 c. hot water
12-oz. can tomato paste
1 T. instant beef bouillon
   granules
1¹/₂ t. dried oregano

16-oz. container cottage
   cheese
8-oz. pkg. shredded mozzarella
   cheese, divided
¹/₂ c. grated Parmesan cheese
1 egg, beaten
24 jumbo pasta shells, cooked

Cook beef, onion and garlic in a large skillet over medium-high heat, stirring until beef crumbles and is no longer pink; drain. Stir in water, tomato paste, bouillon granules and oregano; simmer over medium heat about 30 minutes.

Stir together cottage cheese, one cup mozzarella, Parmesan cheese and egg in a medium bowl; mix well. Stuff cooked shells with cheese mixture; arrange in a greased 13"x9" baking pan. Pour beef mixture over shells.

Cover and bake at 350 degrees for 40 to 45 minutes. Uncover and sprinkle with remaining mozzarella cheese. Bake 5 more minutes or until cheese melts. Serves 6 to 8.

Melanie McNew
Cameron, MO

STUFFED CABBAGE ROLLS

You get your meat and veggies all rolled up in one entrée with these cabbage rolls. The meat mixture that bakes inside resembles mini-meat loaves.

12 leaves cabbage
1¼ lbs. ground beef
1 c. cooked rice
1 onion, chopped
1 egg, beaten
½ t. poultry seasoning or
   dried thyme

2 T. canola oil
2 (8-oz.) cans tomato sauce
1 T. brown sugar, packed
¼ c. water
1 T. lemon juice or vinegar

Cover cabbage leaves with boiling water; let stand 5 minutes or until leaves are limp. Drain and set aside.

Combine ground beef, rice, onion, egg and poultry seasoning or thyme; mix well. Place equal portions of meat mixture in center of each cabbage leaf. Fold sides of each leaf over meat mixture; roll up cabbage leaves and fasten with a wooden pick.

Heat oil in a large skillet over medium heat; add rolls and sauté until golden. Pour tomato sauce into skillet. Combine brown sugar, water and lemon juice or vinegar; stir into tomato sauce. Cover and simmer one hour, basting occasionally. Serves 6.

Alexis Mauriello
Richardson, TX

LASAGNA ROLLS

Double this casserole so you can have one to keep and one to either give away or freeze for holiday company…it freezes for up to one month.

11 lasagna noodles, uncooked
1 lb. Italian sausage, casing
   removed
1 small onion, chopped
1 clove garlic, minced
26-oz. jar spaghetti sauce
1/4 c. dry white wine or chicken
   broth
3 T. fresh parsley, chopped
1/2 t. salt

3 c. ricotta cheese
1 c. shredded mozzarella
   cheese
2 eggs, lightly beaten
1/3 c. fine, dry bread crumbs
2 T. grated Parmesan
   cheese
1 t. Italian seasoning
1/2 c. grated Parmesan
   cheese

Cook lasagna noodles according to package directions; drain. Cut in half crosswise and set aside.

Cook sausage, onion and garlic in a large skillet, stirring until sausage crumbles and is no longer pink; drain. Add spaghetti sauce, wine or broth, parsley and salt, stirring well. Cover and simmer 10 minutes, stirring occasionally. Remove from heat and set aside.

Combine ricotta cheese and next 5 ingredients, stirring well. Spread ricotta mixture evenly over lasagna noodles. Roll up jelly-roll fashion, starting at narrow end.

Place lasagna rolls, seam-side down, in a lightly greased 13"x9" baking dish. Pour meat sauce over rolls and sprinkle with 1/2 cup Parmesan cheese. Bake, covered, at 375 degrees for 30 minutes. Uncover and bake 15 more minutes or until thoroughly heated. Serves 8 to 10.

MEXICAN LASAGNA

We give lasagna a Mexican flavor in this recipe. Corn tortillas take the place of lasagna noodles; Cheddar and Monterey Jack cheese replace mozzarella; and chopped jalapeño, cumin, cilantro and avocado give the lasagna its south-of-the-border flavor.

½ lb. ground mild pork sausage
½ lb. ground beef
1 jalapeño pepper, seeded and finely chopped
⅔ c. canned diced tomatoes and green chiles
1 t. garlic powder
1 t. ground cumin
½ t. salt
½ t. pepper
10¾-oz. can cream of celery soup

10¾-oz. can cream of mushroom soup
10-oz. can enchilada sauce
18 (6-inch) corn tortillas
2 c. shredded Cheddar cheese
1 c. shredded Monterey Jack cheese
1 tomato, seeded and diced
4 green onions, chopped
¼ c. fresh cilantro, chopped
Optional: 1 avocado, chopped

Cook sausage and ground beef in a large skillet over medium-high heat, stirring until meat crumbles and is no longer pink. Drain. Stir in jalapeño and next 5 ingredients; cook until thoroughly heated.

Stir together soups and enchilada sauce in a saucepan; cook until thoroughly heated.

Spoon one-third of sauce onto bottom of a lightly greased 13"x9" baking dish; top with 6 tortillas. Spoon half of beef mixture and one-third of sauce over tortillas; sprinkle with half of Cheddar cheese. Top with 6 tortillas; repeat layers, ending with tortillas. Sprinkle with Monterey Jack cheese and next 3 ingredients.

Bake at 350 degrees for 30 minutes. Top with avocado, if desired. Serves 6 to 8.

BEEF IN ROSEMARY-MUSHROOM SAUCE

*Add some roasted redskin potatoes and a simple tossed salad
for an oh-so-elegant yet easy dinner!*

1-lb. boneless top sirloin steak,
    about ³/₄-inch thick
8-oz. pkg. sliced mushrooms
1 c. white wine or chicken broth
10¹/₂-oz. can beef broth
8-oz. can tomato sauce

1 c. green onions, chopped
¹/₄ c. fresh parsley, chopped and
    divided
1 ¹/₂ t. fresh rosemary, chopped
1 ¹/₂ t. balsamic vinegar
4 cloves garlic, minced

    Place steak in a large plastic zipping bag; top with mushrooms and wine or broth. Refrigerate 30 minutes, turning occasionally. Remove steak from bag, reserving mushrooms and marinade.

    Lightly spray a large non-stick skillet with non-stick vegetable spray and place over medium-high heat. Add steak and cook 6 minutes or to desired degree of doneness, turning after 3 minutes. Remove steak from skillet; keep warm.

    Combine beef broth, tomato sauce, green onions, 2 tablespoons parsley and next 3 ingredients in a medium bowl. Add parsley mixture, mushrooms and marinade to skillet; bring to a boil. Cook until reduced to 2 cups, about 15 minutes, stirring frequently. Thinly slice steak diagonally across the grain and place on a serving platter. Spoon sauce over steak; sprinkle with remaining 2 tablespoons parsley. Serves 4.

Sharon Demers
Dolores, CO

GREEN PEPPER STEAK

Slicing meat across the grain yields tender results. Place an electric knife or sharp chef's knife at an angle against the grain of the meat.

1-lb. round steak
¼ c. soy sauce
1 clove garlic, diced
1½ t. fresh ginger, peeled and
    grated
2 T. canola oil

1 c. green onions, thinly sliced
1 c. green pepper, thinly sliced
1 stalk celery, thinly sliced
1 T. cornstarch
1 c. water
2 tomatoes, coarsely chopped

Slice steak across the grain into thin strips about ⅛ inch thick. Stir together soy sauce, garlic and ginger in a large bowl; add steak and toss well.

Heat oil in a deep skillet; add steak and cook over medium-high heat 6 minutes or until browned. Cover and simmer 25 minutes over medium heat. Adjust heat to medium-high; add green onions, green pepper and celery. Cook 10 minutes or until vegetables are crisp-tender.

Whisk together cornstarch and water until smooth; add to pan. Stir and cook 4 minutes or until thickened; add tomatoes and heat thoroughly. Serves 4.

Kendall Hale
Lynn, MA

STEAK & SPINACH PINWHEELS

If you're using wooden skewers, be sure to soak them first in water for about 30 minutes to prevent any flare-ups on the grill.

"Such a pretty presentation for special occasions."
Vickie

1- to 1¼-lb. flank steak or top
   round steak, halved lengthwise
¾ t. lemon-pepper seasoning
¼ t. salt
8 slices bacon, partially cooked

10-oz. pkg. frozen chopped spinach,
   thawed and drained
2 T. fine, dry bread crumbs
½ t. dried thyme

With a sharp knife, score both pieces of steak in a diamond pattern with cuts one inch apart. Repeat on other side. Place one piece of steak between 2 lengths of heavy-duty plastic wrap; pound lightly into a 10"x6" rectangle. Repeat with second piece. Blend seasoning and salt; sprinkle each steak evenly with half of seasoning mixture. Arrange 4 slices of bacon lengthwise on each steak; set aside.

Combine spinach, bread crumbs and thyme in a bowl; spread half of spinach mixture over each steak. Starting at a short end, roll up each steak. Place wooden picks at one-inch intervals on rolled-up steaks to form 6 one-inch pinwheels from each steak. Slice between wooden picks. Slide 2 pinwheels carefully onto each of 6 skewers. Cook on grill over medium-high heat (350 to 400 degrees) about 6 to 7 minutes or to desired degree of doneness. Serves 6.

Vickie
Gooseberry Patch

SLOW-COOKER BEEF STROGANOFF

1 ³/₄ lbs. boneless beef round steak, cubed
1 T. canola oil
¹/₂ c. red wine or beef broth
2 T. all-purpose flour
¹/₂ t. garlic powder
¹/₂ t. pepper
¹/₄ t. paprika
¹/₄ t. dried oregano
¹/₄ t. dried thyme
¹/₄ t. dried basil

10³/₄-oz. can cream of mushroom soup
.9-oz. pkg. onion-mushroom soup mix
8-oz. pkg. sliced mushrooms
¹/₂ c. sour cream
8-oz. pkg. wide egg noodles, cooked
2 T. butter, softened
Garnish: fresh minced parsley

Brown meat in one tablespoon oil in a Dutch oven over medium-high heat 8 to 10 minutes. Add wine or broth to pan, stirring to loosen particles from bottom of pan. Combine flour and seasonings in a 3- to 4-quart slow cooker. Place browned meat and mixture from pan on top; toss to coat. Add mushroom soup and soup mix; stir until blended. Stir in mushrooms.

Cover and cook on high setting 3 to 3¹/₂ hours or on low setting 6 to 7 hours or until meat is tender. Stir in sour cream; cover and cook until thoroughly heated. Serve over noodles tossed with butter; sprinkle with parsley, if desired. Serves 6.

Jacque Zehner
Modesto, CA

SLOW-COOKED SUPPER
menu on page 463

PERFECT PRIME RIB

This succulent cut of meat doesn't need a lot of help in the flavor department, but a serving of horseradish sauce is always a welcome addition.

¼ c. Worcestershire sauce
2 t. garlic powder
2 t. seasoned salt

2 t. pepper
6-lb. bone-in beef rib roast

Combine all ingredients except roast in a small bowl. Rub mixture over roast; place in a large plastic zipping bag. Refrigerate 8 hours or overnight, turning often.

Place roast, fat-side up, in a lightly greased large roasting pan; pour mixture from bag over roast. Cover with aluminum foil; bake at 350 degrees for 1½ hours. Uncover and bake 1½ more hours or until a meat thermometer inserted into thickest portion registers 145 degrees (medium rare) or to desired degree of doneness. Let stand for 15 minutes before slicing. Serves 6 to 8.

Paula Smith
Ottawa, IL

garnish, if desired

Use simple garnishes to dress up main dishes throughout the year. Fresh mint sprigs add coolness and color to summertime dishes, while rosemary sprigs and cranberries arranged to resemble holly add a festive touch to holiday platters.

MOM'S SICILIAN POT ROAST

Rotini pasta adds to the Sicilian twist of this pot roast…as do the other Italian flavors. It would be just as yummy served over hot cooked rice or savory mashed potatoes.

4-lb. rolled rump beef roast
2 T. garlic-flavored olive oil
2 (28-oz.) cans whole tomatoes
2 (8-oz.) cans Italian tomato sauce
1/2 c. water
1 T. garlic, minced
1 t. dried oregano
1 t. dried basil

1 t. dried parsley
1 1/2 t. salt
1/2 t. pepper
Optional: 1/4 c. all-purpose flour,
   2 c. hot water
hot cooked rotini pasta
Garnish: fresh oregano sprigs

Brown roast slowly in oil over medium heat in a Dutch oven. Add tomatoes, tomato sauce, water, garlic and seasonings to Dutch oven. Bring to a boil; cover, reduce heat and simmer 2 1/2 hours or until tender, turning occasionally.

Cut roast into serving-size slices. Return meat to Dutch oven; simmer, uncovered, 30 more minutes. If sauce is not thick enough, combine flour and water, stirring until dissolved. Gradually stir flour mixture into sauce, a little at a time, until sauce thickens. To serve, place prepared pasta on a large platter; top with sauce and sliced meat. Garnish with fresh oregano sprigs, if desired. Serves 8 to 10.

Barbara Rannazzisi
Gainesville, VA

"We start this dish early in the morning so it's cooking while we nibble on appetizers during football games. Serve it with a crisp salad and garlic bread. Life doesn't get any better than this!"

Barbara

PEPPER-CRUSTED ROAST BEEF

A caramelized onion sauce is spooned over slices of roast beef.

2- to 3-lb. boneless beef rib roast
¼ c. garlic, minced
½ t. salt
3 T. peppercorns
¼ c. Worcestershire sauce

2 red onions, thinly sliced
1 T. canola oil
1 T. brown sugar, packed
2 T. balsamic vinegar

Rub roast with garlic and salt; coat fat side of roast with peppercorns. Drizzle roast with Worcestershire sauce. Place in a roaster pan. Bake at 350 degrees for 2 hours and 15 minutes or until a meat thermometer inserted into thickest portion registers 145 degrees (medium rare) or 160 degrees (medium). Shield with aluminum foil during cooking if roast gets too brown.

Cook onions in oil in a large skillet over medium heat until onions are soft. Add brown sugar and vinegar; cook about 8 to 10 minutes or until onions are caramelized. Let stand 10 minutes; slice roast and serve onions over top. Serves 6 to 8.

Linda Behling
Cecil, PA

EASY HOLIDAY DINNER
menu on page 464

MARINATED BRISKET

The long cook time guarantees tender slices of this lean cut of meat.

¼ c. soy sauce
1 T. celery salt
2 T. smoke-flavored cooking
    sauce
1 T. Worcestershire sauce
2 t. onion salt
2 t. garlic salt
2 t. salt
2 t. pepper

4- to 5-lb. beef brisket,
    trimmed
½ c. catsup
3 T. brown sugar, packed
1 T. soy sauce
1 t. dry mustard
1 t. lemon juice
3 drops hot sauce
⅛ t. nutmeg

    Stir together first 8 ingredients in a small bowl. Pour over brisket and marinate overnight in the refrigerator, turning every few hours.
    Remove from marinade. Bake at 350 degrees for 3½ hours. Stir together catsup and next 6 ingredients and pour over brisket during the last 45 minutes of cooking time. Serves 8.

Neta Jo Liebscher
El Reno, OK

stir dinnertime conversation

    Ask a few questions to encourage conversation at mealtime. What's a favorite childhood memory? What trip would you like to take? Asking questions is a nice way to share sweet memories and catch up with family & friends.

"I like to put my brisket on early Sunday morning so that it will be ready for a houseful after church. Growing up, my children were spoiled with homegrown beef, and brisket was their favorite. Now that they're grown, my husband and I look forward to the Sundays when they and their families come home for their favorite Mom-cooked meal."

Neta Jo

Simple Sloppy Joes,
page 277

fast family suppers

Getting supper to the table fast is a priority for families on-the-go, and most of these recipes can be ready in 30 minutes or less. Try breakfast for dinner one night and serve up hearty Country-Style Supper Skillet (page 244). Don't forget comforting favorites like Momma's Divine Divan (page 261) or Cheesy Tuna Tempter (page 256). Bring the family back to the table with these quick & easy choices.

COUNTRY-STYLE SUPPER SKILLET

Eggs, fresh tomatoes, bacon and potatoes make up this hearty dish you'll serve again and again.

½ lb. bacon, chopped
3 c. potatoes, peeled, cooked and
   diced
1 c. tomato, chopped
½ c. onion, chopped
½ c. green pepper, chopped

1 t. garlic, chopped
½ t. salt
¼ t. pepper
1 ½ c. shredded sharp Cheddar
   cheese
8 eggs

Cook bacon over medium heat in a large deep skillet until crisp; partially drain drippings, reserving some in skillet.

Add vegetables, garlic, salt and pepper; sauté in pan drippings about 5 minutes or until tender. Sprinkle with cheese. Make 8 wells for eggs; crack eggs into wells about 2 inches apart. Reduce heat; cover and cook eggs over medium heat 10 to 12 minutes or to desired degree of doneness. Serves 4 to 6.

Rita Morgan
Pueblo, CO

BREAKFAST FOR SUPPER
menu on page 465

HAM, MUSHROOM & BACON QUICHE

Your entire family will love this quiche…it's loaded with cheese, bacon and ham.

6 eggs, beaten
¾ c. milk
salt and pepper to taste
1 c. shredded Cheddar cheese
2 to 3 slices bacon, crisply cooked
   and crumbled

4 slices deli ham, chopped
4-oz. can sliced mushrooms,
   drained
9-inch unbaked pie crust

   Mix together eggs and milk in a medium bowl. Add salt and pepper; set aside.
   Sprinkle cheese, bacon, ham and mushrooms on top of pie crust; pour egg mixture over top. Bake at 350 degrees for 25 to 30 minutes or until a wooden pick inserted in center comes out clean and top is golden. Serves 4.

Kaitlyn Kiser
Plainwell, MI

"I've made this substituting spinach and sausage or potatoes and broccoli for the ham, mushrooms and bacon. It's fun to experiment with lots of different ingredient combinations!"

Kaitlyn

bacon bits

If you'd like to save time by using precooked bacon, microwave it briefly to crisp it.

SIMPLY SCRUMPTIOUS FRITTATA

Just cook cubed redskin potatoes in 2 tablespoons of oil in a large skillet until tender and golden before adding them to this hearty frittata.

1 T. vegetable oil
½ c. onion, chopped
½ c. green pepper, chopped
1 to 2 cloves garlic, minced
4 redskin potatoes, peeled, cubed and cooked

¾ c. cubed cooked ham
8 eggs, beaten
½ t. salt
pepper to taste
¾ c. shredded Cheddar cheese

Heat oil in a heavy oven-proof non-stick 10" skillet over medium heat. Add onion and green pepper; cook and stir until tender. Add garlic; cook one more minute. Stir in potatoes and ham; cook until thoroughly heated.

Reduce heat to medium-low; add eggs, salt and pepper. Cook about 5 minutes or until eggs are firm on the bottom. Top with cheese; place in oven and bake at 350 degrees for 5 to 10 minutes or until cheese melts. Cut into wedges. Serves 4.

Jill Valentine
Jackson, TN

"A tasty way to use any remaining ham from Sunday dinner...try different cheeses for variety."

Jill

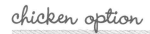

chicken option

Cubed cooked chicken makes a fine substitute for ham in this frittata. If you use chicken, Cheddar is still tasty as the topper, or consider provolone as an option.

LUCKY-7 MAC & CHEESE

Seven varieties of cheese come together in this favorite homestyle dish that stirs up quickly on the cooktop rather than baking in the oven. We consider whoever gets a serving of this…lucky!

1 c. fat-free milk
½ c. extra sharp Cheddar
   cheese, cubed
½ c. Colby cheese, cubed
½ c. pasteurized process
   cheese spread, cubed
½ c. Swiss cheese, cubed

½ c. provolone cheese, cubed
½ c. Monterey Jack cheese, cubed
½ c. crumbled blue cheese
16-oz. pkg. elbow macaroni,
   cooked
salt and pepper to taste

Cook milk and cheeses in a heavy 4-quart saucepan over low heat until cheeses melt, whisking often. Stir in macaroni; season with salt and pepper. Heat thoroughly. Serves 6 to 8.

Tina Vogel
Orlando, FL

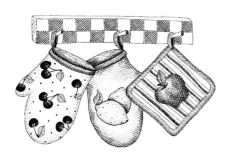

GREEK PIZZA

Mediterranean ingredients like olives, capers, fresh basil and feta cheese make up the flavorful toppings of this Greek-inspired pizza.

13.8-oz. tube refrigerated pizza
   dough
olive oil
2 cloves garlic, minced
8-oz. pkg. shredded mozzarella
   cheese, divided
½ c. canned artichokes, drained
   and chopped

¼ c. sliced green olives
½ c. fresh basil, thinly sliced
¼ c. crumbled feta cheese
3 T. capers
Optional: 6 anchovy fillets, finely
   chopped

Roll out pizza dough on a floured surface to about ¼ inch thick. Place on a lightly greased baking sheet; brush lightly with olive oil.

Spread garlic over dough; sprinkle with half of mozzarella. Top with artichokes, olives, basil, feta, capers and, if desired, anchovies. Sprinkle with remaining half of mozzarella. Bake at 400 degrees for 8 to 10 minutes or until cheese melts. Serves 4.

Sean Avner
Delaware, OH

> "Don't let the anchovies keep you from trying this...they're completely optional!"
>
> **Sean**

pizza party

Almost everyone loves pizza, so why not provide the crust and sauce, then invite friends to visit and share their favorite toppings? You might create a new combination!

VEGETABLE LO MEIN À LA ROB

Lo mein noodles are usually the key ingredient in this Asian dish, but the "à la Rob" version of this dish substitutes rice noodles. We'll let you choose…it's good either way.

8-oz. pkg. rice noodles, cooked
2 T. plus 1 t. sesame oil, divided
½ t. salt
1 onion, halved and sliced into crescents
2 stalks celery, thinly sliced
2 cloves garlic, pressed
1½ t. fresh ginger, peeled and shredded

1 carrot, peeled and shredded
¼ lb. snow peas
1 c. sliced mushrooms
1 c. frozen corn kernels
Optional: dry white wine or vegetable broth
Sauce

> "A savory main dish that's much easier than it looks…chop the veggies and stir up the sauce, and it goes together very quickly."
> **Robbin**

Toss noodles in a bowl with one teaspoon sesame oil and salt; set aside.

Heat remaining 2 tablespoons oil in a skillet over high heat. Add onion and next 7 ingredients, one at a time, in order given; stir-fry each 2 to 4 minutes until crisp-tender. Add a little white wine or vegetable broth to skillet if skillet gets too dry. Pour noodles on top and reduce heat to low. Drizzle Sauce over noodles and toss together. Serves 4 to 6.

SAUCE:

½ c. dry white wine or vegetable broth
¼ c. sugar
1½ T. cornstarch
6 T. soy sauce

4 t. hoisin sauce
2 t. sesame oil
1 t. rice wine vinegar or white vinegar

Combine all ingredients in a small saucepan. Cook over low heat 5 minutes or until thickened. Keep warm. Makes one cup.

Robbin Chamberlain
Worthington, OH

FRESH TOMATO & BASIL LINGUINE

If ripe garden tomatoes are out of season, chopped roma tomatoes or halved cherry tomatoes are good substitutes.

1 ½ lbs. tomatoes, finely chopped
3 cloves garlic, minced
1 red pepper, chopped
1 bunch fresh basil, torn
½ c. olive oil

1 t. salt
pepper to taste
16-oz. pkg. linguine, cooked
Garnish: grated Parmesan
   cheese

Stir together tomatoes, garlic, red pepper and basil in a large bowl; drizzle with oil. Sprinkle with salt and pepper; mix well and toss with hot cooked linguine. Sprinkle with Parmesan cheese, if desired. Serves 6 to 8.

Vickie
Gooseberry Patch

"This is a terrific light meal I like to serve with muffins and fresh fruit."

Nancy

SPINACH PIE

16-oz. container cottage cheese
10-oz. pkg. frozen chopped spinach,
   thawed and drained
8 oz. shredded Cheddar cheese

3 eggs, beaten
¼ c. butter, melted
3 T. all-purpose flour
salt blend to taste

Combine all ingredients in a bowl. Pour into a 9" pie plate. Bake, uncovered, at 325 degrees for one hour. Cool slightly and cut into wedges. Serves 6.

Nancy Burton
Wamego, KS

LEMON-PEPPER FISH

Feel free to substitute either pollock or haddock for the cod in this recipe. Each option is a white fish and a member of the cod family.

1 lb. frozen cod, thawed
16-oz. pkg. frozen stir-fry
   vegetables
salt to taste

1 t. lemon-pepper seasoning
1 t. dried rosemary
1 c. tomato juice
2½ T. grated Parmesan cheese

Line a 13"x9" baking dish with aluminum foil. Place cod on foil and cover with vegetables. Season with salt, lemon-pepper seasoning and rosemary. Pour tomato juice over ingredients in dish; sprinkle with Parmesan cheese. Bake at 400 degrees for 20 to 25 minutes or until fish flakes easily with a fork and vegetables are tender. Serves 4.

Liz Plotnick-Snay
Gooseberry Patch

al fresco dining

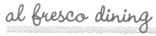

Dinners at home don't have to be in the kitchen...and the outdoors isn't reserved for cookouts. Bake up a tasty dish inside, then lead everyone to the backyard...they'll be so surprised!

FETTUCCINE WITH SMOKED SALMON

Fresh asparagus and dill pair up with creamy fettuccine and smoked salmon for a refreshing springtime meal.

8-oz. pkg. fettuccine, uncooked
1 lb. asparagus, cut into ½-inch
   pieces
1 c. whipping cream
2 T. fresh dill, chopped
1 T. prepared horseradish

4 oz. smoked salmon, cut into
   ½-inch pieces
½ t. salt
¼ t. pepper
freshly squeezed lemon juice

Cook pasta according to package directions; add asparagus during last 3 minutes of cooking time. Drain and set aside.

Heat cream, dill and horseradish in a skillet over low heat about one minute or until hot; add pasta mixture, tossing to mix. Gently toss in salmon; add salt and pepper. Squeeze lemon juice over top. Serves 4 to 6.

Carole Larkins
Elmendorf AFB, AK

> "I like to serve this spooned into a serving bowl ringed with fresh lettuce leaves."
>
> **Carole**

noodle options

Substitute any long slender pasta for fettuccine. Consider linguine, spaghetti or vermicelli. Just take note of the cooking time of the new noodle so you'll know when to add the asparagus.

"I took plain old tuna casserole and punched it up with lots of cheese...now my daughter loves it!"

Charity

CHEESY TUNA TEMPTER

Tuna casserole is the ultimate comfort food. This version is made even more comfy with the addition of two types of cheeses.

½ c. celery, chopped
¼ c. onion, chopped
5 T. butter, divided
10¾-oz. can cream of mushroom
   soup
1½ c. milk, divided
6-oz. can tuna, drained
1 c. finely shredded sharp Cheddar
   cheese

½ c. grated Parmesan cheese
¼ t. salt
¼ t. pepper
8-oz. pkg. medium egg noodles,
   cooked
10 round buttery crackers,
   crushed

Sauté celery and onion in 2 tablespoons butter in a large skillet over medium heat until tender. Add soup, milk, tuna, cheeses, salt and pepper; mix well.

Place noodles in a lightly greased 2-quart baking dish. Pour tuna mixture over top; toss to coat noodles. Sprinkle cracker crumbs on top and dot with remaining 3 tablespoons butter. Bake at 350 degrees for 25 minutes or until hot and bubbly. Serves 4 to 6.

Charity Meyer
Lewisberry, PA

SHRIMPLY DIVINE CASSEROLE

Don't wait for special occasions to serve shrimp. This dish is easy enough to whip up during the week…your family will thank you for it!

8-oz. pkg. spinach egg noodles,
   cooked
3-oz. pkg. cream cheese, cubed
1 1/2 lbs. uncooked medium shrimp,
   peeled and cleaned
1/2 c. butter
10 3/4-oz. can cream of mushroom
   soup

1 c. sour cream
1/2 c. milk
1/2 c. mayonnaise
1 T. fresh chives, chopped
1/2 t. mustard
Optional: 3/4 c. shredded cheese

Place noodles in a lightly greased 13"x9" baking dish. Place cream cheese cubes on hot noodles; set aside.

Sauté shrimp in butter in a large skillet over medium heat until shrimp turn pink; place over noodles and cheese.

Stir together soup and next 5 ingredients; pour over shrimp. Sprinkle shredded cheese on top, if desired. Bake at 325 degrees for 20 to 30 minutes or until bubbly. Serves 6.

Karen Puchnick
Butler, PA

THAI PEANUT NOODLES

If you want to purchase raw shrimp and cook and peel it yourself, start with 2 pounds. Chicken breasts are a nice substitute for shrimp in this peanutty-flavored Asian dish. For 4 servings, use 4 boneless breasts. Cut the chicken into bite-size chunks and sauté in a little oil ahead of time.

1 lb. cooked, peeled medium
   shrimp
1 c. light Italian salad dressing,
   divided
2 T. crunchy peanut butter
1 T. soy sauce
1 T. honey
1 t. ground ginger

3/4 t. red pepper flakes
1 carrot, peeled and shredded
1 c. green onions, chopped
1 T. sesame oil
8-oz. pkg. angel hair pasta,
   cooked
2 T. fresh cilantro, chopped
Optional: 2/3 c. peanuts, chopped

Coat shrimp with 1/2 cup Italian salad dressing; refrigerate 30 minutes.
Whisk together remaining 1/2 cup Italian salad dressing, peanut butter, soy sauce, honey, ginger and red pepper flakes until smooth; set aside.
Sauté carrot, green onions and shrimp in sesame oil about 5 minutes or until shrimp are thoroughly heated. Toss pasta, peanut sauce and shrimp mixture together in a large serving bowl; sprinkle with cilantro and, if desired, peanuts. Serves 4.

Emily Selmer
Sumner, WA

"If you're short on time, use canned chicken instead."

Karen

CHICKEN BURRITOS

These burritos are the perfect solution for what to serve on those busy nights when you need supper in a hurry! Just add Mexican rice or black beans to go along.

4 boneless, skinless chicken breasts, cooked and shredded
1½ c. salsa, divided
1 c. sour cream
6 (10-inch) flour tortillas

10¾-oz. can cream of chicken soup
2 c. shredded Mexican-blend cheese
Toppings: chopped tomatoes, sliced green onions, sour cream

Combine chicken, ½ cup salsa and sour cream in a large bowl. Spoon chicken mixture evenly onto tortillas. Fold up sides and roll up, burrito-style; place in an ungreased 13"x9" baking dish. Blend together soup and remaining one cup salsa; pour over burritos.

Bake, uncovered, at 350 degrees for 30 minutes. Sprinkle with cheese and bake 5 more minutes or until cheese melts. Serve with desired toppings. Serves 6.

Karen Wright
Arnold, MO

FIESTA TIME!
menu on page 461

MOMMA'S DIVINE DIVAN

Choose rotisserie chicken from your supermarket deli to add more flavor to this family favorite. Generally, one rotisserie chicken will yield 3 cups of chopped meat, so you'll need 2 rotisserie chickens to get the 4 to 5 cups needed for this recipe. Add cooked rice, and you have a complete meal!

½ lb. broccoli flowerets, cooked
4 to 5 boneless, skinless chicken
    breasts, cooked and cubed
salt to taste
1 c. seasoned bread crumbs
1 T. butter, melted

10¾-oz. can cream of chicken soup
½ c. mayonnaise
1 t. curry powder
½ t. lemon juice
1 c. shredded Cheddar cheese

Arrange broccoli in the bottom of a lightly greased 13"x9" baking dish. Sprinkle chicken with salt to taste; place on top of broccoli and set aside.

Toss together bread crumbs and butter; set aside.

Combine soup, mayonnaise, curry powder and lemon juice in a small bowl; spread over chicken and broccoli. Top with cheese; sprinkle with bread crumb mixture. Bake, uncovered, at 350 degrees for 25 minutes. Serves 8 to 10.

Margaret Vinci
Pasadena, CA

FAMILY NIGHT
menu on page 458

CHICKEN CHIMIES

Add a bit of heat to this Mexican favorite by using pepper Jack cheese in place of regular Monterey Jack.

"Why go out to eat when this is just as good as any restaurant?"

Diana

2 boneless, skinless chicken breasts, cooked and shredded
salt, pepper and garlic salt to taste
1 T. butter
10 (8-inch) flour tortillas
8-oz. pkg. shredded Monterey Jack cheese

6 green onions, sliced
1 T. vegetable oil
Toppings: sour cream, guacamole, salsa
Optional: lettuce leaves

Sprinkle chicken with salt, pepper and garlic salt to taste. Heat butter in a large skillet over medium heat; add chicken and sauté about 3 minutes.

Spoon chicken evenly onto tortillas. Top with cheese and green onions; fold up sides and roll up, burrito-style. Heat oil in a large skillet over medium-high heat. Add rolled-up tortillas and sauté until golden. Serve with your choice of toppings and over lettuce leaves, if desired. Serves 6 to 8.

Diana Duff
Cypress, CA

clever condiments!

When serving a Mexican meal with a trio of toppings, such as these chimichangas, slice the tops off 3 bell peppers, rinse and remove seeds. Then fill one pepper each with guacamole, sour cream and salsa. Cover with reserved tops and refrigerate until ready to serve. Works great for cookouts, too...fill with mustard, mayo and catsup.

"No leftover turkey on hand? Use chicken instead."

Sandy

GOBBLER COBBLER

There's no such thing as boring leftovers when you serve dishes like this!

3 c. cooked turkey, cubed
2½ c. turkey gravy
1½ c. frozen peas, partially thawed
1½ c. sliced mushrooms
⅔ c. sun-dried tomatoes, chopped
¼ c. water

2 T. fresh parsley, chopped and divided
1 t. poultry seasoning, divided
2¼ c. buttermilk biscuit baking mix
¼ t. pepper
¾ c. plus 2 T. milk

Combine turkey, gravy, peas, mushrooms, tomatoes, water, one tablespoon parsley and ½ teaspoon poultry seasoning in a large stockpot. Cook over medium heat until mixture comes to a boil, stirring occasionally.

Stir together baking mix, remaining one tablespoon parsley, remaining ½ teaspoon poultry seasoning, pepper and milk in another bowl. Pour turkey mixture into a lightly greased 2-quart baking dish; drop biscuit mixture on top in 6 equal mounds. Place dish on a baking sheet; bake at 450 degrees for 20 minutes or until topping is golden. Serves 6.

Sandy Rowe
Bellevue, OH

casserole topper

Create a topper for your favorite casserole. Unroll 2 refrigerated pie crusts; sprinkle one with pecans and sun-dried tomatoes (or any other goodies) and top with remaining crust. Roll crusts together and cut into shapes with cookie cutters. Bake at 425 degrees for 8 minutes and arrange on the baked casserole before serving.

MAPLE-CRANBERRY TURKEY

For a small holiday gathering, this recipe is just the ticket. Turkey breast tenderloins yield enough for 4 servings. Cranberries, cinnamon and sweet potatoes give you all the flavors of the season.

1-lb. pkg. turkey breast tenderloins	1/4 c. orange juice
1 T. olive oil	1 T. butter
1/3 c. sweetened dried cranberries	1/4 t. cinnamon
1/3 c. maple syrup	29-oz. can cut sweet potatoes

Brown turkey in oil in an 11" skillet over medium heat 6 to 7 minutes on each side; set aside.

Bring cranberries, syrup, orange juice, butter and cinnamon to a boil in a saucepan; remove from heat. Add sweet potatoes to turkey in skillet; pour cranberry mixture on top.

Cook over medium heat 30 minutes or until turkey is done and sauce thickens. Serves 4.

Delinda Blakney
Bridgeview, IL

year-round Thanksgiving

Remind your family throughout the year of all they have to be thankful for by serving this skillet supper full of Thanksgiving flavor.

SANTA FE PORK CUTLETS

Salsa, corn and cilantro give this tenderloin its Santa Fe flair. Let your taste buds be the judge regarding whether you go for mild or spicy salsa.

3 T. all-purpose flour
¼ t. salt
⅛ t. pepper
1-lb. pork tenderloin, sliced ¼ inch
    thick
3 t. vegetable oil, divided

½ c. salsa
½ c. thawed frozen corn kernels
¼ c. water
Toppings: sour cream, chopped
    fresh cilantro

Combine flour, salt and pepper; dredge pork in flour mixture. Heat 2 teaspoons oil over medium heat in a non-stick skillet. Sauté half the cutlets one to 1½ minutes per side. Transfer to a plate. Repeat with remaining one teaspoon oil and cutlets. Cover to keep warm.

Add salsa, corn and water to skillet. Simmer over medium heat one minute. Remove from heat. Spoon salsa mixture over cutlets. Top with sour cream and chopped cilantro, if desired. Serves 4.

Beverly Ray
Brandon, FL

"What a delicious way to serve pork, and it's so fast!"

Beverly

leftover salsa

Serve the rest of the salsa with chips as an appetizer while this southwestern supper simmers.

LEMONY PORK PICCATA

Serve over quick-cooking angel hair pasta to enjoy every drop of the lemony sauce.

1-lb. pork tenderloin, sliced into
    8 portions
2 t. lemon-pepper seasoning
3 T. all-purpose flour
2 T. butter

¼ c. dry sherry or chicken broth
¼ c. lemon juice
¼ c. capers
4 to 6 thin slices lemon

Pound pork slices to ⅛-inch thickness, using a meat mallet or rolling pin. Lightly sprinkle pork with lemon-pepper seasoning and flour. Melt one tablespoon butter in a large skillet over medium-high heat. Add half of pork and sauté 2 to 3 minutes on each side until golden, turning once. Repeat procedure with remaining butter and pork. Remove pork to a serving plate; set aside.

Add sherry or chicken broth, lemon juice, capers and lemon slices to skillet. Cook 2 minutes or until slightly thickened, scraping up browned bits. Add pork and heat thoroughly. Serves 4.

Melody Taynor
Everett, WA

COMPANY'S COMING
menu on page 459

HONEY-PECAN PORK CUTLETS

A touch of honey in the pecan sauce adds a hint of sweetness to these pork cutlets.

1 lb. boneless pork loin cutlets
¹/₂ c. all-purpose flour
3 T. butter, divided

¹/₄ c. chopped pecans
¹/₄ c. honey

Pound pork to ¹/₄-inch thickness, using a meat mallet or rolling pin. Coat cutlets with flour.

Heat one tablespoon butter in a large skillet over medium heat. Add pork and sauté about 5 to 6 minutes or until browned on both sides.

Soften remaining 2 tablespoons butter in a small mixing bowl and combine with pecans and honey; add to skillet, stirring gently. Cover and simmer 7 to 8 minutes or until done. Remove to a serving platter and spoon sauce over pork. Serves 2 to 3.

Kathy Grashoff
Fort Wayne, IN

> *"You won't believe that something so good could be so simple."*
>
> **Kathy**

quick table setting

You don't have to spend a lot of time setting the table for casual gatherings. Just wrap colorful napkins around silverware and slip one bundle into a glass at each place setting. It's so charming…and you don't have to remember where the forks, knives and spoons go!

HEARTY RED BEANS & RICE

In New Orleans, beans go hand in hand with rice. It's the official Monday meal there as well. But no matter which day you choose to serve this version of the classic dish, family & friends will leave the table happy.

"A big bowl of this down-home favorite really hits the spot."

Kerry

1 green pepper, chopped
1 onion, chopped
½ c. green onions, chopped
½ c. celery, chopped
2 T. fresh parsley, chopped
3 slices bacon, crisply cooked
   and crumbled, drippings
   reserved
½ lb. Polish sausage, sliced
2 (15-oz.) cans kidney beans,
   drained and rinsed

1 c. chicken broth
6-oz. can tomato paste
2-oz. jar chopped pimentos,
   drained
2 T. catsup
1 t. chili powder
1 ½ t. Worcestershire sauce
3 c. cooked rice

Sauté green pepper, onions, celery and parsley in reserved bacon drippings in a skillet over medium heat until tender.

Stir in bacon, sausage and next 7 ingredients. Reduce heat; cover and simmer 30 minutes, stirring occasionally. Serve over cooked rice. Serves 4.

Kerry Mayer
Denham Springs, LA

BACON FLORENTINE FETTUCCINE

*Creamed spinach gets a makeover in this recipe when it's paired
with crispy bacon and fettuccine.*

16-oz. pkg. refrigerated fettuccine,
    uncooked
2 (10-oz.) pkgs. frozen creamed
    spinach
½ lb. bacon, crisply cooked and
    chopped

⅛ t. garlic powder
½ c. plus 2 T. grated Parmesan
    cheese, divided
pepper to taste

    Prepare fettuccine according to package directions; drain, reserving
¾ cup of cooking liquid. Return fettuccine and reserved liquid to saucepan.
    Microwave spinach according to package directions. Add spinach, bacon
and garlic powder to fettuccine in saucepan, stirring to combine. Transfer to
a serving dish and stir in ½ cup cheese. Season with pepper and sprinkle with
remaining 2 tablespoons cheese. Serves 4.

Barbara Adamson
Oviedo, FL

garlic substitution

    No garlic powder? No problem! Substitute 1 teaspoon bottled minced garlic or 1 clove
garlic, minced, instead of ⅛ t. garlic powder, if you'd like.

TANGY BROWN SUGAR HAM

These thick slices of ham steak are brushed with a sweet-hot sauce and grilled for a pleasing smoky taste.

1 c. brown sugar, packed
1/3 c. prepared horseradish
1/4 c. lemon juice

4 slices cooked ham, cut 1 inch
    thick (about 1 lb.)

Combine sugar, horseradish and lemon juice in a saucepan; bring to a boil. Brush over ham.

Grill ham over high heat (400 to 500 degrees) 4 to 6 minutes on each side or until thoroughly heated. Serves 4.

Alyce Leitzel
Hegins, PA

double-duty grilling

Roast vegetables alongside the meat…brush slices of squash, potatoes, bell peppers or eggplant with olive oil and grill until tender. They're delicious warm or cold, so be sure to grill plenty for sides now and salads later.

MINI MEAT LOAVES

This recipe can also be baked in 6 ungreased muffin cups. Spoon mixture evenly into cups and bake at 350 degrees for 35 minutes.

1 lb. ground beef	1 egg, beaten
1 small onion, finely chopped	10³/₄-oz. can vegetable soup,
2 slices bread, cubed	undiluted

Combine all ingredients in a large mixing bowl. Shape into 6 oval loaves. Place on an ungreased rimmed baking sheet. Bake at 350 degrees for 20 minutes. Serve with barbecue sauce, chili sauce, salsa or catsup. Serves 6.

Roxanne Bixby
West Franklin, NH

"For extra fun, use large cookie cutters to shape the meat, then simply place the meat on a cookie sheet to bake."

Roxanne

doubly good!

Double this recipe if you'd like to have extras on hand in the freezer. Thaw however many you'd like to serve overnight in the refrigerator and reheat them on high in the microwave.

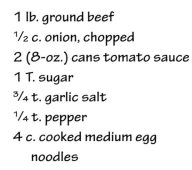

HAMBURGER-NOODLE BAKE

This one-dish meal is easy to make ahead of time and refrigerate or freeze for later…just heat it up when hunger hits! If frozen, let it thaw in the refrigerator overnight.

1 lb. ground beef
1/2 c. onion, chopped
2 (8-oz.) cans tomato sauce
1 T. sugar
3/4 t. garlic salt
1/4 t. pepper
4 c. cooked medium egg
   noodles

1 c. cottage cheese
8-oz. pkg. cream cheese,
   softened
1/4 c. sour cream
1/4 c. grated Parmesan
   cheese

    Cook ground beef and onion in a skillet over medium-high heat, stirring until beef crumbles and is no longer pink; drain. Stir in tomato sauce, sugar, garlic salt and pepper; heat thoroughly and remove from heat.

    Gently combine noodles, cottage cheese, cream cheese and sour cream; spread half of noodle mixture in a lightly greased 11"x7" baking dish. Layer with half of meat mixture; repeat both layers. Sprinkle with Parmesan cheese; bake at 350 degrees for 30 minutes. Serves 8.

Kate Conroy
Bethlehem, PA

SIMPLE SLOPPY JOES
(pictured on page 242)

These sandwiches will be a winner with the family for their flavor and with Mom for their ease!

1 lb. ground chuck
1 onion, chopped
1 c. catsup
¼ c. water

2 T. Worcestershire sauce
¼ t. salt
¼ t. pepper
6 to 8 sandwich buns

Cook ground chuck and onion in a large skillet over medium-high heat, stirring until beef crumbles and is no longer pink; drain. Stir in catsup, water, Worcestershire sauce, salt and pepper; simmer 20 minutes, stirring frequently. Spoon onto buns. Serves 6 to 8.

Jennifer Catterino
Pasadena, MD

love of cooking

After graduating from college, I found that I could only "cook" frozen pizza. My idea of a gourmet meal was when I opened up a jar of spaghetti sauce and poured it over pasta. When I got my first job out of school, I met my dear friend, Barbara. Barb would often invite me over for dinner because she loved to cook. I was impressed with her cooking and thought I would give it a try and invite her over for dinner. Well, it didn't work out as I'd hoped. I burned dinner, so we ordered out! That was the beginning of many cooking lessons and wonderful recipes Barb shared with me.

Barb instilled in me a love of cooking and I have no one else to thank but her. She's still the best cook, even though I continue to bake a frozen pizza now and then!

Gina Bass-Yurevich
Springfield, IL

NACHO GRANDE CASSEROLE

Turn this chunky casserole into a hearty appetizer by providing tortilla chips for dipping.

2 lbs. ground beef
1 onion, chopped
2 (16-oz.) cans spicy chili beans
16-oz. pkg. frozen corn kernels, thawed
15-oz. can tomato sauce
1¼-oz. pkg. taco seasoning mix

3 c. finely shredded Cheddar Jack cheese, divided
3 c. nacho cheese tortilla chips, crushed and divided
Toppings: chopped tomatoes and green onions

Cook ground beef and onion in a Dutch oven over medium-high heat, stirring until beef crumbles and is no longer pink; drain. Add beans, corn, tomato sauce and seasoning mix; stir until blended. Simmer over medium heat 10 minutes.

Pour half of beef mixture into a lightly greased 13"x9" baking dish. Top with 1½ cups each of cheese and crushed chips; top with remaining beef mixture and remaining 1½ cups each of cheese and chips. Bake at 350 degrees for 25 to 30 minutes or until bubbly and golden. Sprinkle with chopped tomatoes and green onions, if desired. Serves 8 to 10.

Carol Hickman
Kingsport, TN

SPAGHETTI PIE

Spaghetti and pie are top choices of kids and adults alike. This version is a fun way to serve the recipe…in a pie plate, cut into wedges!

8-oz. pkg. spaghetti, cooked
4 eggs, beaten and divided
²/₃ c. grated Parmesan cheese
2 c. cottage cheese, drained
1 lb. ground beef

1 c. green pepper, chopped
1 c. onion, chopped
1½ c. spaghetti sauce
1 c. shredded mozzarella cheese

Combine spaghetti with half of beaten eggs and Parmesan cheese; spread in a lightly greased 9" pie plate. Combine cottage cheese and remaining eggs; spread over spaghetti.

Cook ground beef, green pepper and onion in a large skillet over medium-high heat, stirring until beef crumbles and is no longer pink; drain. Stir sauce into beef mixture; spread over cottage cheese mixture.

Bake at 350 degrees for 30 minutes. Top with mozzarella cheese and bake 5 more minutes or until cheese melts. Cut into wedges to serve. Serves 4 to 6.

Susann Kropp
Cairo, NY

sauce things up!

Bottled spaghetti sauce provides much of the flavor in this Italian pie, so pick a flavor to suit your fancy…heavy on the garlic, heavy on the herbs, and with roasted red pepper are flavor options for bottled sauce.

SKILLET ENCHILADAS

These tortillas are stuffed with cheese and olives, then served with a loaded sauce of ground beef and green chiles…yum!

¼ c. vegetable oil
8 (8-inch) corn tortillas
3 c. shredded Cheddar cheese, divided

½ c. chopped olives
Enchilada Sauce

"Try diced potatoes in place of ground beef for a vegetarian twist."

Julie

Heat oil in a 10" skillet over medium heat; add one tortilla, heating until just softened. Remove to a paper towel; pat dry. Repeat with remaining tortillas.

Fill tortillas evenly with 2½ cups cheese and olives; roll up and place seam-side down in skillet. Pour Enchilada Sauce over tortillas; cook, covered, over medium heat 5 minutes. Sprinkle with remaining ½ cup cheese; cook, uncovered, until cheese melts. Serves 4 to 8.

ENCHILADA SAUCE:

1 lb. ground beef
½ c. onion, chopped
10¾-oz. can cream of mushroom soup

10-oz. can enchilada sauce
⅓ c. milk
2 T. chopped green chiles

Cook ground beef and onion in a large skillet over medium-high heat, stirring until beef crumbles and is no longer pink; drain. Stir in soup and remaining ingredients; simmer 20 to 25 minutes.

Julie Coles
Boise, ID

Roasted Corn with Rosemary
Butter, page 297

savory sides

Rounding out your meal is a snap with this selection of side dishes. Choose Cuban Black Beans (page 288) to accompany any of the south-of-the-border main dishes. Share the bounty of your garden with savory Tomato Pie (page 315). And when the weather turns cooler, Mom's Red Cabbage (page 296) offers side-dish comfort. With over 25 delectable choices, you can't go wrong!

ASPARAGUS WITH TOMATO VINAIGRETTE

It's best to remove the woody stem ends of asparagus before cooking. Holding a stalk of asparagus by both ends, bend the cut end until it snaps…it will naturally break where the most tender part begins.

1 lb. fresh asparagus, trimmed
1/2 t. salt
3 T. olive oil

1 1/2 T. white wine vinegar
1/2 t. honey
2 large tomatoes, chopped

Add one inch of water to a medium saucepan; bring to a rolling boil. Add asparagus and salt; boil over low heat 3 to 5 minutes or until tender. Drain.

Heat olive oil over low heat in another saucepan; stir in vinegar and honey. Add tomatoes; heat thoroughly. To serve, pour vinaigrette over asparagus. Serves 4 to 6.

CELEBRATE SPRING!
menu on page 459

BROCCOLI PARMESAN

This recipe calls for just broccoli flowerets, but don't discard the leaves and stalks. Instead, dice or shred them to use in salads and stir-fries.

8 c. broccoli flowerets
2 T. butter
3 T. onion, chopped
2 T. all-purpose flour
1 t. chicken bouillon granules
1¾ c. milk
½ c. shredded Parmesan cheese

½ t. salt
½ t. pepper
½ t. dry mustard
¼ t. ground marjoram
Optional: shredded Parmesan
   cheese

Steam broccoli, covered, in a steamer basket over boiling water 5 minutes or until crisp-tender. Keep warm.

Meanwhile, melt butter in a heavy saucepan; add onion and sauté until tender. Add flour and bouillon granules, stirring until blended. Cook, stirring constantly, one minute. Gradually add milk; cook over medium heat, stirring constantly, until thickened and bubbly. Stir in ½ cup cheese and next 4 ingredients; pour over broccoli. Sprinkle with additional cheese, if desired. Serves 6 to 8.

EASY HOLIDAY DINNER
menu on page 464

CANDIED-GLAZED BAKED APPLES

Red cinnamon candies give these apples a little zip and a lot of color!

¾ c. sugar	4 baking apples
⅓ c. red cinnamon candies	2 t. lemon juice
1 c. water	1 T. butter, diced

Combine sugar, cinnamon candies and water in a saucepan; bring to a boil over high heat, stirring until sugar dissolves. Reduce heat; simmer, uncovered, 2 minutes. Remove from heat; set aside.

Peel top third of each apple. Remove and discard core, leaving bottom intact. Brush top of apples with lemon juice; arrange in a lightly greased 8"x8" baking dish. Dot centers of apples with butter; brush generously with sugar glaze. Bake at 350 degrees, uncovered, for one hour; brush frequently with remaining glaze. Serve warm. Serves 4.

Jackie Smulski
Lyons, IL

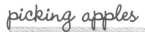

picking apples

Certain varieties of apples hold their shape better than others when they're to be cooked or baked. Look for Granny Smith, Rome, Braeburn, Gala or York apples for this recipe.

CUBAN BLACK BEANS

These black beans are a perfect accompaniment to either Chicken Burritos (page 260) or Chicken Chimies (page 263). Or add smoked sausage to the beans and serve with Mexican rice for a one-dish meal.

1 onion, chopped
1 small green pepper, chopped
3 cloves garlic, pressed
2 T. olive oil
3 (15-oz.) cans black beans
¼ c. water or chicken broth

1 T. white vinegar
½ t. salt
¼ t. black pepper
Garnishes: chopped green onions,
    chopped tomato, sour cream

Sauté onion, green pepper and garlic in hot oil in a Dutch oven over medium-high heat until tender. Add undrained beans and next 4 ingredients; bring to a boil. Cover, reduce heat and simmer 15 to 20 minutes. To serve, sprinkle beans with chopped green onions and tomato; top with sour cream, if desired. Makes 5½ cups.

dressed-up refried beans

Cook 2 seeded and diced pickled jalapeños, 2 chopped cloves garlic and ¼ cup chopped onion in ¼ cup bacon drippings. Add 2 (16-ounce) cans refried beans; heat thoroughly and stir in ½ teaspoon ground cumin.

FIESTA TIME!
menu on page 461

GREEN BEANS AMANDINE

Amandine is the French term for dishes that are garnished with almonds. Here, slivered almonds are sautéed with minced onion in butter and tossed with fresh green beans.

2 lbs. green beans
1 small ham hock
1 c. water
⅔ c. slivered almonds

⅓ c. onion, minced
3 T. butter, melted
1 t. salt

    Wash beans; trim stem ends. Cut beans into 1½-inch pieces. Place in a Dutch oven; add ham hock and water. Bring to a boil; cover, reduce heat and simmer 12 to 15 minutes or until crisp-tender. Drain.

    Sauté almonds and onion in butter in Dutch oven until onion is tender. Add beans and salt; toss lightly. Serves 8.

SUMMERTIME CELEBRATION
menu on page 460

CALICO BEANS

This recipe gets its name from the varied colors of the three types of beans that make up this dish.

½ lb. ground beef
1 c. onion, chopped
1 clove garlic, minced
½ lb. bacon, crisply cooked
   and crumbled
3 (16-oz.) cans baked beans in sauce
2 (16-oz.) cans kidney beans,
   drained and rinsed

15¼-oz. can lima beans,
   drained and rinsed
½ c. catsup
¼ c. brown sugar, packed
1 t. salt
1 t. dry mustard
2 t. white vinegar

Cook ground beef, onion and garlic, stirring until beef crumbles and is no longer pink; drain.

Combine ground beef mixture, crumbled bacon, beans and remaining ingredients in a 3-quart baking dish. Bake, covered, at 350 degrees for 45 minutes. Makes 11½ cups.

Cynthia Rogers
Upton, MA

"This recipe is perfect for summer barbecues...it serves a crowd! I serve it in a slow cooker and let guests help themselves. Many have a second helping, and everyone asks for the recipe. It's much tastier than any baked bean dish you've tasted!"

Cynthia

an instant hit!

Core an apple, then scoop out the insides, leaving at least ¼-inch-thick sides...set each on a serving plate and fill with baked beans.

"This delicious recipe is a wonderful tribute to my Grannie Hobson."

Kristi

GRANNIE HOBSON'S LOUISIANA RED BEANS

If you don't have enough time to soak the beans overnight, try the quick-soak method: Place beans in a Dutch oven; cover with water 2 inches above beans and bring to a boil. Boil one minute; cover, remove from heat and let stand one hour. Drain and proceed with recipe.

1 lb. dried red kidney beans
8-oz. ham hock
6 c. water
3 c. onion, chopped
1 c. green onions, chopped
1 green pepper, chopped
½ c. fresh parsley, chopped
2 cloves garlic, minced

1 t. salt
½ t. black pepper
¼ t. dried oregano
¼ t. dried thyme
⅛ t. hot pepper sauce
1 T. Worcestershire sauce
1 lb. cooked ham, chopped
2 t. vegetable oil

Place beans in a Dutch oven. Cover with water 2 inches above beans and let soak 8 hours or overnight. Drain beans; rinse thoroughly and drain again.

Place beans and ham hock in a large stockpot. Add 6 cups water to beans; bring to a boil. Add onion and next 10 ingredients; cover, reduce heat and simmer 2 hours and 15 minutes, stirring occasionally.

Meanwhile, cook ham in oil until lightly browned. Stir into beans and cook, uncovered, 30 minutes. Remove ham hock before serving. Makes 11 cups.

Kristi Hobson
Grapeland, TX

BAKED BROCCOLI

½ c. celery, chopped
½ c. onion, chopped
2 T. butter
10-oz. pkg. frozen chopped broccoli
2 c. rice, cooked

10¾-oz. can cream of chicken soup
8-oz. jar pasteurized process
   cheese sauce
½ c. milk
¼ c. bread crumbs, buttered

Sauté celery and onion in butter in a large skillet. Add broccoli and stir until broken up and slightly cooked. Mix together remaining ingredients, except bread crumbs, in a separate bowl. Add to broccoli mixture. Place in a 13"x9" casserole dish coated with non-stick vegetable spray. Cover with buttered crumbs. Bake, uncovered, at 350 degrees for 20 to 30 minutes. Serves 4 to 6.

Judy Borecky
Escondido, CA

"You can add sliced water chestnuts if you want a little more crunch...very good."
Judy

ROASTED CAULIFLOWER

Roasting these vegetables adds a subtle sweetness.

1 T. olive oil
½ t. garlic powder
¼ t. salt
¼ t. freshly ground black pepper

1 head cauliflower, cut into
   flowerets
1 red onion, cut into ½-inch-thick
   wedges

Place a large jelly-roll pan in a 500-degree oven for 5 minutes or until hot.
Meanwhile, combine oil and next 3 ingredients in a large bowl. Add cauliflower and onion; stir well until coated. Pour vegetables onto a hot jelly-roll pan and spread into a single layer. Bake at 500 degrees for 15 minutes or until browned, stirring occasionally. Serves 4 to 5.

Karen Puchnick
Butler, PA

"This is a tasty substitute for deep-fried cauliflower!"
Karen

ORANGE-MAPLE GLAZED CARROTS

Fresh orange juice and zest as well as grated fresh nutmeg make everyday carrots extra special. Feel free to use ¼ teaspoon of ground nutmeg in place of the freshly grated nutmeg.

⅓ c. orange juice
12 carrots, peeled and thinly
   sliced
zest of one orange

3 T. maple syrup
2 T. butter
1 t. grated nutmeg

    Microwave orange juice in a microwave-safe baking dish on high for 1½ minutes. Add carrots and orange zest; stir to coat. Cover and microwave on high 7 minutes.

    Stir in syrup, butter and nutmeg; microwave, uncovered, for 2 minutes. Carrots should be crisp-tender; if not, microwave 2 more minutes. Sprinkle with additional nutmeg, if desired. Serves 4.

Elizabeth Blackstone
Racine, WI

"This dish always impresses guests...don't let them know you made it in the microwave."

Elizabeth

MOM'S RED CABBAGE

We used Braeburn apples for their firmness and sweet yet tart flavor. They're a good accompaniment to the red cabbage.

10 slices bacon, diced
1 onion, diced
1 head red cabbage, shredded
1/2 c. sugar
1/3 c. cider vinegar

1 t. chicken bouillon granules
1 bay leaf
1 c. applesauce
1 c. jellied cranberry sauce
2 apples, peeled and sliced

Cook bacon in a large skillet until crisp; reserve 2 tablespoons drippings in skillet. Add onion to drippings in skillet and sauté until tender. Add cabbage, sugar, vinegar, bouillon granules and bay leaf; cook 8 minutes. Add applesauce, cranberry sauce and apples; simmer 10 minutes or until apples are crisp-tender. Remove and discard bay leaf. Makes 7 cups.

Lisa Rubach
Elkhorn, WI

COZY COMFORT FOOD
menu on page 462

ROASTED CORN WITH ROSEMARY BUTTER
(pictured on page 282)

The next time you fire up the grill, make room for this corn on the cob. Nothing could be better than fresh sweet corn roasted in the husk. Peak season for corn is May through September, so enjoy its abundance!

6 ears yellow or white sweet corn,
   in husks

¼ c. butter, softened
1 t. fresh rosemary, chopped

     Pull back corn husks, leaving them attached. Remove and discard silks. Combine butter and rosemary in a small bowl; brush over corn. Pull husks over corn and grill corn over medium-high heat (350 to 400 degrees) for about 15 minutes, turning occasionally. Serves 6.

SOUTHERN SUPPER
menu on page 461

GRANDMA LUCY'S CORN FRITTERS

Showcase the bounty of summer corn with a batch of these delicately fried fritters. When sweet corn is not at its peak, substitute 3 cups of canned or frozen corn kernels.

4 ears sweet corn, cooked
2 eggs, beaten
¼ c. milk
½ c. all-purpose flour
1 t. baking powder

1 t. sugar
½ t. salt
1 T. bacon drippings or vegetable oil
Optional: butter and maple syrup

Cut kernels from corn and place in a medium mixing bowl; stir in eggs and milk. Combine flour, baking powder, sugar and salt in a small bowl; stir into corn mixture, and mix gently.

Heat bacon drippings or vegetable oil in a skillet over medium-high heat. Drop batter by ¼ cupfuls and cook until delicately browned, turning to brown the other side. Serve with butter and maple syrup, if desired. Makes one dozen.

Carole Griffin
Mount Vernon, OH

FAMILY NIGHT
menu on page 458

"These fritters remind me of my childhood and the golden days of summer when my grandmother made them."

Carole

CRACKED PEPPER LINGUINE

This creamy dish is versatile enough to pair with most entrées.

8-oz. pkg. linguine, uncooked
1 T. butter
¼ c. onion, minced
2 cloves garlic, pressed
8-oz. container sour cream
1 T. milk

½ t. salt
2 to 3 t. cracked black pepper
2 T. grated Parmesan cheese
2 T. fresh parsley, chopped
Garnish: fresh parsley sprigs

Cook pasta according to package directions.

Melt butter in a small skillet over medium-high heat. Add onion and garlic and sauté until crisp-tender. Remove mixture from heat and cool slightly.

Stir in sour cream, milk, salt and pepper. Toss with pasta. Sprinkle with cheese and parsley. Garnish, if desired. Serves 4.

COMPANY'S COMING
menu on page 459

VIDALIA ONION PIE WITH MUSHROOMS

A Vidalia onion is a sweet onion, not a hot one. And not every sweet onion can be called a Vidalia…only those grown within a designated area around Vidalia, Georgia.

1 large Vidalia onion, halved and
    thinly sliced
2 c. shiitake mushrooms, sliced
1 T. olive oil
4 eggs, beaten
1 c. whipping cream

1 T. fresh thyme, chopped
1½ t. salt
1 t. pepper
⅛ t. nutmeg
9-inch frozen deep-dish pie crust,
    thawed

Sauté onion and mushrooms in hot oil in a large skillet over medium heat 15 minutes or until tender.

Stir together eggs and next 5 ingredients in a large bowl; stir in onion mixture. Spoon mixture into pie crust and place on a baking sheet.

Bake on lower oven rack at 350 degrees for 45 minutes or until done. Serves 4 to 6.

Note: Feel free to substitute any type of mushroom for the shiitakes.

veggie market

Take the kids along to a farmers' market. Let each choose a vegetable and help prepare it…even picky eaters will want to eat their very own prepared dish.

LOADED MASHED POTATO CASSEROLE

These mashed potatoes are full of great flavor. They'll definitely be a
hands-down winner with the hungry crew who gets invited over to try them.

5½ c. mashed potatoes
½ c. milk
8-oz. pkg. cream cheese, softened
8-oz. container sour cream
2 t. dried parsley

1 t. garlic salt
¼ t. nutmeg
¾ c. shredded Cheddar cheese
6 slices bacon, crisply cooked and
   crumbled

Combine all ingredients except Cheddar cheese and bacon in a large mixing bowl. Beat at medium-high speed with an electric mixer until smooth. Spoon into a lightly greased 13"x9" baking dish; top with Cheddar cheese and bacon. Cover and bake at 350 degrees for 30 minutes. Uncover and bake 10 more minutes or until cheese melts. Serves 12.

Tami Bowman
Gooseberry Patch

"When you're in a pinch for time, speed up the prep for this casserole by using prepackaged mashed potatoes and precooked bacon."

Tami

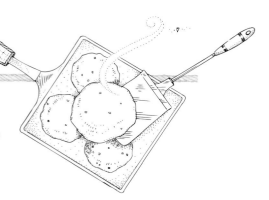

crispy potato pancakes

Making these pancakes is a great way to use up extra mashed potatoes. Stir an egg yolk and some minced onion into 2 cups of potatoes. Form into patties and fry in butter until golden. They're delicious served with grilled sausage.

CREAMED PEAS

Salmon and fresh peas are a traditional New England Independence Day dish. We also like the peas paired with Maple-Curry Pork Roast from our fall menu on page 462.

1 T. butter	4 c. frozen baby sweet peas, thawed
1 T. vegetable oil	1/2 c. whipping cream
1 c. onion, finely chopped	salt and pepper to taste

Melt butter with oil in a large saucepan over low heat. Add onion and cook, stirring frequently, about 11 minutes or until tender and golden. Add peas and cook about 15 minutes or until peas are very tender. Add cream and cook about 5 or 6 minutes until the liquid thickens into a sauce. Season with salt and pepper to taste. Serves 6 to 8.

COZY COMFORT FOOD
menu on page 462

ROSEMARY POTATOES

If you have access to fresh rosemary, substitute an equal amount for the dried.

4 to 6 redskin potatoes,
   peeled and quartered
¼ c. olive oil
2 T. lemon juice

2 cloves garlic, minced
1 to 2 t. dried rosemary,
   crushed
salt and pepper to taste

Toss together all ingredients in a large bowl; spoon into a greased 13"x9" baking pan. Bake at 350 degrees for one hour. Serves 4 to 6.

Gayle Burns
Bloomington, IN

"So simple, yet extraordinarily delicious."

Gayle

keep it hot

If you're taking a casserole to a potluck dinner or picnic, keep it toasty by covering the casserole dish with foil and then wrapping it in several layers of newspaper.

Rice Pilaf with Carrots

RICE PILAF WITH CARROTS

Toasting brings out the full flavor of nuts. Toast the pine nuts in a dry skillet over medium heat for just a few minutes, stirring often.

1 T. vegetable oil
2 c. basmati rice, uncooked
¼ c. onion, chopped
2 cloves garlic, minced
4 c. chicken broth

½ t. salt
1 c. carrots, peeled and finely
   chopped
½ c. green onions, chopped
3 T. pine nuts, toasted

Heat oil in a medium saucepan over medium-high heat. Add rice and onion; sauté 2 minutes. Add garlic; sauté one minute. Add broth and salt; bring to a boil. Cover, reduce heat and simmer 7 minutes. Stir in carrots; cover and cook 7 more minutes or until liquid is absorbed. Remove from heat; stir in green onions and toasted pine nuts. Let stand, covered, 15 minutes; fluff with a fork. Serves 6 to 8.

HERBED RICE PILAF

¼ c. butter
2 c. long-cooking rice, uncooked
1 c. celery, chopped
½ c. onion, chopped
4 c. chicken broth

1 t. Worcestershire sauce
1 t. soy sauce
1 t. dried oregano
1 t. dried thyme

"I often add shredded chicken or turkey if I want a heartier side dish."

Jo Ann

Melt butter in a saucepan; stir in uncooked rice, celery and onion. Sauté until rice is lightly golden and the celery and onion become tender. Transfer to a lightly greased 2-quart casserole dish. Whisk together remaining ingredients and pour over rice mixture. Bake, covered, at 325 degrees for 50 minutes or until rice is tender. Makes 8 servings.

Jo Ann
Gooseberry Patch

RISOTTO IN THE MICROWAVE

Microwave risotto takes about the same amount of time to prepare as traditional risotto, though most of its preparation is hands off, giving you more time for cooking the rest of your dinner.

2 T. butter
2 T. olive oil
½ c. onion, minced
1 c. Arborio rice

3 c. reduced-sodium chicken
   broth
½ c. grated Parmesan cheese
¼ t. pepper

Microwave butter and oil, uncovered, in a microwave-safe 1½-quart glass or ceramic dish on high for one minute and 15 seconds to 2 minutes. Add onion; stir well. Cover and cook on high 45 seconds to one minute. Add rice, stirring well. Cover and cook on high 3 to 4 minutes. Stir in chicken broth; cook, uncovered, on high 9 minutes. Stir well, and cook, uncovered, on high 7 minutes. Remove from microwave oven and let stand 5 minutes. Stir in Parmesan cheese and pepper. Makes 3½ cups.

EASY HOLIDAY DINNER
menu on page 464

COMPANY RICE

Today's grocery stores carry a variety of quick-cooking wild rice blends…choose one if you want a quicker-cooking substitute.

¼ c. butter, cut into pieces
6-oz. pkg. wild rice
8-oz. pkg. sliced mushrooms
14½-oz. can chicken broth
3 green onions, chopped

½ t. salt
Optional: 2 T. dry sherry
Optional: ½ c. sliced almonds, toasted

Melt butter in a 2-quart saucepan over medium heat. Stir in rice; cook 5 minutes, stirring occasionally. Add mushrooms, next 3 ingredients and sherry, if desired; bring to a boil. Cover, reduce heat and simmer one hour and 5 minutes or until rice is done; drain excess liquid, if desired. Fluff rice with a fork; sprinkle with almonds, if desired. Serves 8.

make-ahead slow-cooker method: company rice

Combine first 6 ingredients and, if desired, sherry in a 4-quart electric slow cooker; cover and cook on high setting 3 hours. Drain excess liquid, if necessary. Fluff rice with a fork; sprinkle with almonds, if desired.

SUMMERTIME CELEBRATION
menu on page 460

Honey-Kissed
Acorn Squash

HONEY-KISSED ACORN SQUASH

*Select acorn squash that's firm, unblemished and feels heavy for its size.
A cut squash will keep in the fridge up to one week. Uncut, it will stay fresh
for one month in a cool, dark place.*

2 acorn squash, halved lengthwise
    and seeded
8-oz. can crushed pineapple, drained
¼ c. chopped pecans

¼ c. sweetened dried cranberries
¼ c. plus 2 T. honey
¼ c. butter, melted
Optional: nutmeg

Place squash halves, cut-side up, in a microwave-safe dish; microwave on
high for 8 to 10 minutes until tender. Combine pineapple and next 4 ingredients; spoon into squash halves. Microwave on high 30 to 45 seconds or until
thoroughly heated and lightly glazed. Sprinkle with nutmeg, if desired. Serves 4.

Lynda McCormick
Burkburnett, TX

BAKED ZUCCHINI GRATIN

Double the recipe for a terrific potluck dish!

1 onion, sliced
2 lbs. zucchini, sliced
½ cup butter, melted and divided

2 c. shredded mozzarella cheese
½ c. bread crumbs
¼ c. grated Parmesan cheese

In a lightly greased 2-quart casserole dish, layer onion and zucchini.
Drizzle with ¼ cup butter; sprinkle with mozzarella cheese. In a separate bowl,
combine remaining butter, bread crumbs and Parmesan cheese. Sprinkle crumb
mixture evenly over the top. Bake, uncovered, at 350 degrees for 35 to
40 minutes or until zucchini is tender. Makes 8 servings.

Heather Anne Kehr
Littlestown, PA

PRALINE-TOPPED BUTTERNUT SQUASH

Walnuts replace pecans in this buttery, sweet topping. The squash is a tasty substitute for sweet potato casserole on any fall menu.

2 butternut squash, peeled and cubed
7 T. butter, divided
½ t. salt
⅛ t. pepper

2 eggs, beaten
½ c. brown sugar, packed
½ c. chopped walnuts
½ t. cinnamon
⅛ t. nutmeg

Boil squash in water to cover until soft; drain.

Process squash in a blender until smooth. Transfer to a saucepan; stir in 4 tablespoons butter, salt and pepper. Heat thoroughly; remove from heat.

Stir in eggs; spread into a greased one-quart baking dish. Set aside. Combine brown sugar, walnuts, cinnamon, nutmeg and remaining 3 tablespoons butter; sprinkle over squash mixture. Bake at 350 degrees for 30 minutes. Serves 8.

Nancy Kowalski
Southbury, CT

family comfort

When I was growing up, my very special friend was my Grammy. She lived with us for ten years when she first came to America from Hungary in 1946. Our best times together were when she would cook or bake. I was always fascinated because she never used a recipe and could whip up anything!

I learned her recipes by watching and touching. She made many comfort foods, but the greatest comfort was her friendship of sharing, caring and spending time with me.

Susie Knupp
Somers, MT

SQUASH CASSEROLE

Yellow squash is also known as crookneck squash because of its thin, curved neck. You can substitute equal amounts of zucchini in this recipe, if you prefer.

2½ lbs. yellow squash, sliced
½ c. butter
4-oz. jar diced pimento, drained
½ c. onion, chopped
2 eggs, beaten
¼ c. green pepper, chopped
¼ c. mayonnaise

2 t. sugar
1½ t. salt
Optional: 8-oz. can sliced water chestnuts, drained and chopped
10 round buttery crackers, crushed
½ c. shredded sharp Cheddar cheese

Cook squash, covered, in a small amount of boiling water 8 to 10 minutes or until tender; drain well, pressing between paper towels.

Combine squash and butter in a bowl; mash until butter melts. Stir in pimento, next 6 ingredients and water chestnuts, if desired; spoon into a lightly greased shallow 2-quart baking dish. Sprinkle with crushed crackers.

Bake at 325 degrees for 30 minutes. Sprinkle with cheese; bake 5 more minutes or until cheese melts. Serves 8.

SOUTHERN SUPPER
menu on page 461

TOMATO PIE

Vine-ripened tomatoes are ideal for this summer pie...what flavor!

9-inch unbaked pie crust
1 c. shredded mozzarella cheese,
    divided
4 tomatoes, seeded and chopped
1 onion, chopped

10 to 12 fresh basil leaves,
    chopped
1 c. shredded Cheddar cheese
1 c. mayonnaise
½ c. grated Parmesan cheese

Prick bottom of pie crust several times with the tines of a fork; bake at 425 degrees for 8 to 10 minutes.

Sprinkle bottom of pie crust with ¼ cup mozzarella cheese. Layer with half each of tomatoes, onion and basil; repeat layers. Combine ¾ cup mozzarella cheese, Cheddar cheese and mayonnaise. Spread mixture over top of pie; sprinkle with Parmesan cheese. Bake at 350 degrees on bottom rack of oven for 35 to 40 minutes. Let stand 15 minutes before serving. Serves 6.

Shelia Willis
Annapolis, MD

"Grow your own tomatoes and basil this year and use them in this tasty tomato pie!"

Shelia

beyond the basics

Look past traditional napkins when hosting family & friends. Try using bandanas, colorful dish towels, inexpensive fabrics from the crafts store or, for especially saucy foods, moistened washcloths.

SPICY GRILLED VEGETABLES

Place the vegetables directly on the grill for true smoky flavor.

4 potatoes, sliced diagonally
3 large carrots, peeled and
   sliced lengthwise
2 large zucchini, sliced crosswise
2 T. onion, chopped

⅓ c. olive oil
1 T. lime juice
½ t. salt
½ t. ground cumin
¼ t. pepper

    Place potatoes and carrots in a medium saucepan and cover with water. Boil 10 minutes over high heat. Drain and place in a large bowl; add zucchini slices.

    Combine onion and next 5 ingredients in a small bowl. Pour over vegetables, tossing to coat well. Let stand about 15 minutes, allowing flavors to blend. Grill vegetables over medium-high heat (350 to 400 degrees) for about 3 minutes on each side, turning once. Serve hot. Serves 4 to 6.

eat your veggies!

    Get kids to eat their vegetables! Serve fresh cut-up vegetables with small cups of creamy salad dressing or even peanut butter for dipping.

STUFFED ZUCCHINI

Zucchini is so plentiful that new recipes are always welcome...especially tasty ones like this.

½ c. bread crumbs
2 T. grated Parmesan cheese
4 T. butter, divided
½ c. onion, chopped
1 clove garlic, minced

1 tomato, peeled and chopped
2 zucchini, halved, scooped out
    and pulp and shells reserved
salt and pepper to taste

Toss together bread crumbs, cheese and 2 tablespoons butter in a small dish. Sauté onion and garlic in remaining 2 tablespoons butter until tender. Add tomato and zucchini pulp; mix well and heat thoroughly.

Place zucchini shells in a greased baking dish; fill with stuffing. Top with bread crumb mixture; bake, covered, at 350 degrees for 30 minutes. Season with salt and pepper to taste and serve immediately. Serves 4.

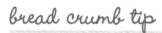

bread crumb tip

Make bread crumbs from leftover buns and loaves using your food processor. They'll store nicely in your freezer up to 6 months.

Roasted Veggie Panini, page 332,
and Cream of Chicken-Rice Soup, page 321

soups,
sandwiches &
salads

Whether served alone or paired together, soups, sandwiches & salads are ideal for lunch or supper. Chicken Stew with Biscuits (page 328) beckons to be served on a cold, blustery day, while Chicken, Artichoke & Rice Salad (page 348) is just right for a springtime luncheon. Whatever the season or occasion, favorites like Roasted Veggie Panini (page 332), Colorful Couscous Salad (page 347) and others inside this chapter are just perfect for sharing with family & friends.

"Drizzle with a little extra half-and-half for an elegant beginning to a holiday meal."

Kathy

CURRIED HARVEST BISQUE

To make peeling and cutting butternut squash a little easier, microwave it on high for one minute.

1 lb. butternut squash, peeled and cut into 1-inch cubes
5 c. chicken broth
1/4 c. butter
1/4 c. all-purpose flour

1 t. curry powder
3/4 c. half-and-half
1 T. lime juice
1/2 t. salt
1/4 t. white pepper

Combine squash and broth in a heavy 4-quart stockpot. Cook about 15 minutes over medium heat until tender. Using a slotted spoon, transfer squash to a blender or food processor; process until smooth. Stir broth into puréed squash; set aside.

Melt butter in stockpot; stir in flour and curry powder. Cook over medium heat, stirring until smooth. Add squash mixture; increase heat to medium-high and stir until soup thickens slightly. Reduce heat to low; add half-and-half and remaining ingredients and heat thoroughly (do not boil). Serves 6.

Kathy Grashoff
Fort Wayne, IN

make-ahead wonders

One reason soups are so popular is you can so easily make them ahead of time. Just chill them overnight and reheat them slowly on the stovetop.

CREAM OF CHICKEN-RICE SOUP

(pictured on page 318)

Don't let a cold be the only reason you serve up this chicken soup…it's perfect year-round!

(pictured on page 318)

4 qts. water
2 boneless, skinless chicken breasts
2 carrots, chopped
2 stalks celery, chopped
1 onion, chopped
¼ c. fresh parsley, minced

¼ c. butter
2 cloves garlic, minced
1 c. rice, uncooked
2 t. salt
2 c. milk
½ c. cornstarch

Bring water to a boil in a Dutch oven. Add chicken and cook until done. Remove chicken from broth to cool, reserving broth in Dutch oven.

Meanwhile, sauté carrots, celery, onion and parsley in butter in a large skillet until tender. Add garlic and cook one minute. Cut chicken into bite-size pieces. Add sautéed vegetables and chicken to reserved broth. Stir in rice and salt and simmer 15 minutes. Mix together milk and cornstarch; add to soup. Stir until thickened. Serves 16 to 20.

Michelle Heurung
Mokena, IL

"Prepare this creamy soup and watch it disappear!"

Michelle

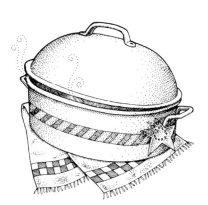

CHICKEN FAJITA CHOWDER

This chunky chowder is full of Mexican flavor! Serve it with a variety of tortilla chips for an added burst of color.

3 T. all-purpose flour

1.4-oz. pkg. fajita or taco seasoning mix, divided

4 boneless, skinless chicken breasts, cubed

3 T. vegetable oil

1 onion, chopped

1 t. garlic, minced

15¼-oz. can sweet corn and diced peppers, drained

15-oz. can black beans, drained and rinsed

14½-oz. can Mexican-style stewed tomatoes

4.5-oz. can chopped green chiles

3 c. water

1 c. instant brown rice, uncooked

10¾-oz. can nacho cheese soup

1¼ c. water

Toppings: sour cream, shredded Cheddar cheese, chopped green onions, tortilla chips

Garnish: fresh cilantro sprigs

Combine flour and 2 tablespoons seasoning mix in a large plastic zipping bag; add chicken. Seal bag and shake to coat.

Sauté chicken in hot oil in a large Dutch oven over high heat about 5 minutes or until golden, stirring often.

Reduce heat to medium-high. Add onion and garlic; sauté 5 minutes. Stir in remaining seasoning mix, corn and next 5 ingredients; bring to a boil. Reduce heat to medium-low; cover and simmer 5 minutes. Add soup and 1¼ cups water; stir until thoroughly heated. Sprinkle with desired toppings; garnish, if desired. Serves 8 to 10.

Kelly Jones
Tallahassee, FL

"This takes a bit of time to prepare, but it's well worth it. You'll have a savory soup that will be a new family favorite."

Kelly

BAKED POTATO SOUP

If your favorite baked potato toppings aren't listed, feel free to add them!

3 lbs. redskin potatoes, cubed
¼ c. butter
¼ c. all-purpose flour
2 qts. half-and-half
16-oz. pkg. pasteurized process
    cheese spread, cubed

1 t. hot pepper sauce
white pepper and garlic
    powder to taste
Toppings: crumbled bacon,
    shredded Cheddar cheese,
    snipped fresh chives

Cover potatoes with water in a large saucepan; bring to a boil. Boil 10 minutes or until tender; drain and set aside.

Melt butter in a large Dutch oven; add flour, stirring until smooth. Gradually add half-and-half, stirring constantly over low heat. Continue to stir until smooth and mixture begins to thicken. Add cheese; stir well. Add potatoes, hot pepper sauce and seasonings. Cover and simmer over low heat 30 minutes. Sprinkle with desired toppings. Serves 8.

Linda Stone
Cookeville, TN

optional toppings

It's the unexpected touches that make the biggest impression. When serving soup or chili, offer guests a variety of fun toppings...fill bowls with shredded cheese, oyster crackers, chopped onions, sour cream and crunchy croutons. Then invite everyone to dig in!

CREAMY WHITE CHILI

Sour cream and whipping cream are stirred into this chili, making it extra rich and creamy. Rotate white chili into your menu as a substitute for chili with beef and kidney beans.

1 T. vegetable oil
1 lb. boneless, skinless chicken
    breasts, cubed
1 onion, chopped
14-oz. can chicken broth
2 (15.8-oz.) cans Great Northern
    beans, drained and rinsed
2 (4.5-oz.) cans chopped green
    chiles, undrained

1 ½ t. garlic powder
1 t. salt
1 t. ground cumin
½ t. dried oregano
8-oz. container sour cream
1 c. whipping cream
2 c. shredded Monterey Jack cheese
Garnish: cilantro sprigs

Heat oil in a large skillet over medium heat; add chicken and onion. Sauté 10 minutes or until chicken is done; set aside.

Combine broth, beans, chiles and seasonings in a large Dutch oven. Bring to a boil over medium-high heat. Add chicken mixture; reduce heat and simmer 30 minutes. Add sour cream and whipping cream, stirring well. Top each serving with shredded cheese; garnish, if desired. Serves 6 to 8.

Janelle Dixon
Fernley, NV

> "This chili has such a fabulous flavor with its blend of green chiles, cumin, sour cream and chicken."
>
> **Janelle**

CHILI NIGHT
menu on page 464

VEGETARIAN CINCINNATI CHILI

Here's a meatless version of Cincinnati chili. Cincinnati is famous for a unique kind of chili that's based on a Greek recipe that traditionally contains cinnamon and is ordered by number. Serve it over cooked spaghetti for 2-way chili or topped with shredded cheese for 3-way chili. Topping it with chopped raw onions makes it 4-way, while a sprinkling of extra beans takes it to 5-way. We show our chili at left as 3-way, since onions and beans are already part of this meatless version.

46-oz. can tomato juice
2 (15-oz.) cans kidney beans,
   drained and rinsed
15-oz. can black beans, drained
   and rinsed
1 onion, chopped
2 T. chili powder
1 1/2 t. white vinegar
1 t. allspice

1 t. cinnamon
1 t. pepper
1 t. ground cumin
1/4 t. Worcestershire sauce
1/8 t. garlic powder
5 bay leaves
Optional: cooked spaghetti,
   shredded Cheddar cheese,
   oyster crackers

Combine first 13 ingredients in a 3-quart slow cooker. Cover and cook on low setting 5 hours. Discard bay leaves before serving. If desired, serve over cooked spaghetti; sprinkle with cheese and serve with oyster crackers. Serves 6.

Leath Sarvo
Cincinnati, OH

"This is one of my family's favorites...my husband and kids always come back for seconds! Very warm and comforting."

Debi

CHICKEN STEW WITH BISCUITS

Your meat, veggies and bread are all combined in one hearty stew!

2 c. water
¾ c. dry white wine or chicken
　broth
2 (.87-oz.) pkgs. chicken gravy mix
2 cloves garlic, minced
1 T. fresh parsley, minced
1 to 2 t. chicken bouillon granules
½ t. pepper
5 small carrots, peeled and cut into
　1-inch pieces

4 boneless, skinless chicken breasts,
　cut into bite-size pieces
1 onion, cut into 8 wedges
3 T. all-purpose flour
⅓ c. cold water
black pepper to taste
16.3-oz. tube refrigerated large
　buttermilk biscuits, baked

　Combine first 7 ingredients in a 3½- or 4-quart slow cooker; stir until blended. Add carrots, chicken and onion; cover and cook on high setting one hour. Reduce heat to low setting and cook 3 to 4 hours.

　Stir together flour and cold water until smooth in a small bowl. Gradually stir into slow cooker; cover and cook one more hour. Pour stew into individual soup bowls; sprinkle with black pepper, if desired, and top with biscuits. Serves 4 to 6.

Debi Piper
Vicksburg, MI

WINTER WARM-UP
menu on page 465

CHICKEN-ANDOUILLE GUMBO

We cut in half the time that it takes to stir up a good roux by first browning it in the oven. It's finished off in a skillet using less oil than normal, but the flavor still maintains its richness.

1 ½ gal. water
4-lb. chicken, cut up
5 bay leaves
5 sprigs parsley
3 cloves garlic
1 lb. andouille or smoked sausage, diced
2 onions, chopped
1 large green pepper, chopped
1 large stalk celery, chopped
3 T. garlic, minced

4 chicken bouillon cubes
1 ½ c. all-purpose flour
¾ c. vegetable oil
1 T. salt
1 t. cayenne pepper
1 t. black pepper
1 bunch green onions, chopped
½ c. fresh parsley, chopped
½ t. filé powder
hot cooked rice

Bring first 5 ingredients to a boil in a large stockpot; cover, reduce heat and simmer one hour. Remove chicken, reserving broth. Skin, bone and coarsely chop chicken; set aside.

Pour broth through a wire-mesh strainer into a large bowl, discarding solids. Measure one gallon broth and return to stockpot. Add sausage and next 5 ingredients; simmer one hour, stirring occasionally.

Meanwhile, place flour in a 15"x10" jelly-roll pan. Bake at 400 degrees for 10 to 15 minutes or until flour is a caramel color, stirring every 5 minutes.

Heat oil in a heavy skillet over medium heat; gradually whisk in browned flour and cook, whisking constantly, until flour is a dark caramel color (about 7 minutes). Stir into sausage mixture and simmer one hour, stirring occasionally. Stir in chicken, salt and cayenne and black pepper; simmer 45 minutes, stirring occasionally.

Stir in green onions and parsley; simmer 10 minutes, stirring occasionally. Remove from heat and stir in filé powder. Serve over hot cooked rice. Serves 12.

MAMMA MIA ITALIAN STEW

This stew is chock-full of flavorful summer produce with a hint of heat from hot Italian sausage.

1 lb. ground hot Italian sausage,
   cooked and drained
1 eggplant, peeled and cubed
1½ c. sliced green beans
2 green peppers, sliced
1 to 2 potatoes, peeled and cubed
1 large zucchini, cubed

1 large yellow squash, cubed
1 c. onion, thinly sliced
15-oz. can Italian-style
   tomato sauce
¼ c. olive oil
2 t. garlic, minced
1 t. salt

Combine all ingredients in a 7-quart slow cooker; stir well. Cover and cook on low setting 8 hours or on high setting 4 hours. Serves 8 to 10.

Connie Bryant
Topeka, KS

seasonal menus

Thinking of a menu for guests? Let the season be your guide! Soups and stews brimming with the harvest's bounty are just right for fall get-togethers, and juicy fruit salads are delightful in the summer. Not only will you get the freshest ingredients when you plan by the season, but you'll also get the best prices at the supermarket!

ROASTED VEGGIE PANINI

(pictured on page 318)

If you don't have a panini press, place the sandwiches in a hot skillet and gently press them with a smaller heavy pan; cook over medium-low heat until the cheese melts.

2 zucchini, sliced
1 yellow squash, sliced
6 oz. portobello mushroom caps, sliced
2 t. olive oil, divided
1 t. balsamic vinegar
1 sweet onion, thinly sliced
1 loaf sourdough bread, sliced

¼ c. olive tapenade
1 red pepper, sliced into rings
1 green pepper, sliced into rings
1 yellow pepper, sliced into rings
1 c. spinach leaves
2 roma tomatoes, sliced
4 slices provolone cheese

Combine zucchini, squash and mushrooms in a large bowl; toss with one teaspoon olive oil and vinegar. Grill, covered, over medium-high heat (350 to 400 degrees) 15 to 20 minutes, turning occasionally; set aside.

Heat one teaspoon olive oil in a skillet over medium heat. Add onion and cook 15 minutes or until caramelized, stirring often; set aside.

Spread tops and bottoms of bread slices with olive tapenade; layer red pepper rings and next 5 ingredients evenly on half the bread slices and top with remaining bread slices. Preheat panini press according to manufacturer's instructions. Place sandwiches in press (in batches, if necessary); cook 3 to 4 minutes or until cheese melts and bread is toasted. Serves 4.

Note: Look for olive tapenade in the deli section of larger supermarkets.

Lynda McCormick
Burkburnett, TX

GREEK SALAD IN A PITA POCKET

You can make a delicious sandwich by stuffing tasty pita bread with almost any vegetable salad. Some pita bread is made with whole wheat, providing extra nutrients in your meal.

1 red pepper, thinly sliced
½ avocado, pitted and sliced
¼ sweet red onion, thinly sliced
5 to 6 black Greek olives, pitted and sliced
crumbled feta cheese to taste

1 t. garlic, crushed
fresh dill, chopped, to taste
½ t. dried oregano
oil and vinegar salad dressing to taste
4 rounds pita bread, split

Gently toss first 8 ingredients with dressing in a medium bowl. Stuff mixture into pita pockets. Serves 4.

sandwich smorgasbord

Whip up several different kinds of sandwiches (or stop at the local deli for a few!) and cut each one into 4 sections. Arrange them all on a large platter with chips and pickles…everyone will love the variety, and the preparation couldn't be easier.

DRESSED OYSTER PO'BOYS

This loaf is piled high with plump fried oysters and slaw...all atop a tangy sauce. Mmm...it's good!

1 1/4 c. self-rising cornmeal
2 T. salt-free Creole seasoning
2 (12-oz.) containers fresh
    Standard oysters, drained
peanut or vegetable oil
1 c. mayonnaise, divided
2 T. Dijon mustard
2 T. white vinegar

6 c. finely shredded multicolored
    cabbage
2 T. catsup
1 T. prepared horseradish
1 t. salt-free Creole seasoning
3/4 t. paprika
4 hoagie rolls, split and
    toasted

Combine cornmeal and Creole seasoning; dredge oysters in mixture.

Pour oil to a depth of 2 inches into a Dutch oven; heat to 375 degrees. Fry oysters, in 3 batches, 2 to 3 minutes or until golden. Drain on wire racks.

Stir together 1/2 cup mayonnaise, mustard and vinegar. Stir in cabbage; set slaw aside.

Stir together remaining 1/2 cup mayonnaise, catsup and next 3 ingredients.

Spread bottom halves of rolls with mayonnaise mixture. Layer with oysters and top with slaw; cover with roll tops. Serves 4.

a New Orleans tradition

Po'boys are as diverse as New Orleans, the city they symbolize. There, you'll find them containing shrimp, crawfish, soft-shell crab or crab, in addition to oysters.

> "This is a family favorite...there are never any leftovers."
>
> **Joanne**

ITALIAN SAUSAGE SANDWICHES

The sausages are flavored with garlic and fennel seeds and are available sweet or hot. Let your taste buds lead you to your choice.

8 Italian sausages
1 Bermuda or Spanish onion, chopped
2 green peppers, quartered and sliced
1 t. salt
1 t. sugar

1 t. Italian seasoning
Optional: 2 tomatoes, chopped
8 hoagie rolls
4 t. butter, divided
16-oz. pkg. shredded mozzarella cheese, divided

Score the sausages every ½ inch. Cook sausages in a large skillet 15 minutes or until browned and cooked through; drain on paper towels. Pour off drippings, reserving 3 tablespoons drippings; place reserved drippings back into skillet.

Add onion to skillet and sauté until tender. Stir in green peppers, salt, sugar and Italian seasoning. Cover and cook 5 minutes; stir in tomatoes, if desired. Place sausages on top. Cook, covered, 5 minutes or until mixture bubbles.

Meanwhile, cut out center of rolls to make boat-shaped shells. Spread ½ teaspoon butter on the inside of each roll; place rolls on a baking sheet and bake at 350 degrees for 10 minutes. Divide mozzarella cheese evenly among hoagie rolls. Place one sausage in each roll; top with onion mixture. Serves 8.

Joanne Ciancio
Silver Lake, OH

SANDWICH NIGHT
menu on page 463

SALAMI SUBMARINE WITH OLIVE SALAD

The olive salad improves with age and is delicious on other sandwiches as well.

18-inch loaf crusty French bread	**¼ lb. Genoa salami, thinly sliced**
Olive Salad	**¼ lb. Swiss cheese, thinly sliced**

Slice bread lengthwise but do not cut all the way through to the other side. Scoop out some of the bread from inside of each half. Pack Olive Salad evenly into each half. Layer salami and cheese in rows down each half of sandwich. Close the halves together and wrap tightly in heavy aluminum foil. Slice to serve. Serves 6 to 8.

OLIVE SALAD:

3 c. green and black olives, coarsely chopped	**¼ c. fresh basil, chopped**
	6 T. olive oil
7-oz. jar roasted red peppers, drained and chopped	**3 T. red wine vinegar**
	2 T. capers
½ c. fresh parsley, chopped	**2 cloves garlic, crushed**

Toss together all ingredients in a large bowl and store in a tightly covered glass jar in the refrigerator.

heat it up

Bake your foil-wrapped sub at 350 degrees for 20 minutes, then unwrap and sprinkle Italian dressing inside the bun for a hot, crisp treat. For extra tang, add banana peppers.

PEPPERONI CALZONES

To save time, prepare this dish using refrigerated pizza dough.

1 c. water
1 pkg. active dry yeast
3 c. all-purpose flour
1 T. sugar
2 T. canola oil
1 t. salt

Tomato-Basil Sauce
1 1/2 c. green pepper, chopped
1 1/2 c. shredded mozzarella
  cheese
1 1/2 c. sliced pepperoni
1 egg, beaten

Heat water until very warm (100 to 110 degrees). Dissolve yeast in warm water; set aside for 5 minutes. Combine one cup flour, sugar, oil and salt in a large mixing bowl; beat at low speed with an electric mixer until blended. Gradually stir in enough remaining flour to make a smooth dough. Turn dough out onto a lightly floured surface; knead until smooth and elastic (8 to 10 minutes). Place in a well-greased bowl, turning to grease top. Cover and let rise in a warm place (85 degrees), free from drafts, 30 minutes or until doubled in bulk.

Punch dough down; divide into 6 equal portions. Roll each portion into a 7-inch circle. Divide one cup Tomato-Basil Sauce evenly over each circle, spreading to within one inch of edge. Sprinkle one half of each circle evenly with green pepper, cheese and pepperoni. Fold each circle in half to cover filling and pinch edges to seal. Place on an ungreased baking sheet; let rest 15 minutes. Brush with egg; bake at 375 degrees for 20 minutes. Serve with remaining Tomato-Basil Sauce. Serves 6.

TOMATO-BASIL SAUCE:

15-oz. can tomato sauce
1/2 c. tomato paste
2 t. dried basil

2 t. dried oregano
2 cloves garlic, minced
8-oz. pkg. sliced mushrooms

Combine first 5 ingredients; mix well. Divide in half; stir mushrooms into half of sauce to use in calzones. Serve calzones with remaining sauce. Makes 2 cups.

Amy Greer
Elkhart, IN

FRENCH DIP SANDWICHES

This brisket is tenderized during its long cook time in the slow cooker. Invite family & friends over to enjoy these savory sandwiches with their dipping juices…they feed a crowd!

6 lbs. beef brisket
1/4 c. mesquite-flavored cooking
    sauce
2 cloves garlic, pressed
1/2 t. dry mustard
1/2 t. seasoning salt
1/2 t. flavor enhancer
1/2 t. meat tenderizer

1/2 t. ground cumin
1/2 t. pepper
1/4 t. onion powder
1/4 t. cayenne pepper
1/4 t. dried marjoram
1/4 t. dried tarragon
2 (10 1/2-oz.) cans beef broth
12 French rolls, toasted

Cut brisket in half; place in a 6- to 7-quart slow cooker. Combine cooking sauce and next 11 ingredients; stir well. Pour mixture over brisket; cover and cook on high setting one hour. Reduce heat to low setting and cook 8 hours.

Remove meat from slow cooker, reserving broth. Skim a few ice cubes across the surface of broth to remove fat, if desired, and discard. Cool brisket slightly and cut into slices; return meat to broth in slow cooker. Add canned beef broth. Increase to high setting and cook 30 to 45 minutes or until meat and liquid are thoroughly heated. Serve on French rolls with a small serving of broth on the side for dipping. Serves 12.

Denise Collins
Canyon Country, CA

GIANT MEATBALL SANDWICH

The combination of ground pork and ground chuck enhances the flavor of these meatballs. If you're pinched for time, though, use already-prepared meatballs, which you can find in your grocer's freezer.

1 lb. ground chuck
½ lb. ground pork sausage
2 c. spaghetti sauce with peppers
   and mushrooms

1 clove garlic, minced
1-lb. loaf unsliced Italian bread
6-oz. pkg. sliced provolone
   cheese

Combine ground chuck and sausage; shape into one-inch balls. Cook meatballs in a large skillet over medium-high heat 8 to 10 minutes or until browned. Drain meatballs on paper towels. Discard drippings.

Combine meatballs, spaghetti sauce and garlic in skillet; bring to a boil. Reduce heat and simmer, uncovered, 12 to 15 minutes or until meatballs are done, stirring mixture occasionally.

While sauce simmers, slice bread in half lengthwise. Place bread, cut-side up, on a baking sheet. Broil 5½ inches from heat one to 2 minutes or until bread is lightly toasted. Spoon meatball mixture over bottom half of toasted bread; arrange cheese on top of meatballs, overlapping as needed. Cover with top of bread. Cut sandwich into 6 pieces; serve immediately. Serves 6.

quick solutions

Easiest-ever sandwiches for a get-together…provide a big platter of cold cuts, a basket of fresh breads and a choice of condiments so guests can make their own. Add cups of hot soup plus cookies for dessert…done!

OPEN-FACED PHILLY SANDWICHES

These sandwiches are great by themselves, but you could add a salad or home fries for a side dish, if you'd like.

3 (8-inch) submarine rolls, unsliced
½ lb. boneless top round steak
2 T. Italian salad dressing
¼ t. red pepper flakes
2 T. butter
1 large onion, thinly sliced

1 green pepper, cut into thin strips
1½ c. sliced mushrooms
1 clove garlic, pressed
1 c. shredded provolone cheese

Make a 1½-inch to 2-inch deep vertical cut around outside edges of each submarine roll, leaving a ½-inch border. Remove tops of rolls and discard. Hollow out about 1½ inches of each bread roll, forming a boat. Set boats aside.

Cut steak diagonally across grain into ⅛-inch-thick strips; place in a small shallow bowl. Add dressing and red pepper flakes, tossing steak to coat well; set aside.

Melt butter in a non-stick skillet over medium-high heat; add onion, green pepper and mushrooms and sauté 15 minutes or until onion is golden brown. Add garlic and sauté one minute. Remove mixture from skillet and set aside.

Stir-fry steak mixture in skillet over medium-high heat 2 to 3 minutes or until steak strips are no longer pink.

Fill bread boats evenly with layers of steak mixture and onion mixture; top with cheese.

Broil 5½ inches from heat 3 minutes or until cheese is lightly browned. Serves 3.

"This recike has been served by my husband's family at Thanksgiving and Christmas since the 1960's. We use wheat, sourdough or whatever bread is on hand to make the croutons... much better than store-bought!"

Taylor

THE BEST SALAD

Oregano and garlic are tasty additions to the homemade croutons that are part of this recipe. Season them according to your family's taste, and you'll have a winner however you flavor them.

3 to 4 slices day-old bread, crusts trimmed
1-lb. pkg. bacon, crisply cooked and crumbled, drippings reserved
1/3 c. sugar
1/3 c. white vinegar
3 egg yolks

8-oz. container sour cream
1 to 2 T. butter
seasonings or herbs to taste
1 head romaine lettuce, torn into bite-size pieces
4 to 5 green onions, chopped

Cut bread into cubes; set aside. Heat 2 tablespoons reserved bacon drippings in skillet; stir together sugar and vinegar and add to skillet. Bring mixture to a boil; boil about 5 minutes.

Blend together egg yolks and sour cream in a small bowl. Add to skillet; cook over medium heat about 7 minutes, stirring constantly, until mixture thickens.

Melt butter in a saucepan and add seasonings to taste for croutons; toss bread cubes to coat. Spread bread cubes on a large ungreased baking sheet and bake at 350 degrees for 10 to 15 minutes or until golden.

Arrange lettuce in a large salad bowl; pour hot dressing over top. Sprinkle with crumbled bacon, croutons and green onions. Toss before serving. Serves 4.

Taylor Driscoll
Beaver Crossing, NE

PARMESAN-CHICKEN SALAD

Serve this versatile salad over lettuce, as a sandwich or by itself with crackers...it's delicious any way you choose.

4 boneless, skinless chicken breasts
1 t. salt
1/2 t. pepper
2 T. vegetable oil
3/4 c. shredded Parmesan cheese
3/4 c. mayonnaise

1/2 c. chopped pecans,
   toasted
1/2 c. celery, chopped
1/3 c. green onions, chopped
1 clove garlic, pressed
2 T. spicy brown mustard

Sprinkle chicken with salt and pepper. Cook chicken in hot oil in a large skillet over medium-high heat 7 to 8 minutes on each side or until done; cool.

Chop chicken. Stir together chicken, cheese and remaining ingredients. Cover and chill at least 2 hours. Serves 4.

a new twist

Use old serving dishes in a new way for a fresh look. Handed-down cream-and-sugar sets can hold sauces, bread sticks can be arranged in gravy boats and a trifle dish can make a great salad bowl.

COLORFUL COUSCOUS SALAD

Couscous is actually a tiny pasta, but it's found in the rice section of supermarkets. It cooks up quickly and is a nice alternative to rice.

10-oz. box couscous, cooked
1 green pepper, diced
1 bunch green onions, diced
4 carrots, shredded
15-oz. can black beans, drained
   and rinsed
15¼-oz. can whole kernel corn,
   drained
¾ c. olive oil
¼ c. lemon juice
⅛ c. white wine vinegar

2 T. sugar
1 T. garlic, minced
3 drops hot pepper sauce
½ t. salt
½ t. pepper
½ t. lemon-pepper seasoning
½ t. seasoned salt
¼ t. ground turmeric
⅛ t. cinnamon
⅛ t. ground ginger

Fluff couscous in a large bowl. Add green pepper and remaining ingredients, stirring well. Refrigerate until ready to serve. Serves 6 to 8.

Donna Cash
Dexter, MI

"Look for flavored couscous in the rice aisle...so tasty and easy!"

Donna

edible "bowls"

Serve up individual portions of this colorful dish in edible bowls! Hollow out fresh green or red peppers and fill 'em up with salad for a tasty lunch.

"Sprinkle with sunflower kernels for extra crunch."

Charlotte

CHICKEN, ARTICHOKE & RICE SALAD

This salad pairs nicely with Raspberry Scones (page 363) for a simple luncheon with friends.

6.9-oz. pkg. chicken-flavored rice
   vermicelli mix, cooked
2 c. diced cooked chicken
6-oz. jar marinated quartered
   artichoke hearts, liquid reserved
1 green pepper, chopped
1 bunch green onions, chopped

8-oz. can water chestnuts,
   drained and chopped
$2/3$ c. mayonnaise
½ t. curry powder
$1/8$ t. salt
$1/8$ t. pepper

Combine rice vermicelli mix and chicken in a serving bowl. Add artichoke hearts and reserved liquid to rice mixture. Add green pepper and remaining ingredients; chill before serving. Serves 3 to 4.

Charlotte Mitchell
Anchorage, AK

LUNCH WITH FRIENDS
menu on page 458

FROSTY FRUIT SALAD

Roll some fresh grapes, strawberries and mandarin oranges in extra-fine sugar for a glittery (and tasty!) garnish.

17-oz. can apricots, chopped and
   juice reserved
17-oz. can crushed pineapple,
   juice reserved
1/2 c. sugar
3 (10-oz.) pkgs. frozen
   strawberries, thawed

6-oz. can frozen orange
   juice concentrate
2 T. lemon juice
2 lbs. grapes, halved
4 bananas, diced

Heat reserved juices and sugar in a heavy saucepan over medium heat; stir until sugar dissolves. Add strawberries, orange juice concentrate and lemon juice. Heat until warmed; remove from heat. Combine apricots, pineapple, grapes and bananas in a large bowl; add juice mixture and toss to coat fruit. Pour into a freezer-safe serving dish; freeze overnight. Remove from freezer about 15 to 25 minutes before serving. Serves 25 to 30.

Lisa Smith
Littleton, CO

> "Made the night before, it's just right for afternoon picnics!"
>
> **Lisa**

memories of friends

Thumbing through the index cards in my little wooden recipe box is more than just a search for something good to eat. Among those smudged and often yellowed cards, there's a history of family & friends.

Pat Ockert
Jonesboro, AR

CRANBERRY-GORGONZOLA GREEN SALAD

Tart dried cranberries and Gorgonzola contribute outstanding flavor to this green salad. For variety, add half each of a Granny Smith apple and your favorite crisp red apple. For a colorful combination, don't peel them.

1/3 c. vegetable oil

1/4 c. seasoned rice vinegar

3/4 t. Dijon mustard

1 clove garlic, pressed

1 small head Bibb lettuce, torn

1 small head green leaf lettuce, torn

1 apple, chopped

1/3 c. coarsely chopped walnuts, toasted

1/3 c. dried cranberries

1/3 c. crumbled Gorgonzola cheese

Whisk together first 4 ingredients in a small bowl; set aside.

Just before serving, combine Bibb lettuce and next 5 ingredients in a large bowl. Pour dressing over salad; toss gently. Serves 8.

glass milk bottles

Antique bottles make fun containers for serving salad dressings. Fill each with a different variety of dressing and set them around the table, or place filled bottles in a wire milk carrier…clever!

GREEN BEAN SALAD WITH FETA

Crumbled feta cheese, toasted walnuts and a sliced red onion make up the basic ingredients for this green bean salad. Leave the green beans whole for a pretty presentation.

¾ c. olive oil

¼ c. white wine vinegar

1 clove garlic, minced

½ t. salt

¼ t. pepper

2 lbs. small green beans

1 small red onion, thinly sliced

4-oz. pkg. crumbled feta cheese

1 c. coarsely chopped walnuts, toasted

Whisk together first 5 ingredients in a small bowl; set aside.

Trim stem end of green beans; cut or snap beans into thirds, if desired, and arrange in a steamer basket over boiling water. Cover and steam 8 to 12 minutes or until crisp-tender. Immediately plunge beans into cold water to stop the cooking process; drain and pat dry.

Combine beans, onion and cheese in a large bowl; toss well. Pour oil mixture over bean mixture; cover and chill one hour. Add walnuts just before serving and toss gently. Serves 8.

FROM THE GARDEN
menu on page 460

BLUE CHEESE POTATO SALAD

Try a variation of this recipe with new potatoes...no need to peel. Garnish with fresh dill.

3½ to 4 lbs. redskin potatoes, peeled, boiled and cubed
½ c. scallions, chopped
½ c. celery, chopped
2 T. fresh parsley, chopped
½ c. slivered almonds, toasted

2 t. salt
½ t. celery seed
¼ t. pepper
2 c. sour cream
½ c. crumbled blue cheese
¼ c. white wine vinegar

Combine potatoes, scallions, celery, parsley, almonds, salt, celery seed, and pepper in a large bowl. Mix together sour cream, blue cheese and vinegar in another bowl. Pour over potato mixture and toss to coat. Chill overnight. Serves 10 to 12.

CELEBRATE SPRING!
menu on page 459

potluck pointer

When toting a salad to a get-together, keep it chilled by placing the salad bowl in a larger bowl that is filled with crushed ice.

Mediterranean Pasta Salad

MEDITERRANEAN PASTA SALAD

For variety, substitute shredded Parmesan cheese for the feta cheese and Italian olive oil dressing for the balsamic vinaigrette.

12-oz. pkg. bowtie pasta, cooked
12-oz. jar marinated artichoke
    hearts, drained and chopped
2¼-oz. can sliced black olives,
    drained
1 cucumber, chopped

1 pt. cherry tomatoes
3 T. sweet onion, chopped
8-oz. bottle balsamic vinaigrette
    salad dressing
6-oz. pkg. crumbled feta
    cheese

Rinse pasta with cold water; drain well. Toss together artichoke hearts and next 5 ingredients with pasta. Chill 2 to 3 hours. Toss with cheese before serving. Serves 8 to 10.

Mary Rose Kulczak
Lambertville, MI

SPINACH PASTA SALAD

1 c. cauliflower flowerets, steamed
1 c. sliced mushrooms
½ c. Italian salad dressing

8 oz. pkg. spinach noodles, cooked
1 c. cooked ham, sliced
½ c. grated Parmesan cheese

In a large bowl, combine cauliflower, mushrooms and dressing. Add noodles and ham; toss lightly. Spoon into bowls, sprinkle with cheese and serve. Serves 6 to 8.

Sandy Benham
Sanborn, NY

Gooey Caramel Rolls, page 366

bountiful breads

Nothing says home quite like the aroma of freshly baked bread. In this chapter, you will discover the comforts of waking up to quick breads like warm Lemony Apple Muffins (page 362) or Gooey Caramel Rolls (page 366). When dinnertime rolls around, share your bounty with slices of hearty Farmhouse Honey-Wheat Bread (page 379) or cheesy Gruyère Rolls (page 377). And you won't want to miss out on Buttermilk Doughnuts (page 367)…especially the fudgy frosting! So yummy, you'll want to start baking now!

PEPPERY BISCUIT STICKS

*Biscuits or bread sticks…these tasty tidbits are great for dipping
in soups, stews and sauces.*

2 c. all-purpose flour	¼ t. garlic powder
2 t. baking powder	6 T. chilled butter
¼ t. baking soda	½ c. shredded Parmesan cheese
2 T. sugar	1 egg, beaten
1¼ t. pepper, divided	½ c. plus 2 T. buttermilk, divided

Combine flour, baking powder, baking soda, sugar, ¼ teaspoon pepper and garlic powder in a large bowl. Cut in butter with a pastry blender or 2 forks until mixture resembles coarse crumbs. Stir in cheese. Make a well in center of mixture. Mix egg and ½ cup buttermilk in a small bowl; stir into flour mixture just until moistened.

Turn dough out onto a lightly floured surface; knead just until dough holds together. Pat into a 12"x6" rectangle. Brush lightly with remaining 2 tablespoons buttermilk; sprinkle with remaining one teaspoon pepper and press lightly into dough. Cut into 24 (6-inch-long) strips. Arrange one inch apart on ungreased baking sheets; bake at 450 degrees for 8 minutes or until golden. Makes 2 dozen.

Virginia Watson
Scranton, PA

SLOW-COOKED SUPPER
menu on page 463

FIESTA CORNBREAD

This moist cornbread is chock-full of flavor thanks to creamed corn, onion, sharp Cheddar cheese and 2 jalapeños!

1 c. yellow cornmeal
¾ t. baking soda
½ t. salt
1 c. buttermilk
8¾-oz. can creamed corn
2 eggs, beaten

2 jalapeño peppers, chopped
1 onion, chopped
¼ c. vegetable oil
1½ c. sharp Cheddar cheese,
   shredded and divided

    Combine first 3 ingredients in a large bowl. Add buttermilk and next 4 ingredients, stirring just until dry ingredients are moistened.
    Heat oil in a 9" cast-iron skillet; spoon in half of batter. Sprinkle with one cup cheese; pour remaining batter over top. Sprinkle with remaining ½ cup cheese; bake at 400 degrees for 40 minutes. Serves 6 to 9.

Kathryn Harris
Lufkin, TX

"If you'd like, shred Pepper Jack cheese and substitute it for the Cheddar... it will add more kick!"

Kathryn

CHILI NIGHT
menu on page 464

STRAWBERRY SURPRISE BISCUITS

Whole strawberries are hidden inside these biscuits, which are sweetened with a powdered sugar glaze.

2 c. all-purpose flour
3 t. baking powder
½ t. salt
2 T. sugar
¼ c. butter

¾ c. plus 1 T. milk, divided
12 strawberries, hulled
⅔ c. powdered sugar
¼ t. vanilla extract

Combine flour, baking powder, salt and sugar in a large bowl. Cut in butter with a pastry blender or 2 forks until mixture is crumbly. Add ¾ cup milk, stirring just until moistened.

Turn dough out onto a lightly floured surface; knead 4 to 5 times. Divide dough into 12 pieces. Pat pieces into 3-inch circles on a floured surface. Place strawberries in centers of circles. Bring dough edges up over strawberries; pinch ends to seal.

Place biscuits on a lightly greased baking sheet. Bake at 425 degrees for 18 to 20 minutes or until golden brown.

Stir together powdered sugar, remaining one tablespoon milk and vanilla for glaze. Cool biscuits and drizzle with glaze. Makes one dozen.

Cheri Henry
Newalla, OK

> "Take your family to a strawberry farm to pick your own strawberries. What fun!"
>
> **Cheri**

LEMONY APPLE MUFFINS

Lemon zest adds citrusy flavor to these apple muffins. Be sure to scrub the lemon well to remove any wax from the fruit. To zest, rub the fruit against a fine grater or pull a zester across the fruit's rind. You want to remove only the colored skin…not the white pith, which is bitter.

2 c. all-purpose flour	1 c. milk
4 t. baking powder	1/3 c. butter, melted
1/8 t. salt	2 eggs, lightly beaten
1/2 c. plus 1 T. sugar, divided	zest of one lemon
1 apple, peeled, cored and chopped	1 t. cinnamon

Combine flour, baking powder, salt and 1/2 cup sugar in a large bowl. Stir in apple and make a well in center of mixture. Combine milk, butter, eggs and lemon zest in a separate bowl; add to flour mixture, stirring just until moistened.

Spoon batter equally into 12 greased muffin cups. Combine remaining one tablespoon sugar and cinnamon; sprinkle over batter. Bake at 425 degrees for 15 minutes or until golden. Cool slightly before removing to a wire rack to cool completely. Makes one dozen.

Vickie
Gooseberry Patch

it's tea time!

One of my favorite things to do, whether it's summer or winter, is to have a tea party with friends! During these tea parties, we're all kids again…giggling, sharing secrets and making memories. Scones are one of my favorite breads to serve and share…they always get rave reviews.

Rhonda Whetstone Neibauer
Wisconsin Rapids, WI

RASPBERRY SCONES

These scones are a nice contribution to breakfast or lunch…or even as a snack! Fresh raspberries are available from May to November, but they can also be purchased frozen or canned.

2 c. all-purpose flour
2 ½ t. baking powder
¼ t. salt
¼ c. plus 1 T. sugar, divided
⅛ t. nutmeg
½ c. chilled butter, sliced

½ c. milk
1 egg, beaten
1 t. lemon zest
¾ c. raspberries
1 T. butter, melted

"These scones are always a hit with overnight guests!"

Marlene

Combine flour, baking powder, salt, ¼ cup sugar and nutmeg in a large bowl. Cut in chilled butter with a pastry blender or 2 forks until mixture resembles coarse crumbs. Combine milk, egg and lemon zest in a separate bowl; add to dry ingredients, stirring just until moistened. Fold raspberries into dough.

Turn dough out onto a lightly floured surface and knead 8 to 10 times. Place dough in the center of a lightly greased baking sheet. Pat into a 9-inch circle about ½ inch thick. With a sharp knife, cut dough into 8 wedges; do not separate. Brush tops of dough with melted butter and sprinkle with remaining one tablespoon sugar. Bake at 425 degrees for 15 minutes or until golden brown. Cool on a wire rack. Makes 8.

Marlene Darnell
Newport Beach, CA

LUNCH WITH FRIENDS
menu on page 458

PEACHES & CREAM FRENCH TOAST

This popular breakfast food is stuffed with a sweet mixture of cream cheese and peach preserves. Don't expect any leftovers…it'll be eaten quickly!

16-oz. loaf French bread, cut into
    8 diagonal slices
8-oz. pkg. cream cheese,
    softened
1/3 c. peach preserves
3 eggs

1/2 c. milk
1/2 t. vanilla extract
1/4 t. cinnamon
Optional: powdered sugar,
    maple syrup

"This is absolutely delicious and makes a great breakfast for company!"

Stephanie

Cut a pocket into each bread slice by cutting from the top crust side almost to the bottom crust. (Be careful not to slice completely through bread.) Combine cream cheese and preserves in a small bowl. Spoon mixture evenly into each pocket.

Beat eggs, milk, vanilla and cinnamon in another small bowl until well combined. Dip stuffed bread slices in egg mixture, letting excess drip off. Spray a griddle or skillet with non-stick vegetable spray. Cook bread slices over medium heat until golden brown, about 2 minutes on each side, turning once. Dust each slice with powdered sugar and drizzle with maple syrup, if desired. Serves 4.

Stephanie Moon
Green Bay, WI

pantry pleasures

Have other flavors of preserves in your pantry? You can vary this French toast by using different flavors.

"Years ago I owned a café where we perfected this simple recipe. The rolls can be prepared the day before and baked the next morning...just be sure to serve them piping hot!"

Maureen

GOOEY CARAMEL ROLLS
(pictured on page 356)

Three ingredients are all it takes to make up these yummy, gooey breakfast rolls!

1½ c. brown sugar, packed
¾ c. whipping cream

2 loaves frozen bread dough, thawed

Whisk together brown sugar and whipping cream in a small bowl; pour into an ungreased 13"x9" baking pan, coating bottom of pan evenly. Set aside.

Roll out one bread dough loaf into a 12"x6" rectangle; roll up, jelly-roll style, beginning at a short end. Slice into 6 one-inch-thick pieces; arrange in baking pan. Repeat with remaining bread dough loaf. Cover dough; let rise in a warm place (85 degrees) until doubled in bulk.

Uncover and bake at 350 degrees for 35 to 45 minutes; let cool slightly. Invert rolls onto a serving plate. Spoon any remaining syrup on top; serve warm. Makes one dozen.

Maureen Seidl
Inver Grove Heights, MN

midnight breakfast

If you're hosting a sleepover, the kids will likely stay up late giggling. Plan to throw a mini breakfast at midnight! Set up a room filled with games, movies and lots of yummy things to eat...breakfast rolls, muffins and doughnuts.

BUTTERMILK DOUGHNUTS

Forget picking up a box of doughnuts at the local store when you can make 4 dozen of your own…plus you get to lick the spoon after you make the fudgy frosting!

2½ c. sugar	2 t. baking soda
2 c. hot mashed potatoes	2 t. baking powder
2 c. buttermilk	½ t. salt
2 eggs	1 t. ground nutmeg
6½ to 7 c. all-purpose flour	vegetable oil
2 T. butter, melted	Frosting

Combine sugar, potatoes, buttermilk and eggs in a large mixing bowl; beat at medium speed with an electric mixer until blended. Combine 6½ cups flour and next 5 ingredients; stir into potato mixture, gradually adding enough remaining flour until a soft dough forms. Turn dough out onto a lightly floured surface and pat to ¾-inch thickness. Using a 2½-inch floured doughnut cutter, cut out dough; repeat procedure with any dough scraps. Pour oil to a depth of one inch in an electric skillet or Dutch oven; heat oil to 375 degrees. Cook doughnuts in batches 2 minutes on each side or until golden brown. Drain on paper towels. Cool on wire racks. Spread Frosting on warm doughnuts. Makes 4 dozen.

FROSTING:

1 lb. powdered sugar	⅓ c. boiling water
½ c. baking cocoa	⅓ c. butter, melted
¼ t. salt	1 t. vanilla extract

Sift together powdered sugar, cocoa and salt in a bowl; stir in water, butter and vanilla until combined.

Jason Keller
Carrollton, GA

BANANA-CHOCOLATE CHIP BREAD

All the toppings of a banana split…bananas, chocolate and cherries…make up the ingredients of this quick loaf bread.

³/₄ c. butter, softened
1¹/₂ c. sugar
3 eggs
3 c. all-purpose flour
1¹/₂ t. baking soda

3 bananas, mashed
10-oz. jar maraschino cherries,
   ¹/₄ c. juice reserved
6-oz. pkg. chocolate chips

"I like to give this bread as a gift to friends, neighbors and teachers!"

Bobbi

Beat butter and sugar at medium speed with an electric mixer until creamy. Add eggs, one at a time, beating just until blended after each addition. Combine flour and baking soda; gradually add to butter mixture, beating at low speed just until blended. Stir in mashed bananas, cherries, reserved juice and chocolate chips. Pour into 2 greased 9"x5" loaf pans. Bake at 350 degrees for one hour. Makes 2 loaves.

Bobbi Carney
Aurora, CO

no time to bake?

Dress up store-bought refrigerated bread sticks in no time. Separate bread stick dough and lay it flat; brush with olive oil and sprinkle sesame seeds and snipped parsley over top. Holding ends of each bread stick, twist 2 times; bake as directed.

PINEAPPLE-ZUCCHINI BREAD

*Enjoying your fruits & veggies couldn't be easier! This bread is brimming
with zucchini, pineapple, raisins and walnuts.*

2 c. sugar

1 c. vegetable oil

3 eggs

3 c. all-purpose flour

2 t. baking soda

1 t. salt

1/4 t. baking powder

1 1/2 t. cinnamon

3/4 t. nutmeg

2 c. zucchini, shredded

8-oz. can crushed pineapple, drained

1 c. raisins

1 c. walnuts, chopped

2 t. vanilla extract

Beat sugar and oil at medium speed with an electric mixer until combined.
Add eggs, one at a time, beating just until blended after each addition.

Combine flour, baking soda, salt, baking powder, cinnamon and nutmeg; gradually add to sugar mixture, beating at low speed just until blended. Stir in zucchini,
pineapple, raisins, walnuts and vanilla. Pour into 2 greased and floured 9"x5" loaf
pans. Bake at 350 degrees for one hour. Makes 2 loaves.

Joyce Wilson
Lonaconing, MD

quick breads

These tasty breads are filled with a bounty
of nuts and fruit. For the tenderest loaves and
muffins, don't overmix...just stir the batter until
moistened. A few lumps won't matter.

COLD TEA GINGERBREAD

Offer ice cream, lemon sauce or whipped cream with each serving of this gingerbread.

½ c. butter, softened	1 t. baking soda
½ c. sugar	½ c. cold tea
1 egg	½ c. molasses
1¾ c. all-purpose flour	

Beat butter and sugar at medium speed with an electric mixer until creamy. Add egg, beating just until blended. Combine flour and baking soda; gradually add to butter mixture, beating at low speed just until blended. Add tea and molasses, beating just until blended. Pour into a greased and floured 9"x5" loaf pan. Bake at 350 degrees for 40 minutes. Makes one loaf.

Michelle Campen
Peoria, IL

no sticking!

Spray your measuring cup with non-stick vegetable spray before measuring molasses, syrup or honey. You'll get a more accurate measurement, and the cup will clean up easily!

APPLE-CHEDDAR BREAD

Apples & Cheddar go together...it's as simple as that!

3 c. all-purpose flour
2 T. baking powder
¾ t. salt
½ c. sugar
1½ c. milk
½ c. vegetable oil

1 egg, beaten
1 egg yolk, beaten
1 small apple, peeled, cored and
   diced
1 c. shredded sharp Cheddar
   cheese

Combine flour, baking powder, salt and sugar in a large mixing bowl. Combine milk, oil, whole egg and egg yolk in a medium bowl; add to flour mixture, stirring just until moistened. Gently fold in apple and cheese.

Divide batter between 2 greased 8"x4" loaf pans. Bake at 350 degrees for about 40 minutes or until a wooden pick inserted in center comes out clean. Cool in pans on a wire rack 10 minutes; remove from pans and cool completely on wire rack. Store in the refrigerator. Makes 2 loaves.

did you know?

Before the introduction of coins, the Egyptians gave loaves of bread as payment for their debts. (This gives new meaning to the word dough!)

BOSTON BROWN BREAD

This old-fashioned, hearty bread is delicious served warm and spread with butter or cream cheese. It's also the traditional accompaniment for Boston baked beans.

1 c. raisins	1 t. salt
1 c. boiling water	1 c. cornmeal
1 c. all-purpose flour	¼ c. brown sugar, packed
1 c. whole-wheat flour	2 c. buttermilk
1½ t. baking soda	1 c. molasses

Put raisins in a small bowl. Cover with boiling water and let stand 15 minutes.

Combine flours and next 4 ingredients in a large mixing bowl; mix well. Drain raisins and pat dry. Combine buttermilk and molasses in a medium bowl; stir in raisins. Add raisin mixture to flour mixture, stirring just until blended. Pour into a greased 9"x5" loaf pan; bake at 350 degrees for one hour. Makes one loaf.

Regina Vining
Warwick, RI

CHEDDAR CHEESE SPOONBREAD

Spoonbread is Southern comfort to the core! This soufflé is baked in a casserole dish and served as a side dish at breakfast, lunch or dinner.

2¼ c. water
1 t. salt
1 c. cornmeal
1 c. milk
1 T. butter

½ t. pepper
4 eggs, beaten
1½ c. shredded sharp
    Cheddar cheese
3 T. scallions, chopped

    Bring water to a boil in a large saucepan. Add salt and reduce heat to simmer. Whisk in cornmeal; cook, stirring constantly, about 2 minutes or until mixture is smooth. Remove from heat and whisk in milk, butter and pepper. Whisk in eggs. Stir in cheese and scallions.

    Pour mixture into a buttered 2-quart baking dish and bake at 400 degrees for 40 minutes or until a wooden pick inserted in center comes out clean. Serves 6 to 8.

EASY CHEESE BREAD

A great accompaniment with your favorite soup or chowder.

2½ c. biscuit baking mix
1 c. shredded cheese, any type
2 t. poppy seed

1 egg, beaten
1 c. milk

    Combine first 3 ingredients. Combine egg and milk and gradually add to biscuit mixture. Stir vigorously until blended. Spoon into a greased 8"x4" loaf pan and bake at 350 degrees for 35 minutes. Makes one loaf.

Katy Bolyea
Naples, FL

GRUYÈRE ROLLS

Yes, these rolls have 3 cups of cheese in them! But the rich, nutty-tasting Gruyère cheese delicately flavors these rolls and does not overpower them.

3 c. all-purpose flour
1 pkg. rapid-rise yeast
3 c. shredded Gruyère
   cheese

1 ½ t. salt
¼ t. sugar
1 ¼ c. water
Optional: melted butter

Combine 2¾ cups flour, yeast and next 3 ingredients in a large mixing bowl. Heat water until very warm (120 to 130 degrees). Gradually add water to flour mixture, beating at high speed with an electric mixer until combined. Beat 2 more minutes at medium speed. Gradually stir in enough remaining flour to make a soft dough.

Turn dough out onto a floured surface and knead until smooth and elastic (about 10 minutes). Place in a well-greased bowl, turning to grease top. Cover and let rise in a warm place (85 degrees), free from drafts, one hour or until doubled in bulk.

Punch dough down; turn out onto a lightly floured surface and knead lightly 4 or 5 times. Divide dough in half. Shape each portion of dough into 8 balls; roll each ball in flour.

Place rolls 2 inches apart on a greased baking sheet. Cover and let rise in a warm place, free from drafts, 30 minutes or until doubled in bulk. Place rolls in oven; spray rolls with water. Bake at 425 degrees for 5 minutes, spraying after 3 minutes without removing rolls from oven. Reduce oven temperature to 350 degrees; continue to bake, without spraying, 13 more minutes or until rolls are golden. Brush with melted butter, if desired. Makes 16 rolls.

brush of herb sprigs

Be sure to place warm melted butter on the table for guests to brush over vegetables or rolls. Make a natural butter brush by bundling sprigs of fresh herbs, such as thyme, oregano, parsley or rosemary, then binding them together with jute. Herbs add extra flavor, too!

LEMON FANS

For a little variety, try using orange zest instead of lemon zest...for Orange Fans!

¼ c. water	2 t. lemon zest
2 pkgs. active dry yeast	1½ t. salt
2 eggs	4 to 4½ c. all-purpose flour
1 c. milk	¼ c. butter, melted and
⅓ c. sugar	divided

Heat water until warm (100 to 110 degrees). Dissolve yeast in warm water in a large bowl; let stand about 5 minutes.

Whisk eggs in a large bowl. Whisk in milk, sugar, lemon zest and salt. Stir in 4 cups flour, ½ cup at a time, until a dough forms. Turn dough out onto a floured surface; knead 6 to 8 minutes or until smooth and elastic, adding more flour, if necessary, to prevent sticking. Place dough in a large, well-greased bowl, turning to grease top. Cover loosely with a damp cloth; let rise in a warm place (85 degrees), free from drafts, 45 minutes to one hour or until doubled in bulk.

Divide dough in half. Roll each half on a lightly floured surface into an 18"x9" rectangle; brush one dough half with one tablespoon butter and cut crosswise into 12 (1½-inch-wide) strips. Then cut lengthwise into 6 (1½-inch-wide) strips, creating 72 squares. Stack 6 squares at a time and place, cut-sides down, in 12 greased muffin cups. Repeat procedure with remaining dough half and one tablespoon butter. Brush tops with remaining 2 tablespoons butter. Cover and let rise in a warm place, free from drafts, until almost doubled in bulk. Bake at 400 degrees for 12 minutes or until golden. Remove from pans and cool completely on wire racks. Makes 2 dozen.

Cindy Neel
Gooseberry Patch

FARMHOUSE HONEY-WHEAT BREAD

This hearty bread is nutritious and delicious, plus it freezes well and makes 2 loaves!

1½ c. water
1 c. small curd cottage cheese
½ c. honey
¼ c. butter
5½ to 6 c. all-purpose flour

1 c. whole-wheat flour
2 T. sugar
3 t. salt
2 pkgs. active dry yeast
1 egg

Heat water, cottage cheese, honey and butter in a saucepan until very warm (about 120 degrees). Combine cottage cheese mixture with 2 cups all-purpose flour, whole-wheat flour and next 4 ingredients in a large mixing bowl; beat at medium speed with an electric mixer 2 minutes. Add enough remaining flour to make a stiff dough. Turn dough out onto a floured surface and knead until smooth and elastic. Place dough in a large, well-greased bowl, turning to grease top; cover and let rise in a warm place (85 degrees), free from drafts, one hour or until doubled in bulk. Punch dough down and shape into 2 loaves; place in 2 greased 9"x5" loaf pans. Cover and let rise 45 minutes or until doubled in bulk. Bake at 350 degrees for 45 minutes or until loaves sound hollow when tapped. Makes 2 loaves.

Mary Murray
Gooseberry Patch

it's done!

To test bread for doneness, thump the crust with your finger. If the loaf sounds hollow, it's done.

BRAIDED COFFEE BREAD

Every morning is a special occasion when you wake up to the scent of this impressive bread. Surprise your family this weekend!

¼ c. water
1 pkg. active dry yeast
3 T. sugar
½ cup milk, scalded and cooled
4 c. all-purpose flour
3 eggs
½ c. unsalted butter, cut into
   small pieces

½ t. salt
2 c. sifted powdered sugar
2 T. milk
2 t. vanilla extract
Garnishes: chopped nuts, chopped
   maraschino cherries

Heat water until warm (100 to 110 degrees). Dissolve yeast in warm water in a large bowl; add sugar. Add milk and ½ cup flour to yeast mixture, beating at medium speed with an electric mixer until smooth. Add eggs, butter and salt, beating until smooth. Stir in remaining 3½ cups flour.

Turn dough out onto a well-floured surface; knead dough until smooth and elastic (about 8 minutes). Place in a large, well-greased bowl, turning to grease top.

Cover and let rise in a warm place (85 degrees), free from drafts, one hour and 15 minutes or until doubled in bulk.

Punch dough down and divide into 6 equal portions; form each portion into a 14-inch-long rope. Braid 3 ropes together, tucking in ends. Repeat with remaining 3 ropes. Place braids on a lightly greased baking sheet and let rise in a warm place, free from drafts, one hour or until almost doubled in bulk. Bake at 375 degrees for 20 minutes. Let cool completely.

Combine powdered sugar, milk and vanilla, stirring well; drizzle over loaves. Garnish, if desired. Makes 2 loaves.

Nancy Molldrem
Eau Claire, WI

> "I make this coffee bread every Christmas Eve just like my mother did when I was a girl. On Christmas morning, the aroma of fresh-baked bread smells so good."
>
> **Nancy**

YANKEE BEAN POT BREAD

One of these loaves could be a meal unto itself with ingredients such as bean and bacon soup and shredded wheat biscuits!

6 to 6½ c. all-purpose flour
2 pkgs. active dry yeast
2 T. brown sugar, packed
1 T. salt
1½ c. water
1 11-oz. can bean and bacon
　soup, undiluted

2 large shredded wheat
　biscuits, crumbled
¼ c. molasses
2 T. butter
2 eggs
Optional: melted butter

Combine 2 cups flour, yeast, brown sugar and salt in a large mixing bowl. Combine water, soup, crumbled shredded wheat biscuits, molasses and butter in a saucepan; heat until warm (butter doesn't need to melt). Stir into flour mixture. Add eggs, one at a time, and mix at low speed with an electric mixer until moistened; beat 3 more minutes at medium speed. Gradually stir in enough remaining flour to make a firm dough. Turn dough out onto a floured surface and knead until smooth and elastic (about 5 minutes). Place in a large, well-greased bowl, turning to grease top. Cover and let rise in a warm place (85 degrees), free from drafts, about one hour or until light and doubled in bulk.

Punch dough down. Divide into 2 portions. Pat each half into a 14"x7" rectangle on a lightly floured surface. Starting with shorter end, roll up tightly, pressing dough into roll with each turn. Pinch edges and ends to seal. Place in 2 greased 9"x5" loaf pans.

Cover and let rise in a warm place, free from drafts, about 45 minutes or until light and doubled in bulk. Bake at 375 degrees for 35 to 40 minutes or until golden brown and loaves sound hollow when tapped. Remove from pans; brush with butter, if desired. Cool. Makes 2 loaves.

Cyndy Rogers
Upton, MA

GREEK STUFFED BREAD

Stuffed with spinach, tomatoes, 2 types of cheese and, of course, olives, this tasty bread is best eaten with a fork and knife…you don't want to miss a bite!

10-oz. pkg. frozen chopped
   spinach, thawed
$2^2/_3$ c. water
2 pkgs. active dry yeast
2 t. sugar
$6^1/_2$ c. bread flour
2 t. salt
$^3/_4$ c. mayonnaise
2 T. dried oregano
1 T. lemon juice
2 t. dried thyme

1 t. dried basil
1 clove garlic, pressed
$^3/_4$ lb. crumbled feta cheese
$1^1/_2$ c. shredded mozzarella
   cheese
$^1/_2$ c. tomato, seeded and
   chopped
1 medium red onion, sliced
20 kalamata olives, pitted and
   chopped
1 egg, lightly beaten

Cook spinach according to package directions. Drain well and press between paper towels to remove excess moisture. Set aside.

Heat water until warm (100 to 110 degrees). Combine warm water, yeast and sugar in a 4-cup liquid measuring cup; let stand 5 minutes.

Combine yeast mixture, $3^1/_4$ cups flour and salt in a large mixing bowl; beat at medium speed with an electric mixer until well blended. Gradually stir in enough of remaining $3^1/_4$ cups flour to make a soft dough. Turn dough out onto a well-floured surface and knead until smooth and elastic (about 8 minutes). Place in a well-greased bowl, turning to grease top. Cover and let rise in a warm place (85 degrees), free from drafts, one hour or until doubled in bulk.

Punch dough down; cover and let rest 10 minutes. Turn dough out onto a well-floured surface and knead 4 or 5 times. Roll dough into a 20-inch circle.

Combine mayonnaise and next 5 ingredients. Spread mayonnaise mixture over dough to within $^1/_2$ inch of edge. Layer cheeses, tomato, onion, olives and spinach over mayonnaise mixture. Fold each side of dough over filling, overlapping edges one inch. Pinch seams to seal. Loaf will be square in shape.

Carefully place loaf, seam-side down, on a greased baking sheet; reshape into a round loaf. Brush with egg. Cut 4 (3-inch-long) slits in top of loaf. Bake at 400 degrees for 35 minutes or until browned. Loaf will be hard but will soften as it cools. Serve warm. Serves 8.

Carrot Cake, page 391

blue-ribbon desserts

Indulge in this yummy collection of made-from-scratch sweet delights. From Mom's Apple Dumplings (page 387) to Peanut Butter & Fudge Pie (page 398) to Candy Bar Fudge (page 423), you'll find that perfect dessert for family get-togethers, a neighborhood potluck, a Sunday dinner, or any occasion… right here. Share these goodies with family & friends today!

FRIENDSHIP DELIGHT

Whip up this easy make-ahead dessert to welcome new neighbors…one bite and your friendship is sealed.

1 c. all-purpose flour
1 c. chopped pecans
½ c. butter, melted
1 c. powdered sugar
12-oz. container frozen whipped topping, thawed and divided
8-oz. pkg. cream cheese

4 c. milk, divided
3.9-oz. pkg. instant chocolate pudding mix
3.4-oz. pkg. instant vanilla pudding mix
Garnish: additional chopped nuts

Combine first 3 ingredients in a small bowl and press evenly into a 13"x9" pan. Bake at 325 degrees for 25 minutes or until lightly browned.

Beat powdered sugar and half of whipped topping at medium speed with an electric mixer until combined; beat in cream cheese until combined. Spread over cooled crust.

Mix 2 cups milk with each pudding mix. Layer chocolate pudding over cream cheese layer; spread to edges. Layer vanilla pudding over chocolate pudding and top with remaining half of whipped topping. Sprinkle with additional chopped nuts, if desired. Refrigerate 3 to 4 hours before serving. Serves 10 to 12.

Lisa Engelhardt
Tavernier, FL

birthday cake

A family favorite was always my mama's birthday pound cake. Back then, before stand mixers, this cake was a two-person job! One of us would beat the eggs, while the other gathered all the other ingredients. We always used a big, green Fire-King bowl to mix the cake in and, later on, Mama gave it to me…I treasure it. Served frosted or with fruit or ice cream, this cake has been loved by four generations of our family over the last 40 years.

Rhonda Jones
Rocky Mount, VA

MOM'S APPLE DUMPLINGS

This classic apple dessert is wrapped in homemade pastry, sprinkled with cinnamon-nutmeg-sugar mixture and topped with cinnamon syrup.

1½ c. sugar
1½ c. water
¼ t. cinnamon
¼ t. nutmeg
8 drops red food coloring
3 T. butter
2 c. all-purpose flour

2 t. baking powder
1 t. salt
⅔ c. shortening
½ c. milk
6 apples
additional sugar, cinnamon, nutmeg
6 T. butter

Prepare syrup by combining sugar, water, cinnamon, nutmeg and food coloring in a saucepan; bring to a boil. Remove from heat and add 3 tablespoons butter; set aside.

Combine flour, baking powder and salt; cut in shortening with a pastry blender or 2 forks until mixture is crumbly. Gradually add milk, stirring with a fork until dry ingredients are moistened. Shape mixture into a ball; roll pastry on a lightly floured surface, shaping into an 18"x12" rectangle.

Peel and core apples. Cut pastry into 6 (6-inch) squares and place an apple on each square. Sprinkle generously with additional sugar, cinnamon and nutmeg; dot each apple with one tablespoon butter. Moisten edges of each pastry square with water; bring corners to center, pressing edges to seal. Place in an ungreased pan and pour syrup over dumplings. Bake at 375 degrees for 35 minutes. Serves 6.

Sharon Gibbons
Knoxville, TN

"These apple dumplings always remind me of growing up and the happiness of home."

Sharon

ICE-CREAM TACOS

The next time you want tacos, make them the dessert kind! These sweet treats are stuffed with ice cream, drizzled with hot fudge and finished with a cherry on top.

8 frozen round waffles, thawed
1 qt. chocolate ice cream,
   softened
½ c. mini marshmallows

½ c. hot fudge sauce,
   warmed
8 maraschino cherries
   with stems

    Warm waffles; do not toast. Gently fold each waffle in half; set in a 13"x9" baking dish, open-side up, keeping the rows tight so taco shape is maintained.
    Combine ice cream and marshmallows in a large mixing bowl; spoon evenly into waffle shells. Cover and freeze until firm. Before serving, drizzle with warmed hot fudge sauce and top each with a cherry. Serves 8.

Kathy Unruh
Fresno, CA

DOUBLE TROUBLE

Chocolate frosting coats this two-layer chocolate cake, giving the lucky recipients double trouble…of the chocolate-indulgence kind!

1³/₄ c. all-purpose flour
1¹/₂ t. baking soda
¹/₂ t. salt
¹/₂ c. butter, softened
³/₄ c. brown sugar, packed
²/₃ c. sugar
2 eggs

1¹/₂ t. vanilla extract
¹/₂ c. sour cream
4 (1-oz.) squares unsweetened baking chocolate, melted and cooled
1 c. buttermilk
Frosting

Combine flour, baking soda and salt in a small bowl; set aside. Beat butter in a large bowl at medium speed with an electric mixer until creamy. Add sugars and beat one minute. Add eggs, one at a time, beating well after each addition; stir in vanilla. Add sour cream; beat 30 seconds. Stir in melted chocolate, mixing well. Add flour mixture to chocolate mixture alternately with buttermilk, beginning and ending with flour mixture; beat well.

Pour batter into 2 greased and floured 8" round cake pans. Bake at 350 degrees for 25 to 35 minutes or until a wooden pick inserted in center comes out clean. Cool in pans on a wire rack 10 minutes; remove from pans and cool completely on wire rack.

Spread Frosting between layers and on top and sides of cake. Serves 12.

FROSTING:

14-oz. can sweetened condensed milk
¹/₂ c. butter

3 (1-oz.) squares unsweetened baking chocolate
2 t. vanilla extract

Heat milk, butter and chocolate in a saucepan over low heat, stirring constantly, until butter and chocolate melt and frosting thickens, about 3 minutes. Remove from heat; stir in vanilla. Let cool 5 minutes before frosting cooled cake.

Jennifer Licon-Conner
Gooseberry Patch

CARROT CAKE
(pictured on page 384)

Crushed pineapple adds extra moistness to this scrumptious carrot cake.

3 c. all-purpose flour
2 t. baking powder
2 t. baking soda
1 t. salt
2 t. cinnamon
4 eggs
2 1/2 c. sugar

1 1/2 c. vegetable oil
1 t. vanilla extract
2 large carrots, grated
15 1/4-oz. can crushed pineapple, drained
1 1/2 c. chopped nuts
Frosting

Stir together first 5 ingredients in a medium bowl. Beat eggs and next 3 ingredients in a large mixing bowl at medium speed with an electric mixer until smooth. Add flour mixture, beating at low speed until blended. Fold in carrots, pineapple and nuts.

Pour batter into 3 greased and floured 9" round cake pans. Bake at 350 degrees for 25 to 30 minutes or until a wooden pick inserted in center comes out clean. Cool in pans on wire racks 10 minutes. Remove from pans and cool completely on wire racks. Spread Frosting between layers and on top and sides of cake. Serves 16.

FROSTING:

2 (8-oz.) pkgs. cream cheese, softened
1/2 c. butter
2 (16-oz.) pkgs. powdered sugar, sifted

2 t. vanilla extract
1 c. chopped nuts

Beat cream cheese and butter at medium speed with an electric mixer until smooth. Gradually add powdered sugar, beating at low speed until light and fluffy. Stir in vanilla and nuts. Makes 6 3/4 cups.

Karen Moran
Navasota, TX

"I remember my mother baking this for my father's birthday...it was his favorite cake!"

Karen

BUTTERY POUND CAKE

The sweet brown sugar glaze pairs perfectly with the apples!

½ c. plus ⅓ c. brown sugar, packed
    and divided
⅓ c. chopped pecans, toasted
1 t. cinnamon
1 t. nutmeg
¾ c. plus 2 T. butter, softened and
    divided
1½ c. sugar
3 eggs

3 c. all-purpose flour
1½ t. baking powder
1½ t. baking soda
½ t. salt
1½ c. sour cream
2 t. vanilla extract, divided
1½ c. apple, peeled, cored and
    thinly sliced
2 T. milk

Combine ⅓ cup brown sugar, pecans, cinnamon and nutmeg in a small bowl; set aside.

Beat ¾ cup butter at medium speed with an electric mixer until creamy. Gradually add 1½ cups sugar, beating 5 to 7 minutes. Add eggs, one at a time, beating just until yellow disappears.

Combine flour, baking powder, baking soda and salt in another bowl. Add sour cream and flour mixture alternately to butter mixture, beginning and ending with flour mixture; beat at low speed after each addition just until mixture is blended. Stir in one teaspoon vanilla.

Spoon half of batter into a greased and floured 12-cup Bundt® pan. Arrange apple slices over batter, then spoon half of brown sugar mixture over apples; gently press into batter. Top with remaining batter, then sprinkle with remaining brown sugar mixture. Bake at 350 degrees for one hour or until a wooden pick inserted in center comes out clean. Cool in pan on a wire rack 15 minutes; remove from pan and cool completely on wire rack.

Heat 2 tablespoons butter in a small saucepan over medium heat until butter starts to brown. Remove from heat and stir in remaining ½ cup brown sugar, milk and one teaspoon vanilla. Stir until smooth; drizzle glaze evenly over cake. Serves 16.

Cheryl Bierley
Miamisburg, OH

WHITE TEXAS SHEET CAKE

A nice change from the chocolate version…and just as delicious!

1 c. butter	2 c. sugar
1 c. water	2 eggs, beaten
2 c. all-purpose flour	½ c. sour cream
1 t. baking soda	1 t. almond extract
1 t. salt	Frosting

Bring butter and water to a boil in a large saucepan. Remove from heat and whisk in flour, baking soda, salt, sugar, eggs, sour cream and almond extract until smooth. Pour into a greased 15"x10" baking pan. Bake at 375 degrees for 20 to 22 minutes or until a wooden pick inserted in center comes out clean. Cool in pan on a wire rack 20 minutes. Spread Frosting on top of cake. Serves 12.

FROSTING:

½ c. butter	½ t. almond extract
¼ c. milk	1 c. chopped walnuts
4½ c. powdered sugar	

Combine butter and milk in a saucepan; cook over low heat until butter melts. Bring to a boil over medium heat.

Remove from heat and add powdered sugar and almond extract; beat at medium speed with an electric mixer until spreading consistency. Stir in walnuts.

Sandra Warren
Friendship, OH

RED VELVET CAKE

(pictured on page 461)

This cake makes a stunning appearance with its reddish cake layers and white frosting…perfect for any festive occasion.

½ c. shortening	1 t. baking soda
1½ c. sugar	¾ t. salt
2 eggs	3 T. baking cocoa
1 t. vanilla extract	1 c. buttermilk
1½ T. red food coloring	1 T. white vinegar
2 c. all-purpose flour	Best-Ever Soft Icing

Beat shortening and sugar at medium speed with an electric mixer until fluffy. Add eggs, one at a time, beating just until yellow disappears. Stir in vanilla and food coloring.

Combine flour, baking soda, salt and cocoa. Stir together buttermilk and vinegar; add to shortening mixture alternately with flour mixture, beginning and ending with flour mixture. Beat just until blended after each addition. Pour batter into 2 greased and floured 9" round cake pans; bake at 350 degrees for 25 minutes or until a wooden pick inserted in center comes out clean. Cool in pans on a wire rack 10 minutes; remove from pans. Cool completely on wire racks. Spread Best-Ever Soft Icing between layers and on top and sides of cake. Serves 12.

BEST-EVER SOFT ICING:

¼ c. all-purpose flour	1 t. vanilla extract
1 c. milk	1 c. sugar
1 c. butter, softened	

Whisk together flour and milk in a small saucepan over low heat until thickened. Pour into a mixing bowl; allow mixture to cool. Add butter and remaining ingredients to flour mixture; beat at high speed with an electric mixer until fluffy, about 8 minutes. Makes 3½ cups.

Marion Pfeifer
Smyrna, DE

"I've found that the men in our family just love this cake! It's always requested for birthdays, graduations or any special gathering."

Marion

ICE-CREAM CONE CAKES

Surprise the birthday honoree with cake made in ice-cream cones. Everything is edible, and there are no forks & plates to clean up!

²/₃ c. all-purpose flour
1 t. baking powder
¹/₈ t. salt
¹/₃ c. baking cocoa
2 T. butter, softened
¹/₂ c. sugar
²/₃ c. buttermilk

¹/₂ t. vanilla extract
1 egg white
10 flat-bottomed ice-cream cones
Frosting
Optional: colored sprinkles,
    10 maraschino cherries
    with stems

Combine first 4 ingredients in a small bowl; set aside.

Beat butter and sugar in a large mixing bowl at medium speed with an electric mixer until creamy. Add flour mixture and buttermilk alternately to butter mixture, beginning and ending with flour mixture; beat at low speed after each addition just until blended. Stir in vanilla. Add egg white, mixing well.

Fill cones to within ¹/₂ inch of the top; carefully place on an ungreased baking sheet. Bake at 375 degrees for 35 minutes; cool completely on wire racks. Spread evenly with Frosting. Top with colored sprinkles and a cherry, if desired. Serves 10.

FROSTING:

2 T. butter, softened
1¹/₂ c. powdered sugar

2 T. buttermilk
1¹/₂ t. vanilla extract

Beat butter and sugar at medium speed with an electric mixer until creamy. Add buttermilk; beat until spreading consistency. Stir in vanilla. Makes about ²/₃ cup.

Kris Lammers
Gooseberry Patch

PEANUT BUTTER & FUDGE PIE

This pie is like an ice-cream sundae…full of the same toppings but with a hint of peanut butter.

½ c. creamy peanut butter
¼ c. honey
1 qt. vanilla ice cream,
　softened
9-oz. graham cracker pie crust
½ c. cashews, chopped

½ c. fudge ice-cream topping,
　warmed
Garnishes: whipped topping,
　additional warmed fudge
　ice-cream topping and chopped
　cashews

Combine peanut butter and honey; stir in ice cream. Spoon half of ice-cream mixture into pie crust; sprinkle with half of cashews. Drizzle half of fudge ice-cream topping over cashews; spoon remaining ice-cream mixture over top. Sprinkle with remaining cashews and drizzle with remaining fudge ice-cream topping. Freeze about 8 hours or until firm. Garnish with whipped topping, additional warmed fudge ice-cream topping and chopped cashews, if desired. Serves 8.

Coli Harrington
Delaware, OH

LEMON CHESS PIE

An old-fashioned favorite we love!

½ c. butter, softened
1⅓ c. sugar
3 jumbo eggs
2 T. cornmeal

1 t. lemon extract
1 T. white vinegar
⅓ c. milk
9-inch unbaked pie crust

Blend butter and sugar together. Stir in eggs and cornmeal. Blend in lemon extract, vinegar and milk; pour into pie crust. Bake at 350 degrees for 45 to 60 minutes or until center is set. Serves 8.

HONEY-CRUNCH PECAN PIE

A splash of bourbon and a measure of golden honey add to this impressive nut-filled dessert. Chopped pecans flavor the filling, while glazed pecan halves crown the surface.

4 eggs, lightly beaten
1 c. light corn syrup
¼ c. sugar
¼ c. brown sugar, packed
2 T. butter, melted
1 T. bourbon
1 t. vanilla extract
½ t. salt

1 c. chopped pecans
9-inch unbaked pie crust
¼ c. plus 3 T. brown sugar, packed
¼ c. butter
⅓ c. honey
2 c. pecan halves

Combine first 8 ingredients in a large bowl; stir well with a wire whisk until blended. Stir in chopped pecans. Spoon pecan mixture into pie crust. Bake at 350 degrees for 35 minutes. Cover with aluminum foil after 25 minutes to prevent excessive browning, if necessary.

Meanwhile, combine ¼ cup plus 3 tablespoons brown sugar, ¼ cup butter and honey in a medium saucepan; cook over medium heat 2 minutes or until sugar dissolves and butter melts, stirring mixture often. Add pecan halves and stir gently until coated. Spoon pecan mixture evenly over pie. Bake 10 more minutes or until topping is bubbly. Cool completely on a wire rack. Serves 10.

MILE-HIGH LEMON MERINGUE PIE

This lemon pie is piled high with a layer of billowy meringue.

½ (14.1-oz.) pkg. refrigerated
   pie crust
8-oz. container sour cream
5 eggs, separated
2.9-oz. pkg. cook-and-serve lemon
   pudding mix

1 c. milk
½ c. plus 2 T. lemonade
   concentrate, thawed
¼ t. cream of tartar
½ t. vanilla extract
½ c. plus 2 T. sugar

Unroll pie crust according to package directions. Fit into a 9" pie plate. Fold edges under and flute. Prick bottom and sides with a fork. Bake at 450 degrees until golden. Remove from oven and let cool on a wire rack. Reduce oven temperature to 350 degrees.

Whisk together sour cream and egg yolks in a medium saucepan; stir in lemon pudding mix, milk and lemonade concentrate. Cook over medium heat, whisking constantly, until thickened. Reduce heat to low and cook 2 minutes or until very thick. Remove from heat; cover and keep hot.

Beat egg whites, cream of tartar and vanilla at high speed with an electric mixer until foamy. Beat in sugar, one tablespoon at a time, until stiff peaks form. Pour hot filling into prepared crust. Dollop meringue onto hot filling. Lightly spread dollops together in decorative swirls, completely sealing meringue to pie crust. Bake at 325 degrees for 22 to 25 minutes or until golden. Cool completely on a wire rack. Serves 8.

Scott Harrington
Boston, MA

> "This pie brings back memories of my grandmother in Alabama. I enjoyed many wonderful Sunday dinners at her home. She was a cook at the Purefoy Hotel for several decades. Her meals at the hotel and those she prepared for her family were fabulous! Grandmother and the hotel are gone now, but her memory lives on in this pie."
>
> **Sandra**

CHOCOLATE SUNDAY PIE

Make any day of the week exceptional when you offer this thick & rich chocolatey pie for dessert.

1½ c. sugar	1 T. butter
¼ c. all-purpose flour	1 t. vanilla extract
5 T. baking cocoa	9-inch pie crust, baked
2 c. milk	Meringue
3 egg yolks, lightly beaten	

Combine sugar, flour and cocoa in a medium saucepan. Gradually add milk, stirring well. Gradually add egg yolks to chocolate mixture; add butter. Cook mixture over medium heat about 20 minutes or until thickened, stirring often. Remove from heat and stir in vanilla. Pour into pie crust and dollop Meringue onto hot pie filling. Lightly spread dollops together in decorative swirls, completely sealing Meringue to pie crust. Bake at 350 degrees for 10 minutes or until Meringue is golden. Cool completely on a wire rack. Serves 8.

MERINGUE:

3 egg whites	¼ c. sugar
¼ t. cream of tartar	

Beat egg whites and cream of tartar at high speed with an electric mixer until foamy. Beat in sugar, one tablespoon at a time, until stiff peaks form.

Sandra Crook
Jacksonville, FL

BLACKBERRY COBBLER

Use fresh blackberries when they're at their peak during May and June. And if time allows, churn some homemade vanilla ice cream to top off this ultimate comfort food!

1 c. butter, divided
1 c. plus 2 T. sugar, divided
1 c. water
1½ c. self-rising flour

⅓ c. milk, room temperature
2 c. fresh or frozen
    blackberries
1 t. cinnamon

Melt ½ cup butter in a 10" round or oval baking dish; set aside.

Heat one cup sugar and water in a saucepan until sugar dissolves; set aside. Place flour in a large mixing bowl and cut in remaining ½ cup butter with a pastry blender or 2 forks until mixture is crumbly. Add milk and stir with a fork to form a dough. Continue stirring until dough leaves the sides of the bowl.

Turn out dough onto a lightly floured surface; knead 3 or 4 times and roll to ¼-inch thickness, shaping into an 11"x9" rectangle. Sprinkle berries over dough; sprinkle with cinnamon and roll up, jelly-roll style. Cut into ¼-inch-thick slices and carefully place slices in baking dish over melted butter. Pour sugar syrup around slices. Bake at 350 degrees for 45 minutes. Sprinkle remaining 2 tablespoons sugar over top and bake 15 more minutes. Serve warm or cold. Serves 8.

Pat Habiger
Spearville, KS

"My grandmother made this cobbler when I was a little girl. I would play on Grandpa and Grandma's farm, which had a large garden, a goldfish tank and a tree swing that would almost touch the sky! Grandma would crochet, quilt and make the greatest desserts."

Pat

GLAZED STRAWBERRY TART

Really show off this tart on special occasions…drizzle it with melted chocolate or dust it with powdered sugar!

1 ½ c. all-purpose flour
½ c. almonds, ground
⅓ c. sugar
½ t. salt
6 T. chilled butter, sliced
1 egg
1 t. almond extract

¾ c. strawberry jam
1 t. lemon juice
2 pts. strawberries, hulled and
   halved
Optional: whipped topping
Garnish: whole strawberry

Combine flour, almonds, sugar and salt in a large mixing bowl; cut in butter with a pastry blender or 2 forks until mixture is crumbly. Whisk together egg and almond extract in another bowl; add to flour mixture, stirring until a dough forms. Shape into a flattened ball; wrap in plastic wrap and refrigerate overnight.

Place dough in center of a greased and floured baking sheet. Pat into a 10-inch circle; form a ¾-inch-high rim around the outside edge. Prick bottom of dough with a fork; bake at 350 degrees for 25 minutes or until golden. Cool 10 minutes on baking sheet on a wire rack; remove crust from baking sheet and cool completely on wire rack.

Heat jam and lemon juice in a small saucepan over low heat until spreadable; spread ½ cup jam mixture over crust. Arrange berry halves on top, cut-sides down; brush with remaining jam mixture. Serve with whipped topping and garnish, if desired. Serves 8.

Jo Ann
Gooseberry Patch

vintage finds

Look for vintage pie tins, servers and cake plates at flea markets…add them to your collection or make them part of the gift when sharing a favorite sweet treat.

BABY CAKES

Use your favorite shaped cookie cutter or a variety of shapes to make these creamy butter cookies.

2 c. all-purpose flour	sugar to taste
1 c. butter, softened	Creamy Filling
1/3 c. whipping cream	

Beat flour, butter and cream at medium speed with an electric mixer until combined; chill one hour.

Roll dough to 1/8- to 1/4-inch thickness on a lightly floured surface. Cut with tiny cookie cutters; place close together on ungreased baking sheets. Pierce each cookie several times with a fork; sprinkle lightly with sugar. Bake at 375 degrees for about 8 minutes or until golden. Remove to wire racks to cool completely. Spread Creamy Filling between cookies, forming sandwiches. Makes about 4 1/2 dozen.

CREAMY FILLING:

1/4 c. butter, softened	1 t. vanilla extract
3/4 c. powdered sugar	

Beat butter at medium speed with an electric mixer until creamy; gradually add sugar, beating well. Stir in vanilla.

Renée Spec
Crescent, PA

BROWN SUGAR COOKIES

A hint of maple syrup makes these cookies appealing!

2 1/3 c. brown sugar, packed
1 c. butter, softened
2 eggs
1 t. vanilla extract

1/2 t. maple syrup
2 c. all-purpose flour
2 c. pecan halves

Beat first 5 ingredients at medium speed with an electric mixer until well blended. Gradually add flour, mixing well. Fold in nuts. Drop dough by tablespoonfuls onto ungreased baking sheets. Bake at 375 degrees for 8 to 13 minutes. Cookies will flatten and spread. Let sit one minute on baking sheet before removing. Remove to wire racks to cool. Makes 3 dozen.

Lisa Watkins
Williamsport, OH

storage containers

Search flea markets, yard sales or antique shops for unique biscuit or pickle jars and old-style bottles. They're just right to fill with sweet treats for friends or to set on your counter filled with after-school snacks!

CHOCOLATEY PUMPKIN COOKIES

With its pumpkin flavor and hint of cinnamon, these cookies will make you reminisce about cool fall days.

1 c. sugar
1 c. shortening
1 c. canned pumpkin
1 egg
1 t. vanilla extract
2 c. all-purpose flour

1 t. baking soda
½ t. salt
1 t. cinnamon
1 c. semi-sweet chocolate chips
Frosting

Beat sugar and shortening at medium speed with an electric mixer until creamy. Add pumpkin, egg and vanilla, beating until blended; set aside.

Combine flour, baking soda, salt and cinnamon in a small bowl; gradually add to shortening mixture, beating well. Fold in chocolate chips.

Drop by tablespoonfuls onto ungreased baking sheets. Bake at 350 degrees for 15 to 20 minutes or until golden and browned on bottom. Remove to wire racks to cool. Drizzle cookies with Frosting. Makes 2 dozen.

FROSTING:

½ c. brown sugar, packed
3 T. butter

3 T. milk
1½ c. powdered sugar

Combine brown sugar, butter and milk in a small saucepan. Bring mixture to a boil over medium heat; boil 2 minutes. Remove from heat. Add powdered sugar. Beat at medium speed with an electric mixer until mixture is smooth.

Susan Whitney
Fountain Valley, CA

lunch-box surprise

Surprise 'em at lunch by slipping cookies inside vellum envelopes and tying them closed with shoestring licorice!

"These snowy cookies look beautiful layered in a gift box lined with red tissue paper...what a sweet surprise."

Kathy

SUGARED PECAN COOKIES

These log-shaped cookies are just perfect when dipped in a tall glass of cold milk!

½ c. butter, softened	1 T. sugar
½ c. cream cheese, softened	⅛ t. salt
1 t. vanilla extract	1 c. pecan halves, ground
1¾ c. all-purpose flour	1 c. powdered sugar

Beat butter and cream cheese at medium speed with an electric mixer until creamy. Stir in vanilla and set aside.

Combine flour, one tablespoon sugar and salt; gradually add to butter mixture, beating well. Stir in pecans. Shape each tablespoonful of dough into a 2-inch log. Place 2 inches apart on ungreased baking sheets; bake at 375 degrees for 12 to 14 minutes. Roll warm cookies in powdered sugar; cool on wire racks. Makes 2 dozen.

Kathy McLaren
Visalia, CA

great gift containers

Keep your eyes open year-round at tag sales and flea markets for anything that you might be able to tuck your sweets into for gift giving. Vintage pie tins, mugs, jelly jars and enamelware pails would all be perfect!

FROSTED ORANGE COOKIES

These light-tasting, citrus-flavored cookies are eye-catching at baby or wedding showers.

1 c. shortening	4 t. baking powder
1½ c. sugar	1 t. baking soda
2 eggs	⅛ t. salt
1 T. orange zest	1 c. milk
⅓ c. orange juice	1 T. lemon juice
4 c. all-purpose flour	Frosting

Beat shortening and sugar at medium speed with an electric mixer until creamy; add eggs, beating until blended. Add zest and orange juice, beating until combined. Combine flour, baking powder, baking soda and salt. Stir together milk and lemon juice; add to shortening mixture alternately with flour mixture, beginning and ending with flour mixture. Drop by tablespoonfuls onto parchment paper-lined baking sheets; bake at 350 degrees for 9 to 10 minutes. Remove to wire racks. Spread with Frosting while still warm. Makes about 4 dozen.

FROSTING:

1-lb. pkg. powdered sugar	4 to 5 T. orange juice
1 T. orange zest	

Beat sugar, one tablespoon orange zest and 4 tablespoons orange juice at medium speed with an electric mixer until creamy; add enough remaining orange juice to reach desired spreading consistency.

Laura Lett
Gooseberry Patch

WHITE CHOCOLATE-CRANBERRY COOKIES

Dried cranberries taste surprisingly sweet. When paired with white chocolate, they make these cookies a favorite choice.

½ c. butter, softened
¾ c. sugar
½ c. brown sugar, packed
1 egg, beaten
1 t. vanilla extract

1 ¾ c. all-purpose flour
1 t. baking powder
½ t. baking soda
1 c. sweetened dried cranberries
½ c. white chocolate chips

Beat butter in a large bowl at medium speed with an electric mixer until creamy; gradually add sugars, beating until combined. Add egg and vanilla; beat until smooth.

Combine flour, baking powder and baking soda; gradually add to sugar mixture, beating well. Stir in cranberries and chocolate chips.

Shape dough into 1 ½-inch balls; place 2 inches apart on ungreased baking sheets. Bake at 375 degrees for 14 minutes or until golden. Remove to wire racks to cool. Makes about 2 ½ dozen.

Shawna Brock
Eglin AFB, FL

cranberry creation

For a personal gift tag, string fresh cranberries onto wire and shape into the recipient's initial.

"Everyone loves peanut butter and chocolate!"

Julie

PEANUT BUTTER JUMBOS

These cookies are big on flavor. They're loaded with peanut butter, oats, chocolate chips and chocolate candy!

¼ c. butter, softened
1 c. brown sugar, packed
1 c. sugar
1½ c. creamy peanut butter
3 eggs
1 t. vanilla extract

4½ c. quick-cooking oats, uncooked
2 t. baking soda
1 c. chocolate chips
1 c. candy-coated chocolate mini-baking bits

Beat butter, sugars and peanut butter at medium speed with an electric mixer until creamy. Add eggs and vanilla, beating until blended. Combine oats and baking soda; add to butter mixture, beating just until blended. Fold in chocolate chips and mini-baking bits.

Drop by tablespoonfuls onto greased baking sheets. Bake at 350 degrees for 15 to 20 minutes. Remove to wire racks to cool. Makes about 1½ dozen.

Julie Anthony
Homeworth, OH

decorating tip

Add chocolate or peanut butter chips to a plastic zipping bag and microwave until the chips are melted. Then just snip off one small corner of the bag and pipe designs onto the cooled cookies.

ICE BOX BROWNIES

These chewy brownies are almost like eating fudge…wonderful!

¼ c. butter
1 ½ squares unsweetened
   chocolate
1 c. brown sugar, packed
1 egg, beaten
½ c. all-purpose flour

¼ t. baking powder
¼ t. salt
¼ t. vanilla extract
½ c. chopped walnuts
Mint Filling
Glaze

Microwave butter and chocolate in a one-quart glass bowl on high for one minute or until melted. Add sugar and egg, stirring until blended. Combine flour, baking powder and salt; stir into chocolate mixture. Stir in vanilla and walnuts. Pour into a greased 8"x8" pan and bake at 350 degrees for 15 to 18 minutes. Remove from oven and cool completely on a wire rack.

Spread Mint Filling over brownies. Chill 30 minutes. Spread Glaze over filling. Cut into squares to serve and store brownies in the refrigerator. Makes 16.

MINT FILLING:

2 c. powdered sugar
¼ c. butter, softened
2 T. milk

¾ t. peppermint extract
½ t. vanilla extract
few drops green food coloring

Beat all ingredients at medium speed with an electric mixer 2 to 3 minutes or until smooth. Chill about 30 minutes.

GLAZE:

2 squares unsweetened chocolate   1 T. butter

Melt chocolate and butter in a small saucepan over low heat, stirring until smooth.

Tami Bowman
Gooseberry Patch

CREAM CHEESE BAR COOKIES

Coconut is a flavorful surprise in these creamy bar cookies!

2¼ c. all-purpose flour, divided
1 c. butter, softened
½ c. sugar
½ c. cornstarch
4 eggs
16-oz. pkg. brown sugar

½ t. baking powder
2 t. vanilla extract
½ c. chopped walnuts
½ c. sweetened flaked
   coconut
Cream Cheese Topping

Combine 2 cups flour, butter, ½ cup sugar and cornstarch with a pastry blender or 2 forks until mixture resembles fine crumbs. Press mixture evenly into an ungreased jelly-roll pan; bake at 350 degrees for 18 minutes.

Beat eggs, brown sugar, remaining ¼ cup flour, baking powder and vanilla at medium speed with an electric mixer until blended; stir in walnuts and coconut. Spread on top of crust.

Bake at 350 degrees for 30 minutes or until set. Let cool in pan on a wire rack; spread with Cream Cheese Topping. Cut into bars. Makes 3½ to 4 dozen.

CREAM CHEESE TOPPING:

8-oz. pkg. cream cheese, softened
½ c. butter, softened

1 t. vanilla extract
16-oz. pkg. powdered sugar

Beat first 3 ingredients at medium speed with an electric mixer until creamy; gradually add sugar, beating until blended. Makes 3½ cups.

Amy Prather
Longview, WA

"My mother-in-law always made these delicious cookies... now I'm carrying on the tradition."

Amy

LEMON-OATMEAL BARS

The zest of two fruits adds extra flavor to these oatmeal bars. Zest each fruit before juicing it by pulling a zester across or down the fruit's rind or by rubbing the fruit against a fine grater. Only remove each fruit's colored skin, not the bitter white part.

1 c. butter, softened
1 c. sugar
2 c. all-purpose flour
1¼ c. long-cooking oats,
   uncooked

zest and juice of 2 lemons
zest and juice of 1 orange
14-oz. can sweetened condensed
   milk

Beat butter and sugar at medium speed with an electric mixer until creamy. Add flour and oats, stirring to make a crumbly dough. Press two-thirds of dough into a greased 13"x9" baking pan; set aside. Stir zests and juices into condensed milk; spread evenly over dough in pan. Sprinkle remaining dough over top. Bake at 350 degrees for 30 to 35 minutes or until golden. Cool completely on a wire rack; cut into squares to serve. Makes 2½ to 3 dozen.

Carrie Kiiskila
Racine, WI

recipe place card

Here's a cookie swap table tent with a holiday feel…jot each cookie's name on a piece of cardstock, then tuck each card into a pinecone.

AUNT MARY'S PRALINE PECANS

Aunt Mary had the right idea when she passed down this recipe for quick & easy pralines…they're made in the microwave!

2 c. sugar
1 c. brown sugar, packed
1 c. evaporated milk
2 c. chopped pecans

2 T. butter
1 t. vanilla extract
⅛ t. salt

Combine sugars and evaporated milk in a 4-quart microwave-safe glass measuring cup. Microwave on high for 6 minutes; stir well. Add nuts, butter, vanilla and salt; microwave on high 6 more minutes. Stir until thickened. Working rapidly, drop by heaping teaspoonfuls onto wax paper; let cool. Makes about 3 dozen.

Sandy White
Elmer, LA

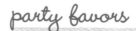

party favors

Package treats, such as candied nuts, fudge, almond brittle, cookies or brownies, in airtight containers and then slip them into gift bags tied with ribbon or raffia. Set them in a basket by your door so there will always be a treat waiting for guests to take home.

ROCKY ROAD-PEANUT BUTTER CANDY CUPS

"Rocky road" gets its name from the combination of chocolate, miniature marshmallows and nuts.

11-oz. pkg. peanut butter and milk
    chocolate chips
2 T. creamy peanut butter
1 c. crispy rice cereal

1 c. miniature marshmallows
3/4 c. unsalted roasted peanuts,
    chopped

Microwave peanut butter and milk chocolate chips in a large glass bowl on high for one to 2 minutes or until melted, stirring every 30 seconds. Stir in peanut butter until well blended.

Stir in rice cereal, miniature marshmallows and chopped peanuts. Spoon mixture by heaping tablespoonfuls evenly into miniature paper candy cups. Chill one hour or until firm. Makes about 3 dozen.

← Copy & attach!

Nothing's Better Than home♥made

...something sweet... ...a bake sale treat

COLA CANDY

Substitute your favorite dark soft drink in the candy and frosting.

3½ c. vanilla wafer crumbs
2 c. powdered sugar
1 c. chopped pecans

½ c. cola
2 T. butter, melted
Cola Frosting

Stir together first 5 ingredients; shape mixture into one-inch balls. Cover and chill at least 30 minutes.

Dip balls in Cola Frosting; chill until ready to serve. Makes 2 dozen.

COLA FROSTING:

¾ c. powdered sugar
⅓ c. cola

¼ c. butter, softened
¼ t. vanilla extract

Stir together all ingredients in a small bowl. Makes one cup.

chocolate cutouts

Mini cookie cutters are just the right size to make chocolate cutouts. Pour melted semi-sweet chocolate onto wax paper-lined cookie sheets and spread to ⅛-inch thickness. Refrigerate until firm and then cut shapes with cookie cutters. Remove from wax paper and chill…a sweet garnish on a frosted cake!

CANDY BAR FUDGE

Caramels, peanuts and two kinds of chocolate make up this candylike fudge.

½ c. butter, softened
⅓ c. baking cocoa
¼ c. brown sugar, packed
¼ c. milk
2½ c. powdered sugar
1 t. vanilla extract
30 caramel candies, unwrapped

2 T. water
2 c. unsalted peanuts
½ c. semi-sweet chocolate chips
½ c. milk chocolate chips

"This fudge is more like a candy bar...everyone loves it!"

Susan

Combine first 4 ingredients in a microwave-safe bowl; microwave on high for 3 minutes or until mixture boils, stirring after one minute. Stir in powdered sugar and vanilla; pour into a buttered 8"x8" baking dish and set aside.

Heat caramels and water in another microwave-safe bowl on high 2 minutes or until melted, stirring after one minute; stir in peanuts. Spread over chocolate mixture; set aside.

Microwave chocolate chips in a microwave-safe bowl on high one minute, stirring until melted. Pour evenly over caramel layer. Refrigerate until firm. Cut into squares. Makes 2½ pounds.

Susan Brzozowski
Ellicott City, MD

Master Cookie Mix, page 455

gifts
from the kitchen

There's always a reason for giving, and the best gifts come from the heart or, in our case…the kitchen! For your next gift-giving occasion, tie up bags of Angie's Chai Tea Mix (page 426), can some fresh Pear Honey (page 433) or whip up some White Chocolate Fudge (page 454). These and our other selections of homemade treats will be welcomed by all!

ANGIE'S CHAI TEA MIX

This Indian tea is quickly becoming popular throughout our country. Keep this mix on hand to stir up for soothing moments during your day.

2 1/2 c. powdered sugar
1 c. instant tea mix
1 c. powdered milk
1 c. powdered non-dairy creamer
1/2 c. vanilla-flavored powdered
   non-dairy creamer

1 1/2 t. pumpkin pie spice
1/2 t. ground ginger
1/2 t. cinnamon
1/2 t. ground cardamom
1/4 t. ground cloves

   Combine all ingredients in a large bowl; store in an airtight container. Attach gift tag with instructions. Makes 5 cups.

Angie Reedy
Mackinaw, IL

Instructions:
   Add 1/3 cup tea mix to 1/2 cup boiling water in a mug; stir well. Makes one serving.

← Copy & attach!

Chai Tea Mix

Instructions:

Add 1/3 cup tea mix to 1/2 cup boiling water in a mug. Makes 1 serving.

HOMEMADE LEMONADE MIX

This summertime favorite is perfect year-round.

3 c. sugar   3 c. lemon juice
1 c. boiling water   2 T. lemon zest

Combine sugar and water in a stockpot, stirring until sugar dissolves; cool. Add lemon juice and zest; mix well. Cover and refrigerate. Use mix within one week. Attach gift tag with instructions. Makes about 6 cups.

Instructions:

Combine ⅓ cup lemonade mix with ¾ cup cold water; stir well. Makes one serving.

← Copy & attach!

Homemade Lemonade Mix

Combine ⅓ cup lemonade mix with ¾ cup cold water; stir well.

Makes 1 serving.

Peppermint
Coffee
Mix

PEPPERMINT COFFEE MIX

Tie chocolate-coated Candy Cane Stirrers onto the bags of coffee mix for an extra chocolatey treat.

1 1/3 c. sugar
1 c. powdered non-dairy creamer
1 c. instant coffee granules

1/2 c. baking cocoa
1/2 c. peppermint candy, crushed
Candy Cane Stirrers

Combine first 4 ingredients in a large bowl. Place in an airtight container; top with crushed candy. Give with Candy Cane Stirrers and attach instructions. Makes about 4 cups.

CANDY CANE STIRRERS:

A handy stirrer hangs right on the edge of a cocoa mug!

6-oz. pkg. semi-sweet chocolate chips, divided

50 mini peppermint candy canes

Microwave 3/4 cup chocolate chips in a small microwave-safe bowl on low (50%) for 1 1/2 minutes. Stir chocolate until smooth; microwave 20 more seconds, if necessary. Add remaining chocolate and stir until smooth. Set bowl in a pan of hot water to keep chocolate soft, making sure water does not mix with chocolate.

Dip straight end of each candy cane into chocolate to coat; place on wax paper to cool. Makes 50.

Instructions:

Combine 2 tablespoons mix with 1/2 cup boiling water; mix well. Makes one serving.

EASIEST CHEESE BALL

Make 'em mini...just roll into 6 small balls, wrap individually and give with some crackers.

2 (8-oz.) pkgs. cream cheese,
    softened
2 (8-oz.) pkgs. shredded sharp
    Cheddar cheese

1-oz. pkg. ranch dressing mix
¼ t. hot pepper sauce
10-oz. pkg. chopped pecans

Combine cream cheese, Cheddar cheese, dressing mix and hot pepper sauce; form into one large ball. Roll ball in chopped pecans to cover. Refrigerate overnight before serving. Serves 12.

a special friend

I have a special friend who's always done favors for me for no special reason. When we met, we were both stay-at-home moms. I went back to work when my oldest child entered college and, needless to say, I didn't have the time to put into meal preparation as I had before.

One hectic night, my friend showed up on my doorstep. There was no special occasion...she just said she was thinking about me. Though her company was always welcome, she'd brought along a freshly baked pie, my family's favorite! Now that's a special friend.

Judy Bozarth
Fort Wayne, IN

CREAMY ARTICHOKE SPREAD

This spread is always a party pleaser. Be sure to make extra for your hostess!

2 (8-oz.) pkgs. cream cheese,
   softened
2 t. garlic, chopped
1 1/2 t. salt
14-oz. can artichoke hearts, drained
   and chopped

1/3 c. sliced black olives
7 green onions, chopped
6 T. sun-dried tomatoes,
   chopped
1/4 c. fresh parsley, chopped
1 t. fresh chives, chopped

Combine cream cheese, garlic and salt in a medium bowl; stir in artichoke hearts and olives. Add green onions and remaining ingredients, stirring gently. Refrigerate overnight. Serves 6.

creative containers

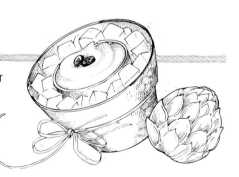

Line a small flowerpot with parchment paper and fill with Creamy Artichoke Spread. Place it in a larger flowerpot and fill the gap with ice cubes…the spread will stay cold while you transport it to a friend or neighbor.

PEAR HONEY

Most people with pear trees will gladly share their harvests.
Return the favor with a jar of this sweet honey.

8 lbs. pears, cored and peeled
6 lbs. sugar
1 T. butter

20-oz. can crushed pineapple
16 (½-pt.) canning jars and lids,
    sterilized

Grate pears; place in a large heavy saucepan. Add sugar and butter; mix well. Bring to a boil; boil gently 2 hours. Stir in pineapple; boil 5 more minutes. Spoon into hot sterilized jars, leaving ¼-inch headspace. Remove air bubbles; wipe jar rims. Cover at once with metal lids and screw on bands. Process in a boiling water bath 10 minutes; set jars on a towel to cool. Makes 16 jars.

Ann Rennier
Columbia, MO

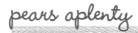

pears aplenty

With 16 jars of Pear Honey, you'll have plenty for gifts all year! Pack a gift basket with fresh pears, a jar or two of honey, and some homemade biscuits.

"Freezer jams are a snap to make and taste amazing!"

Connie

STRAWBERRY FREEZER JAM

Spread this jam over biscuits or a toasted slice of Farmhouse Honey-Wheat Bread (page 379) for your morning breakfast. If the jam is frozen, let it thaw overnight in your refrigerator and stir it before serving.

2 c. strawberries, hulled and crushed
4 c. sugar
1³/₄-oz. pkg. powdered pectin

³/₄ c. water
5 (¹/₂-pt.) freezer-safe airtight plastic containers, sterilized

Combine strawberries and sugar in a large mixing bowl; set aside.

Whisk together pectin and water in a small saucepan; bring to a boil. Boil, stirring constantly, one minute; remove from heat. Pour pectin mixture over strawberry mixture; stir until sugar dissolves, about 3 minutes.

Spoon into containers, leaving ¹/₂-inch headspace and secure lids. Set aside in refrigerator until set, up to 24 hours. Freeze up to one year. Makes 5 containers.

Connie Bryant
Topeka, KS

CHAMPAGNE MUSTARD

This tasty gift is sure to delight any hostess when it's packed along with seasoned toasts or crunchy bagel chips.

²/₃ c. dry mustard
²/₃ c. champagne vinegar
3 eggs

³/₄ c. sugar
¹/₂ t. dried tarragon or dried basil

Whisk together mustard and vinegar; whisk in eggs and sugar. Pour into a heavy saucepan; cook, stirring constantly, until thickened. Remove from heat; stir in tarragon or basil. Spoon into an airtight container. Refrigerate up to one week. Makes about 2 cups.

celebrate!

Use a paint marker to write "Happy New Year" on an ice bucket filled with a jar of Champagne Mustard, breadsticks for dipping, noisemakers and confetti…a ready-made celebration!

ALL-PASTA SAUCE

One taste of this homemade pasta sauce and you won't be tempted to use the store-bought sauce again! Use in place of tomato or spaghetti sauce all year long.

11 lbs. tomatoes, chopped
2 green peppers, chopped
1 1/2 lbs. onions, chopped
24-oz. can tomato paste
1 c. vegetable oil
3/4 c. sugar
1/4 c. canning salt
2 cloves garlic, chopped

2 bay leaves
1 1/2 T. dried basil
1 T. dried parsley
1/2 T. dried oregano
4 (1-qt.) canning jars and lids,
   sterilized
1/4 c. balsamic vinegar, divided

Process tomatoes, green peppers and onions in batches in a blender; add to a large stockpot. Bring to a boil; boil gently for one hour. Stir in tomato paste and next 8 ingredients; boil one more hour. Remove and discard bay leaves.

Spoon into hot sterilized jars, leaving 1/2-inch headspace. Add one tablespoon balsamic vinegar to each jar. Remove air bubbles; wipe jar rims. Cover at once with metal lids and screw on bands. Process in a boiling water bath 20 minutes; set jars on a towel to cool. Makes 4 jars.

Vickie
Gooseberry Patch

give a pail of pasta!

Fill an enamelware pail with a jar of homemade pasta sauce, a package of noodles, and a loaf of freshly baked bread for gift giving any time of year.

BEST-DAD-IN-THE-LAND BARBECUE RUB

Rub about ⅓ cup of this mix onto beef brisket at least 2 hours before cooking…an easy mix to add to a Father's Day grilling gift.

16-oz. bottle seasoned salt
1 c. brown sugar, packed
⅔ c. chili powder
¼ c. paprika
2 T. garlic salt
1½ T. pepper

2 t. dry mustard
1 t. ground ginger
1 t. nutmeg
1 t. ground cloves
1 t. mesquite-flavored
    seasoning mix

Combine all ingredients in a mixing bowl; stir well. Store in an airtight container in a dry, cool place for up to 6 weeks. Makes about 3 cups.

happy father's day!

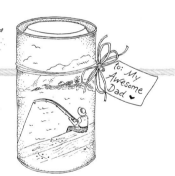

Pick up a photo tube at any camera shop and slip this spicy barbecue rub into it. Make a black & white photocopy of one of Dad's favorite photos, scale it to fit the tube and secure with spray adhesive. He'll love it!

BACKYARD-BARBECUE MANGO CHUTNEY

Add this chutney to your menu for your next outdoor barbecue party.
It's so tasty on chicken, pork chops and even fish!

6 c. sugar
6 c. brown sugar, packed
3 c. white vinegar
1½ T. allspice
2 t. cinnamon
2 t. ground ginger
2 t. nutmeg
1½ t. ground cloves
1 t. kosher salt
4 red hot chili peppers, seeded and
   chopped

2 onions, chopped
3 cloves garlic, chopped
1 c. golden raisins
1 c. raisins
16 c. mangoes, peeled
   and sliced
½ c. sliced almonds
4 (1-qt.) canning jars and lids,
   sterilized

    Combine first 10 ingredients in a large saucepan; bring to a boil and boil 30 minutes. Add onions, garlic, golden raisins and raisins; boil 30 more minutes. Reduce heat; stir in mangoes and almonds. Simmer 30 minutes; pour into jars, leaving ½-inch headspace. Remove air bubbles; wipe jar rims. Cover at once with metal lids and screw on bands. Store in refrigerator. Makes 4 jars.

for the grilling enthusiast

    A jar of fresh Backyard-Barbecue Mango Chutney makes a nice gift for a griller…add tongs, an oven mitt and a grill brush.

CARAMEL APPLES

It's just not October without these chewy, sweet treats! Keep 'em around for snacks or hand them out as party favors during a fall festival.

2 (14-oz.) pkgs. caramels, unwrapped
1 ½ t. vanilla extract
2 T. water

9 wooden craft sticks
9 tart apples, washed and patted dry

Combine caramels, vanilla and water in a heavy saucepan; cook, stirring constantly, over medium heat until caramels melt. Cool slightly.

Insert craft sticks into apples; dip apples in caramel mixture. Place on a buttered, wax paper-lined baking sheet; refrigerate until firm. Makes 9.

fall treats

After wrapping each apple in cellophane, nestle it inside a small orange gift sack. Add a pumpkin face to the sack using a black permanent marker, then gather the sack around the stick and tie on green curling ribbon.

FROSTED PECANS

Candied pecans are a welcome treat any time of year. Make someone's day with a batch of these goodies.

1 ½ c. sugar
½ c. sour cream

1 ½ t. vanilla extract
1 lb. pecan pieces

Combine sugar and sour cream in a large saucepan; bring to a boil over medium heat and simmer, stirring constantly, 5 minutes. Add vanilla and pecans; stir until pecans are well coated.

Spread on wax paper; break into pieces when cool. Store in an airtight container. Makes 4 to 5 cups.

Lisa Johnson
Hallsville, TX

SUGARED NUTS

Caution! These could be addictive!

1 egg white
½ c. sugar
½ t. cinnamon

2 11-oz. cans lightly salted
mixed nuts

Beat egg white until foamy. Stir in sugar, cinnamon and nuts, coating nuts well. Spread on a greased 15"x10" jelly-roll pan. Bake at 225 degrees for one hour, stirring every 15 minutes. Remove from oven. Cool. Store in an airtight container. Makes about 6 cups.

CHOCOLATE-PEANUT POPCORN

Satisfy your savory & sweet cravings with a batch of this popcorn…all you need with this is a good movie!

12 c. popped popcorn or 2.9-oz. bag
    microwave popcorn, popped
2¼ c. salted peanuts

1¾ c. milk chocolate chips
½ c. corn syrup
¼ c. butter

   Combine popcorn and nuts in a lightly greased roasting pan; set aside. Combine chocolate chips, corn syrup and butter in a heavy saucepan; cook, stirring constantly, until chips and butter melt. Bring mixture to a boil; pour over popcorn mixture, tossing well to coat.

   Bake at 300 degrees for 30 minutes, stirring every 10 minutes. Remove from oven; stir and allow to cool slightly in pan. Remove popcorn to a baking sheet lined with lightly greased wax paper to cool completely. Store in an airtight container. Makes 11 cups.

sweet little favors

   Package this sweet & crunchy popcorn treat by the cupful in cellophane gift bags and tie with ribbon to match the season.

PATCHWORK SOUP MIX

Add a bag of Herbed Oyster Crackers to go along with this hearty soup mix. The pair offers just the right combination for chasing the chill away!

1/3 c. dried yellow split peas
1/3 c. dried green split peas
1/3 c. dried lima beans
1/3 c. dried pinto beans
1/3 c. dried kidney beans
1/3 c. dried Great Northern beans
1/4 c. dried minced onion

1 T. chicken bouillon granules
1/4 t. ground cumin
1/4 t. garlic powder
1/4 t. pepper
1/8 t. dried oregano
Herbed Oyster Crackers

Combine all ingredients except crackers in an airtight container. Give with Herbed Oyster Crackers and attach instructions. Makes 2 cups.

HERBED OYSTER CRACKERS:

2 (10-oz.) pkgs. oyster crackers
1 c. vegetable oil
1 1/2 T. ranch dressing mix

1 t. garlic salt
1 t. lemon-pepper seasoning
1 t. dried dill weed

Toss together crackers and oil until completely coated. Add dressing mix and remaining 3 ingredients, stirring well. Spread in a single layer on an ungreased baking sheet; bake at 250 degrees for 10 minutes. Store in an airtight container. Makes 10 cups.

Instructions:

Combine 8 cups water and soup mix in a large stockpot; bring to a boil. Cover, remove from heat and let sit one hour.

Return pan to heat; stir in 2 cups chopped carrots and 1 1/2 cups chopped celery. Add 1 1/2 pounds smoked ham hock; bring to a boil. Cover, reduce heat and simmer 2 hours or until beans are tender; skim fat as necessary. Remove ham hock from soup; remove meat from bone. Chop meat and return to soup. Stir in 1/4 teaspoon pepper. Heat thoroughly and serve. Serves 10.

PAINTED DESERT CHILI IN A JAR

*The painted desert effect comes from the rippled appearance, like sand art.
Bring out the beautiful colors by spooning each ingredient around the edges
of the jar, then filling the center.*

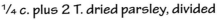

¼ c. plus 2 T. dried parsley, divided
¼ c. dried minced garlic, divided
1.25-oz. pkg. taco seasoning mix,
   divided
2 T. dried minced onion
2 T. ground cumin
2 T. paprika

2 T. white cornmeal
2 T. chili powder
1 c. dried pinto beans
¼ c. dried navy beans
¼ c. dried black beans
1 c. dried kidney beans

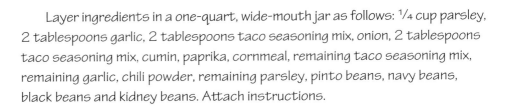

Layer ingredients in a one-quart, wide-mouth jar as follows: ¼ cup parsley,
2 tablespoons garlic, 2 tablespoons taco seasoning mix, onion, 2 tablespoons
taco seasoning mix, cumin, paprika, cornmeal, remaining taco seasoning mix,
remaining garlic, chili powder, remaining parsley, pinto beans, navy beans,
black beans and kidney beans. Attach instructions.

Instructions:

Cook 2 pounds ground beef in a 12-quart stockpot, stirring until beef
crumbles and is no longer pink; drain. Add contents of jar, ¾ cup chopped
onion, 4 (14½-ounce) cans diced tomatoes, 12-ounce can tomato paste,
½ cup cider vinegar, ½ cup packed brown sugar, 46-ounce bottle tomato juice
and 10 cups water to ground beef in stockpot. Bring to a boil; reduce heat and
simmer, partially covered, 2½ to 3 hours, stirring occasionally. Add salt and
pepper to taste. Serves 12.

Amy Conrad
Enid, OK

NUTTY GINGER RICE MIX

Sometimes thoughtful notes are the best way to keep in touch. This cinnamony rice mix is a sweet addition tucked into a gift box with card-making supplies. See our suggestions for making the box below the recipe.

1 c. long-grain rice, uncooked
½ c. roasted peanuts
1 t. cinnamon

1 t. ground ginger
1 cube chicken bouillon,
   crumbled

Combine all ingredients in a medium bowl; place in an airtight container. Seal and attach instructions. Makes 1½ cups.

Instructions:

Combine 2 cups water, ¼ cup butter and ¼ cup honey in a saucepan; bring to a boil. Reduce heat; add rice mix, cover and simmer 20 minutes. Serves 6.

made by hand

Fill a mini box with all the essentials for making handmade cards…scraps of vintage floral fabrics, buttons, colorful card stock, ribbon, a glue stick, envelopes and stamps. Tie up this pretty package with a ribbon threaded through a decorative buckle or brooch.

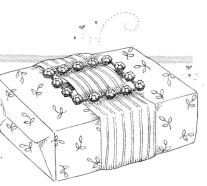

Cappuccino
Waffle
Mix

CAPPUCCINO WAFFLE MIX WITH COFFEE SYRUP

Give this mix along with a jar of Coffee Syrup. They'll be a welcome eye-opener for breakfast!

1 ¹/₃ c. all-purpose flour
¹/₃ c. powdered milk
¹/₃ c. powdered non-dairy creamer
2 t. baking powder

¹/₂ t. salt
2 T. instant coffee granules
¹/₂ t. cinnamon
Coffee Syrup

Combine first 5 ingredients in a medium bowl. Combine coffee granules and cinnamon in a small bowl. Spoon half of flour mixture into a pint-size jar.

Layer coffee mixture over flour mixture. Spoon remaining flour mixture over coffee mixture. Seal container. Give with Coffee Syrup and attach instructions. Makes 2 cups.

COFFEE SYRUP:

1 c. brewed coffee

2 c. sugar

Combine both ingredients in a heavy saucepan; cook over medium-high heat, stirring constantly, until sugar dissolves. Bring to a boil, without stirring; boil 2 minutes. Remove from heat; cool to room temperature. Store in an airtight container in the refrigerator. Makes 1 ³/₄ cups.

Instructions:

Beat ¹/₂ cup softened butter, one cup sugar and 1 ¹/₂ teaspoons vanilla extract at medium speed with an electric mixer until creamy. Gradually blend butter mixture into waffle mix with a pastry blender or 2 forks until crumbly. Place mixture in a mixing bowl; add ³/₄ cup water and 2 eggs, stirring until just combined. Bake according to waffle iron manufacturer's directions. Serve with warm Coffee Syrup. Makes 5 to 6 waffles.

TAKE-A-BREAK MOCHA MUFFIN MIX

Surprise a good friend with a special gift of this muffin mix...just because.

1¾ c. all-purpose flour
¾ c. plus 1 T. sugar, divided
2 T. plus ½ t. baking cocoa, divided
2½ t. baking powder

2 t. instant coffee granules
½ t. salt
½ c. mini chocolate chips

Stir together flour, ¾ cup sugar, 2 tablespoons baking cocoa, baking powder, coffee granules and salt. Spoon into a one-quart jar; set aside. Place chocolate chips in a small plastic zipping bag; seal and place on top of mix. Place remaining one tablespoon sugar and remaining ½ teaspoon cocoa in a mini plastic zipping bag; place in jar. Secure lid; attach instructions. Makes 3 cups.

Instructions:

Combine muffin mix with one cup milk, ½ cup melted butter, one beaten egg and one teaspoon vanilla extract; mix until just moistened. Fold in chocolate chips; spoon equally into 12 greased or paper-lined muffin cups. Sprinkle with sugar-cocoa mixture in small packet; bake at 375 degrees for 15 to 18 minutes. Cool on a wire rack. Makes one dozen.

box of love

Tell a best friend no one else can fill her shoes! Cover the lid of a plain shoe box with pictures of shoes cut from magazines or catalogs. Fill the box with bags of the muffin mix, chocolate chips and the sugar-cocoa topping; wrap the box with pretty cotton string.

TERRIFIC TRUFFLE CAKE MIX

Show appreciation for the friends next door by giving them this chocolatey mix on Good Neighbor Day. It's always the fourth Sunday in September.

3 c. all-purpose flour
3 c. sugar
1/2 c. baking cocoa

1 t. baking soda
1/2 t. vanilla powder

Combine all ingredients; place in a plastic zipping bag. Attach instructions. Makes 6 1/2 cups.

Instructions:

Beat ¾ cup softened butter at medium speed with an electric mixer until creamy; add 5 eggs, one at a time, mixing well after each addition. Add one cup milk; mix well. Add cake mix; beat 3 minutes. Pour into a greased 9-cup Bundt® pan; bake at 325 degrees for 60 to 70 minutes or until a wooden pick inserted in center comes out clean. Cool in pan 25 minutes on a wire rack; remove from pan and cool completely on wire rack. Serves 15 to 18.

good neighbor surprise

Make a cone shape from pretty scrapbook paper. Glue in place. Punch a hole in each side of the cone and slide ribbon or rickrack through to make a handle; tie each end to secure. Place a bag filled with your favorite goodies into the cone. Slipped over a doorknob, it's sure to be a welcome Good Neighbor Day surprise!

BROWNIES BAKED IN A JAR

Slide these brownies out of their jars, slice and enjoy with scoops of your favorite ice cream and chocolate sauce. Be sure to use widemouthed jars, or the brownies can't slide out!

1 c. all-purpose flour
1 c. sugar
1/2 t. baking soda
1/4 t. cinnamon
1/3 c. butter, softened
1/4 c. water

1/4 c. buttermilk, room temperature
3 T. baking cocoa
1/2 t. vanilla extract
1 egg, beaten
3 (1-pt.) widemouthed canning jars
   and lids, sterilized

Combine first 4 ingredients in a medium bowl. Beat butter at medium speed with an electric mixer until creamy; add water and next 4 ingredients, beating until combined. Add flour mixture, mixing until just blended. Divide batter equally among buttered jars; wipe rims. Each jar should be slightly less than half full.

Place jars on a jelly-roll pan in center of oven; bake, uncovered, at 325 degrees for 40 minutes. Wipe rims; cover with metal lids and screw on bands. Set aside to cool. Makes 3 pints.

an ooey-gooey treat

Give Brownies Baked in a Jar with whimsical sundae dishes, colorful spoons and a sampling of ice-cream toppings...a treat to beat the summer heat!

WHITE CHOCOLATE FUDGE

No candy thermometer needed for this quick fudge! You can make it in less than 25 minutes.

6 oz. premium white chocolate, chopped
½ (8-oz.) pkg. cream cheese, softened

3 c. sifted powdered sugar
½ t. vanilla extract
1 c. chopped pecans
25 pecan halves

Place white chocolate in top of a double boiler; bring water to a boil. Reduce heat to low; cook until white chocolate melts, stirring occasionally. Remove from heat.

Beat cream cheese at high speed with an electric mixer until creamy. Gradually add sugar; beat at medium speed until smooth. Stir in melted white chocolate and vanilla; beat well. Stir in chopped pecans.

Press mixture into a lightly buttered 8"x8" pan. Cover and chill. Cut into squares. Gently press a pecan half on each square of fudge. Store in an airtight container in the refrigerator. Makes 25 squares (1½ pounds).

cookie cutter trick

Purchase cookie cutters in desired shapes and make several batches of fudge in pans the depth of the cookie cutters. Then cut out the fudge, leaving it inside the cutters; decorate the fudge with nuts, cherries or peppermints, if desired, and wrap the fudge, cutter and all, in cellophane gift bags tied with ribbon.

MASTER COOKIE MIX

(pictured on page 424)

Attach a gift card with recipes for Coconut Bites and Best Chocolate Chip Cookies…this mix makes both flavors of cookies!

5 c. all-purpose flour
3¾ c. sugar
2 T. baking powder

1½ t. salt
1½ c. plus 2 T. butter,
    softened

Combine flour, sugar, baking powder and salt in a large bowl. Cut in butter with a pastry blender or 2 forks until mixture resembles coarse crumbs. Store in an airtight container in the refrigerator. Attach recipes. Makes 11½ cups.

COCONUT BITES:

3 c. Master Cookie Mix
2 eggs
1 T. lemon zest
1 c. sweetened flaked coconut

¾ c. chopped pecans
½ c. red candied cherries,
    chopped
Garnish: sugar

Beat cookie mix, eggs and lemon zest at medium speed with an electric mixer until combined; stir in coconut, pecans and cherries. Spread mixture in a well-greased 13"x9" baking pan. Bake at 350 degrees for 20 to 25 minutes or until center springs back when lightly pressed. Sprinkle with sugar while warm, if desired; cool and cut into squares. Makes 4 dozen.

BEST CHOCOLATE CHIP COOKIES:

2 c. Master Cookie Mix
½ c. brown sugar, packed
1 egg

1 t. vanilla extract
1 c. semi-sweet chocolate chips
½ c. chopped walnuts

Beat cookie mix, brown sugar, egg and vanilla at medium speed with an electric mixer until combined; stir in chocolate chips and nuts. Drop by rounded teaspoonfuls onto greased baking sheets. Bake at 375 degrees for 12 to 15 minutes or until golden; cool on wire racks. Makes 3 dozen.

HAPPY BIRTHDAY COOKIES

With alphabet cookie cutters, you can spell out a greeting
or a friend's name for a birthday surprise!

¾ c. butter, softened	4 c. all-purpose flour
1 c. powdered sugar	⅛ t. salt
1 egg	Icing
1½ t. almond extract	colored sprinkles

Beat butter and sugar at medium speed with an electric mixer until creamy. Add egg and almond extract; beat until smooth. Combine flour and salt in a separate bowl; add to butter mixture, stirring until a soft dough forms. Divide dough in half; wrap in plastic wrap and chill one hour.

Roll dough to ¼-inch thickness on a lightly floured surface. Use alphabet cookie cutters to cut out "happy birthday" cookies; place on greased baking sheets. Bake at 350 degrees for 8 to 10 minutes; cool on wire racks with wax paper underneath racks. Spoon Icing over letters and top with decorator sugar or colored sprinkles. Makes 3 to 5 sets of cookies.

ICING:

¼ c. water	1¼ t. almond extract
2 T. corn syrup	2 to 3 t. whipping cream
4 c. powdered sugar	

Combine water and corn syrup in a heavy saucepan. Add sugar, stirring until well blended; use a pastry brush to scrape down any sugar on sides of pan. Cook over low to medium heat until a candy thermometer registers 100 degrees; remove from heat. Stir in almond extract and 2 teaspoons cream; cool 5 minutes. Add enough remaining cream to make desired consistency. Makes about one cup.

MENUS *of spring*

FAMILY NIGHT

serves 8 to 10

Momma's Divine Divan
(page 261)

*Grandma Lucy's Corn
Fritters (page 299)

Cream Cheese Bar Cookies
(page 417)

LUNCH WITH FRIENDS

serves 3 to 4

Chicken, Artichoke &
Rice Salad (page 348)

Raspberry Scones
(page 363)

Glazed Strawberry Tart
(page 405)

*Double recipe.

CELEBRATE SPRING!

serves 12

COMPANY'S COMING

serves 4

MENUS *of summer*

FROM THE GARDEN

serves 4 to 6

*Garlic & Lemon Roasted Chicken
(page 208)*

*Green Bean Salad with Feta
(page 352)*

SUMMERTIME CELEBRATION

serves 8

**Lime & Ginger Grilled Salmon
(page 205)*

Company Rice (page 309)

*Green Beans Amandine
(page 289)*

*Double recipe.

SOUTHERN SUPPER

serves 4

Dixie Fried Chicken (page 207)

Squash Casserole (page 313)

Roasted Corn with Rosemary Butter (page 297)

Red Velvet Cake (page 395)

FIESTA TIME!

serves 6

Chicken Burritos (page 260)

Cuban Black Beans (page 288)

Garden-Fresh Salsa (page 177)

**Mexican Coffee (page 162)

***Quadruple recipe.*

MENUS *of fall*

COZY COMFORT FOOD

serves 6

Maple-Curry Pork Roast
(page 217)

Mom's Red Cabbage
(page 296)

Creamed Peas (page 304)

GAME-DAY HUDDLE

serves 6 to 8

The Cheesy Bowl (page 183)

Blue-Ribbon Chicken Fingers
(page 194)

Celebration Snack Mix
(page 170)

Peanut Butter Jumbos
(page 414)

SANDWICH NIGHT

serves 8

Italian Sausage Sandwiches
(page 336)

Ice Box Brownies
(page 415)

SLOW-COOKED SUPPER

serves 6

Slow-Cooker Beef Stroganoff
(page 236)

Peppery Biscuit Sticks
(page 358)

MENUS *of winter*

CHILI NIGHT

serves 6

Creamy White Chili
(page 325)

Fiesta Cornbread
(page 359)

EASY HOLIDAY DINNER

serves 6

Pepper-Crusted Roast Beef
(page 240)

Risotto in the Microwave
(page 308)

Broccoli Parmesan (page 285)

Honey-Crunch Pecan Pie
(page 399)

WINTER
WARM-UP

serves 4 to 6

Chicken Stew with Biscuits
(page 328)

White Texas Sheet Cake
(page 394)

BREAKFAST FOR
SUPPER

serves 6

Country-Style Supper Skillet
(page 244)

Buttermilk Doughnuts
(page 367)

HANDY TIPS *for entertaining*

STRESS-FREE PARTY PLANNING

Make entertaining a breeze with our quick & easy suggestions for no-fuss events.

• **Plan ahead.** Anything that can be done before the party will make things much easier on the day of the party. Nothing makes guests feel more at ease than a relaxed hostess.

• **Create simple centerpieces.** Oh-so simple… the prettiest centerpieces can be created in just minutes. Candles tucked inside a Mason jar and flowers inside an ironstone pitcher are such easy-to-create ideas. Check out other fun suggestions in the tip box on the facing page.

• **Follow an easy menu plan.** Beginning on page 458, we've given you lots of ideas for menus, no matter what the season. Or create your own menus using the recipes within this book. Be creative…

host a lunch, a family reunion or an afternoon plant swap and brunch with girlfriends.

• **Remember the little touches.** Fresh flowers and scented candles always add a nice feel in any room of your house.

• **Keep it simple and have fun!** You can still host a wonderful get-together and not spend a lot of time in the kitchen. See our tips on the facing page for inspiring no-cook appetizers.

• **In the unlikely event of leftovers…**our Country Friends© like to send each guest home with a paper tote bag that has a pinwheel tied to the handle and a little "thank you" surprise inside.

countdown to party time

Follow this time line to make entertaining a breeze.

Four to six weeks ahead:
• Set the date and time.
• Make your guest list.
• Plan your menu.
• Select invitations (if using them).

Three weeks ahead:
• Mail holiday invitations. For informal events, mailing invitations two weeks in advance is fine.

One to two weeks ahead:
• Check your supply of chairs, serving dishes, flatware and glassware.
• Make your grocery list; shop for nonperishables.
• Add welcome touches to the front porch.

no-cook appetizers

• Dress up a softened block of cream cheese with colorful hot pepper jelly.

• Serve salsa and chips.

• Pick up chicken fingers from the deli or your favorite restaurant and serve with honey mustard, ranch, honey or sweet & sour sauce.

• Offer different selections of cheese and bread and arrange on a plate or in a basket. Add grapes, apples and other fruits to serve alongside the cheese.

sweetie-pie Centerpieces:

SPRAY-PAINT A VINE CORNUCOPIA BRIGHT PINK & SPILL ALL KINDS OF CANDIES OUT OF IT, RIGHT DOWN THE CENTER OF THE TABLE — REALLY LOAD IT UP!

MAKE A HUGE NEST OF CURLING RIBBONS & PUT A GIANT FISHBOWL FULL OF BRIGHT JAWBREAKERS RIGHT IN THE MIDDLE OF THE TABLE.

MAKE AN EASY GUMDROP TOPIARY!

SUPPLIES:
• CLAY POT - SPRAY-PAINTED WHITE
• STYROFOAM™ BALL & FOAM BLOCK
• DOWEL ROD
• GUMDROPS, HARD CANDIES
• HOT-GLUE GUN

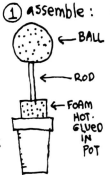

① assemble: ← BALL
← ROD
← FOAM HOT-GLUED IN POT

② NOW HOT-GLUE ALL KINDS OF HARD CANDIES & GUMDROPS ALL OVER THE BALL — COVER THE ENTIRE THING! WORK IN ROWS.

③ WRAP DOWEL ROD WITH LICORICE WHIPS.

④ HOT-GLUE MORE CANDY ON POT.

Two or three days ahead:
• Get out the china, serving dishes and utensils.
• Shop for perishables.
• Tidy up the house.
• Make place cards (if using them).

One day ahead:
• Plan the centerpiece.
• Prepare any make-ahead dishes.
• Chill beverages. Make extra ice.
• Arrange furniture for best seating and so it's easy to move around.

Day of the event:
• Set the table. Arrange the centerpiece.
• Finish preparing the food and arrange on serving dishes.
• Relax and enjoy your party!

Party Planner

Photocopy these pages and use them throughout the year to coordinate menu items for your seasonal celebration, as well as a reminder of who's bringing what.

guests	what they're bringing (appetizer, beverage, bread, main dish, side dish, dessert)	serving pieces needed

Party Guest List

....
....
....
....
....
....
....
....

Pantry List

....
....
....
....
....
....
....

Party To-Do List

....
....
....
....
....
....
....

Family Memories

Remember the best parts of the seasonal celebrations
by jotting down your family's highlights on these pages.

Treasured Traditions

Write your family's favorite holiday traditions on these lines.

Special Activities

List events you attended this year and the ones you want to check out next year.

Favorite Ideas

Clothing & Accessories . . . .

. . . .

. . . .

Gardening . . . .

. . . .

. . . .

. . . .

Gift Giving . . . .

. . . .

. . . .

Gift Wrapping . . . .

. . . .

. . . .

. . . .

Holidays . . . .

. . . .

. . . .

. . . .

Home Decorating . . . .

. . . .

. . . .

. . . .

. . . .

Favorite Recipes

Appetizers & Snacks . . . .

. . . .

Beverages . . . .

. . . .

Breakfast Entrées . . . .

. . . .

Cakes . . . .

. . . .

Casseroles . . . .

. . . .

Condiments . . . .

. . . .

Cookies & Candies . . . .

. . . .

Desserts . . . .

. . . .

Entrées . . . .

. . . .

Food Gifts . . . .

. . . .

Pies & Pastries . . . .

. . . .

Salads & Side Dishes . . . .

. . . .

Soups & Stews . . . .

. . . .

project index

recipe index

METRIC EQUIVALENTS

The recipes that appear in this cookbook use the standard United States method for measuring liquid and dry or solid ingredients (teaspoons, tablespoons, and cups). The information on this chart is provided to help cooks outside the U.S. successfully use these recipes. All equivalents are approximate.

METRIC EQUIVALENTS FOR DIFFERENT TYPES OF INGREDIENTS

A standard cup measure of a dry or solid ingredient will vary in weight depending on the type of ingredient.
A standard cup of liquid is the same volume for any type of liquid. Use the following chart when converting standard cup measures to grams (weight) or milliliters (volume).

Standard Cup	Fine Powder (ex. flour)	Grain (ex. rice)	Granular (ex. sugar)	Liquid Solids (ex. butter)	Liquid (ex. milk)
1	140 g	150 g	190 g	200 g	240 ml
¾	105 g	113 g	143 g	150 g	180 ml
⅔	93 g	100 g	125 g	133 g	160 ml
½	70 g	75 g	95 g	100 g	120 ml
⅓	47 g	50 g	63 g	67 g	80 ml
¼	35 g	38 g	48 g	50 g	60 ml
⅛	18 g	19 g	24 g	25 g	30 ml

USEFUL EQUIVALENTS FOR DRY INGREDIENTS BY WEIGHT

(To convert ounces to grams, multiply the number of ounces by 30.)

1 oz	=	¹⁄₁₆ lb	=	30 g
4 oz	=	¼ lb	=	120 g
8 oz	=	½ lb	=	240 g
12 oz	=	¾ lb	=	360 g
16 oz	=	1 lb	=	480 g

USEFUL EQUIVALENTS FOR LENGTH

(To convert inches to centimeters, multiply the number of inches by 2.5.)

1 in		=	2.5 cm
6 in = ½ ft		=	15 cm
12 in = 1 ft		=	30 cm
36 in = 3 ft = 1 yd		=	90 cm
40 in		= 100 cm	= 1 meter

USEFUL EQUIVALENTS FOR LIQUID INGREDIENTS BY VOLUME

¼ tsp =						1 ml
½ tsp =						2 ml
1 tsp =						5 ml
3 tsp =	1 tbls			= ½ fl oz	=	15 ml
	= 2 tbls	= ⅛ cup		= 1 fl oz	=	30 ml
	= 4 tbls	= ¼ cup		= 2 fl oz	=	60 ml
	= 5⅓ tbls	= ⅓ cup		= 3 fl oz	=	80 ml
	= 8 tbls	= ½ cup		= 4 fl oz	=	120 ml
	= 10⅔ tbls	= ⅔ cup		= 5 fl oz	=	160 ml
	= 12 tbls	= ¾ cup		= 6 fl oz	=	180 ml
	= 16 tbls	= 1 cup		= 8 fl oz	=	240 ml
	= 1 pt	= 2 cups	= 16 fl oz	=	480 ml
	= 1 qt	= 4 cups	= 32 fl oz	=	960 ml
			33 fl oz	= 1000 ml	= 1 liter

USEFUL EQUIVALENTS FOR COOKING/OVEN TEMPERATURES

	Fahrenheit	Celsius	Gas Mark
Freeze Water	32° F	0° C	
Room Temperature	68° F	20° C	
Boil Water	212° F	100° C	
Bake	325° F	160° C	3
	350° F	180° C	4
	375° F	190° C	5
	400° F	200° C	6
	425° F	220° C	7
	450° F	230° C	8
Broil			Grill

Credits

We want to extend a warm thank you to the people who allowed us to photograph some of our projects at their homes: Joan Adams, Sandra Cook, Thomas Hankins, Brenda Hogan, the Kymer family, Beth Morgan, Ellison Poe, Nancy Gunn Porter, Catherine Smith, Becky Thompson, Leighton Weeks and the Westerguard family. We especially want to thank Cindy George for allowing us to photograph our section introductions at her home.

To Chris Olsen, we extend a special word of thanks for creating the beautiful front porch décor shown on pages 8-9, 38-39, 66-67 and 90-91. Chris is a talented landscape designer, and the owner of Horticare Landscape Management Company, Inc., of Little Rock, Arkansas.

Our sincere thanks also goes to The Good Earth Garden Center and Nurseries of Little Rock, Arkansas, for providing many of the beautiful plants shown in our photographs.

We want to especially thank photographers Ken West of The Peerless Group, Jerry R. Davis of Jerry Davis Photography and Andrew Uilkie of Uilkie Photography, all of Little Rock, Arkansas, for their excellent work. Photography stylists Sondra Harrison Daniel, Karen Smart Hall and Charlisa Erwin Parker also deserve a special mention for the high quality of their collaboration with the photographers.

We extend a special word of thanks to Terrece Beesley, who designed the *Cross-Stitched Bouquet* shown on page 33; Mary Ayres, who designed the *Framed Stitched Pieces* and *Embroidered Pillows* shown on page 50; Judy Patterson, who designed the *Pumpkin Pins* shown on page 77; and Kathie Rueger, who designed the *Collector's Shelf* shown on page 92.

We would like to recognize Viking Husqvarna Sewing Machine Company of Cleveland, Ohio, for providing the sewing machines used to make many of our projects, and Design Master Color Tool, Inc., of Boulder, Colorado, for providing the wood-tone spray used on some of our projects. We also thank East Side Mouldings of Lititz, Pennsylvania, for providing the moulding used for the *"Thanks" Wall Hanging* shown on page 86.

A special word of thanks to Karla Edgar, Kathy Elrod, Rose Glass Klein, Jo Nortier, Glenda Taylor and Nora Faye Taylor for assisting with making and testing many of the projects and recipes in this book.

All's well that ends well. ~ old adage

FAMILY KEEPSAKES

The antique Christmas ornaments you hung on your tree as a child, the colorful birdhouses you helped your granddad make…your home wouldn't be complete without displaying several of your family's cherished keepsakes to add to any season's sweet memories.

Arranging family ornaments is a quick & easy thing to do; just place holiday greenery in an old tin bucket about two-thirds of the way up; then carefully nestle the ornaments with an eye for size and color variety to fill the bucket. Tuck a few sprigs of greenery to peek out among the ornaments to complete the display.

At the sight of the season's first daffodil, group colorful birdhouses like these on a porch table or line them up on a mantel to add a bit of delightful whimsy. If you place them outdoors, just be sure they're protected from inclement weather. If you'd like to make birdhouses like these for your feathered friends, follow the directions below.

FARM-STYLE BIRDHOUSES

To give your feathered friends a taste of farm living, add a little paint, glue, and jumbo craft sticks to purchased birdhouses. Cut shutters, trim, and picket fence pieces from the craft sticks. Glue trim to the shutters and rails to the pickets. Paint the houses, shutters, and fence; then lightly brush them with a dry paintbrush dipped in white paint. Spot-sand areas for a timeworn look. Glue the fence and shutters to the houses and glue a piece of whitewashed tin tile to one of the roofs. Finish them with a coat of poly or marine varnish so they'll be durable for years to come.